B.J. Summers' Guide to Coca-Cola

FOURTH EDITION

Identifications
Current Values

COLLECTOR BOOKS

A Division of Schroeder Publishing Co., Inc.

Collector Books
P.O. Box 3009
Paducah, Kentucky 42002-3009
www.collectorbooks.com

Copyright © 2003 B.J. Summers

The current values in this book should be used only as a guide. They are not intended to set prices, which vary from one section of the country to another. Auction prices as well as dealer prices vary greatly and are affected by condition as well as demand. Neither the author nor the publisher assumes responsibility for any losses that might be incurred as a result of consulting this guide.

Searching for a publisher?

We are always looking for people knowledgeable within their fields. If you feel that there is a real need for a book on your collectible subject and have a large comprehensive collection, contact Collector Books.

Contents

Boy - oh Boy!

ICE COLD

DRINK Coca-Cola

Dedication & Acknowledgments

A great part of any hobby is getting to meet, and become friends with, some of the most interesting people. It has been my extreme pleasure to know Mr. Alfred Mitchell, who recently passed away. "Mr. Al," as I called him, was a walking storehouse of information about Coca-Cola. He could tell you the value of most Coke items, and then give a history of the item. Whenever I was stumped for information, I knew I could call "Mr. Al" for help. He was always eager to talk about his longtime hobby of collecting Coca-Cola. Even when I asked a simple (a nicer way of saying *stupid*) question, "Mr. Al" always had a sincere desire to help.

He will be greatly missed by a wonderful lady, his wife Earlene, all their immediate family, and his extended Coca-Cola family.

I would like to extend my sincere thanks to the following people and businesses without whose help this book would have been impossible.

Alfred and Earlene Mitchell
c/o Collector Books
P.O. Box 3009
Paducah, KY 42002-3009

Still one of the nicest couples you'll ever meet. They have been collecting since the 1960s, and are a constant source of information. They remain very active collectors.

Gary Metz's Muddy River Trading Co.
P.O. Box 1430
Salem, VA 24153
Ph. 540-387-5070
Fax 540-387-3233\e-mail: mudauction@aol.com

Gary Metz remains a mainstay in the advertising auction world. Gary's primary emphasis is Coca-Cola, but his auctions always have a broad spectrum of collectible advertising.

Antiques, Cards, and Collectibles
203 Broadway
Paducah, KY 42001
Ph. 270-443-9797\e-mail: ray@haylan.net

Located in historic downtown Paducah, Kentucky, the old Michael Hardware Store is a great place for an afternoon of browsing. Ray Pelley and his friendly staff offer a full line of antiques and collectibles.

Charlie's Antique Mall
303 Main St., P.O. Box 196
Hazel, KY 42049
Ph. 270-492-8175/e-mail: charlies10@aol.com

Located in the historic community of Hazel, Kentucky, on Main Street, this place has it all. The manager, Ray Gough, has some great dealers with a wide variety of antiques and collectibles and some of the friendliest help you'll find. This border town mall can keep even the pickiest collector busy for the better part of a day.

Farmer's Daughter Antiques
6330 Cairo Rd.
Paducah, KY 42001
Ph. 270-444-7619

This is a neat shop full of primitives and advertising. Easily located one mile west off I-24 at exit 3.

Chief Paduke Antiques Mall
300 S. 3rd St.
Paducah, KY 42003
Ph. 270-442-6799

This full-to-overflowing mall is located in an old railroad depot in downtown Paducah with plenty of general line advertising, including good Coke pieces, plus a good selection of furniture. Stop by and see Charley or Carolyn if you're in this area.

Collectors Auction Service
Rt. 2 Box 431, Oakwood Dr.
Oil City, PA 16301
Ph. 814-677-6070

CAS offers a great phone and mail auction. Call and get one of their full-color catalogs. You'll be hooked on their services after just one auction.

Gene Harris Antique Auction Center, Inc.
203 South 18th Avenue, P.O. Box 476
Marshalltown, IA 50158
Ph. 515-752-0600

If you have been collecting for any time at all, you probably know about this auction house. It seems like there is always an ad in the antique papers for one of their sales. Not only will you find advertising offered but watches and clocks, china, dolls, and almost anything else you can imagine.

Eric Reinfeld
87 Seventh Avenue
Brooklyn, NY 11217
Ph. 718-783-2313

Eric is an avid collector of Whistle and Coca-Cola. He's always interested in selling and buying, so give him a call.

Riverbend Auction Company
103 South Monroe St.
P.O. Box 800
Alderson, WV 24910

Sam and Vivian Merryman
14627 N 300 E
Covington, IN 47932

Sam and Vivian live on the banks of the Wabash River (frozen when I was there) with a nice Coke collection. Sam is a retired Coke employee who still works when needed. This gracious couple was nice enough to allow us to spend a couple of days photographing their collection. They are very active in collecting, and extremely informative about Coca-Cola. Thanks Sam and Vivian.

Patrick's Collectibles
612 Roxanne Dr.
Antioch, TN 37013
Ph. 615-833-4621

If you happen to be around Nashville, Tennessee, during the monthly flea market at the state fairgrounds, be certain to look for Mike and Julie Patrick. They have some of the sharpest advertising pieces you'll ever hope to find. And if Coca-Cola is your field, you won't be able to walk away from the great restored drink machines. Make sure to look them up — you certainly won't be sorry.

Pleasant Hill Antique Mall & Tea Room
315 South Pleasant Hill Rd.
East Peoria, IL 61611
Ph. 309-694-4040

Bob Johnson and the friendly staff at this mall welcome you for a day of shopping. And it'll take that long to work your way through all the quality antiques and collectibles here. When you get tired, stop and enjoy a rest at the tea room where you can get some of the best home cooked food found anywhere. All in all, a great place to shop for your favorite antiques.

Creatures of Habit
406 Broadway
Paducah, KY 42001
Ph. 270-442-2923

This business will take you back in time with its wonderful array of vintage clothing and advertising. If you are ever in western Kentucky, stop and see Natalya and Jack.

The Illinois Antique Center
308 S.W. Commercial
Peoria, IL 61602
Ph. 309-673-3354

This is a day-long stop. Dan and Kim have restored an old, very large warehouse overlooking the river in downtown Peoria. It's full of great advertising and collectibles. Stop by and see Dan and Kim and their very friendly staff and plan on being amazed.

Rare Bird Antique Mall
212 South Main St.
Goodlettsville, TN 37072
Ph. 615-851-2635

If you find yourself in the greater Nashville, Tennessee, area stop by this collectors' paradise. Jon and Joan Wright have assembled a great cast of dealers who run the gamut of collectible merchandise. So step back to a time when the general store was the place to be, and be prepared to spend some time.

Riverside Antique Mall
P.O. Box 4425
Sevierville, TN 37864
Ph. 423-429-0100

Located in a new building overlooking the river, this is a collectors' heaven, full of advertising, with lighted showcases and plenty of friendly help. You need to allow at least half a day for a quick look through this place that sits in the shadows of the Smokey Mountains.

Bill and Helen Mitchell
226 Arendall St.
Henderson, TN 38340
Ph. 901-989-9302

Bill and Helen have assembled a great variety of advertising with special emphasis on Coca-Cola, and they are always searching for new finds. So if you have anything that fits the bill, give them a call or drop them a letter.

Richard Opfer Auctioneering, Inc.
1919 Greenspring Drive
Timonium, MD 21093
Ph. 410-252-5035

Richard Opfer Auctioneering, Inc. provides a great variey of antiques and collectibles auctions. Give his friendly staff a call for his next auction catalog.

Wm. Morford
RD #2
Cazenovia, NY 13035
Ph. 315-662-7625

Wm. Morford has been operating one of the country's better cataloged phone auction businesses for several years. He doesn't list reproductions or repairs that are deceptive in nature. Each catalog usually has a section with items that are for immediate sale. Try out this site and tell him where you got his name and address.

If I have omitted anyone who should be here, please be assured it is an oversight on my part and was not intentional.

Much of our world has changed since September 11, 2001 — also a "day that will live in infamy." I was watching *The Today Show* that morning, like so many others, in a state of disbelief. Although I could see what was taking place, my mind couldn't fully comprehend the staggering loss of life and the billions of dollars of damage. The face of New York City had changed forever. And as Americans we were changed in that moment of destruction by a madman. All of us seem to be looking for that "warm and fuzzy feeling" again. That search has taken some of us back to basics such as family, friends, worship, and community.

However, as we seek safety and comfort in familiar surroundings, we realize some things haven't changed, and that helps us draw the strength we seek. Walking into your house and smelling bread baking ... hot dogs cooking over a picnic fire with family and friends ... Thanksgiving dinner with the family ... and Christmas Eve with all its sounds, wrapping paper flying, and small kids that can't wait for Santa. And who has helped define that image of Santa more than Coca-Cola with the smiling, warm-hearted, rosy-cheeked old elf created by Haddom Sundblom? What could be more familiar and comforting than a summer ball game and an icy cold bottle of Coca-Cola? Coca-Cola, an American icon, helps us reflect on a slower, friendlier time of life.

Coca-Cola started in a backyard kettle. Since that time it's been with us through good times and bad: wars, depression, development of mind-staggering advances in medicine, computers, and a man on the moon. Many of us married the girl that shared a cherry Coke with us at the local hamburger hangout.

So Coca-Cola really needs no introduction. It's certainly interwoven with the thread of American life. It's a treat to see some of the great advertising that has been produced by Coca-Cola, and the prices it now commands.

I've attempted to help both the advanced and beginning collector with this book. I don't attempt to set prices on any Coke memorabilia, but only report values. *These values are meant to be only a guide, not absolute.* If you're buying, you will no doubt like that sentence. But if you're selling, it won't be as appealing. When you look at the caption, or listing, you will see that I have keyed the prices so you'll know the origin of the value. You'll see the following key codes throughout this book:

"Look up America — It's the real thing. Coke." See page 132.

    C – a value given to me by a collector(s);
    B – a value determined by an auction price (Remember on auction values that two determined bidders can run a price far past fair market value. Likewise, lack of interest will sometimes let a collectible sell for less than it should);
    D – a value determined by a dealer;

Condition will be graded by the following key:
    NOS – refers to new old stock, usually found in a warehouse or store closed for some time;
    NRFB – never removed from box;
    MIB – absolutely mint, still in the original container;
    M – mint condition; however, has been out of the container;
    NM – almost mint, nothing to detract from display;
    EX – excellent; very minor distractions, such as shelf ware, don't detract from the focal point;
    VG – may have light scratches on the edges or back, but nothing to detract from the face;
    G – the usual used condition, with scratches and nicks on the item front, but still desirable;
    F – some bad detractions;
    P – poor; pick it up only because of its rarity or because it is a piece you don't have in your collection.

Of course, other factors will affect price, such as location. Generally speaking, an item with a $100 price in my area (the Midwest and the South) may sell in the $150 – 175 range on the East Coast and in the Northeast; and in the $200 – 225 range on the West Coast.

How tough is the demand in my area? I'm a long-time collector of items from my hometown of Paducah, Kentucky. Fortunately for me, the city has a very colorful and rich history with some great memorabilia. Unfortunately for me, there are several die-hard collectors like myself, and among us, we keep the prices artificially high due to the demand for those few items that are always surfacing.

Probably the last item on pricing is condition. This is the place where I find the most problems. If an item in the price guide is labeled as mint at $200, and you see one in a store in fair condition at $200, it's overpriced. Don't buy it! I've attempted to make sure all of the listings in this book have the condition listed. This should help when it's time to buy or haggle. It's extremely difficult to find a seller and a buyer that agree on an item's value. A buyer shouldn't be hesitant about making an offer, and a seller shouldn't be offended by an offer. Good luck buying, selling, and collecting.

Many collectors have contacted me in the past. Some have gotten to me and some — unfortunately — haven't. Please mail correspondence to:

Collector Books
ATTN: B.J. Summers
P.O. Box 3009
Paducah, KY 42002-3009

Please realize it might take some time to receive and answer the mail. I'm sometimes guilty of allowing it to pile up on my desk. Also, some questions require some research on my part. Phone calls aren't very good because I'm rarely where I can take them. If left on the recorder, they will probably not be returned due to the volume of calls and the associated long distance charges. Probably the best method would be via e-mail at bjsummers@apex.net.

Cardboard stand up Santa Claus. See page 259.

❧∶ My Hometown Bottler ∶❧

As a collector of Coca-Cola memorabilia I'm always interested in the great designs of the bottling plants. With this book, we'll begin a new feature titled "My Hometown Bottler." I'd like to hear from you about your hometown bottler, and later I'll detail how to do this.

The Paducah, Kentucky, bottling plant, opened in 1939, is a fantastic building with strong Art Deco influences. Construction on the building was started shortly after the devastating flood of 1937, which had left the existing bottling plant swimming in the frigid Ohio River flood waters. The building was designed by Coca-Cola architect S. Lester Daly. The exterior of the two-story building is of concrete and brick construction, while the interior is an awesome continuation of Art Deco design. As can be seen in the photos, the interior has a great rotunda with offices situated in a circular arrangement. The ceiling of this area rises to a dome of glass bricks and concrete that allows light in during the day, and at night, when lit, provides a great light show for the community. In the center of this area is an enormous one-of-a-kind chandelier of cut glass plates in the likeness of the hobbleskirt bottle made especially for this plant.

A head-on shot of my hometown plant shows the heavy Art Deco styling that was so popular in the 1930s when this building was erected. The unusual shape of the property dictated the trapezoid-shaped building. This is a busy four-way intersection with two approaches at angles. The dome at the top allows light in during the day, and when lit at night provides a fantastic light show.

(Left) The close-up on the front doors reveals a dramatic entrance for those having business with Coca-Cola. (Right) As you enter the lobby of the bottling plant, your eye is immediately drawn to the fantastic floor design and the old manual machine that was used in the early years of Coke production by Mr. Carson, our "Mr. Coca-Cola" around this area. Mr. Carson started his Coca-Cola business here in 1903, and in later years, everyone knew if they saw his car outside a soda shop, he would be buying Coca-Cola for those inside.

One awesome feature of this building is a chandelier that is hung from the top of the dome. It was designed especially for this plant, and is one of a kind. The photograph doesn't do this justice. It has large glass panels that are cut into the exact shape of a hobbleskirt bottle. Tall clear tubes produce a light that is hard to forget.

A great view of the first floor swirl design can be seen in this photo, taken from the second floor landing. The strong Art Deco influence is evident again in the circular stairway with its sleek railing. As on the first floor, all offices on the second floor open off the rotunda.

This view of the rotunda dome is shot from the first floor. The light shining through the glass bricks helps to illuminate the area during the day. The neon tubes that light up the dome can't be seen in this photograph, but have for years provided a great light show. Sadly, the dome has been dark for the last few years due to the aging process of the wiring and lights. It's still a sight to behold.

Do you have a bottling plant you would like to share with other collectors? Send a few good 35 mm photographs that do not have to be returned, along with a description of the building, its history, and any other pertinent information. Those selected will be featured in future books. Send to the address below:

Collector Books
ATTN: B.J. Summers
P.O. Box 3009
Paducah, KY 42002-3009

What is your favorite piece of Coca-Cola memorabilia? For most collectors, that question is difficult at best. It's almost like asking which child is your favorite, or which brother you like the most. For some the answer is easy, but others find it next to impossible.

With this book, a new, and hopefully regular, feature has been added. It is called, "My Favorite Coca-Cola Collectible." Let me hear from you about your favorite piece. Why is it your favorite? What, if any, is the story behind how it came to be yours? Is there any history to it? Send your photos (they will not be returned) and information to the address below.

The first collectible to be featured here is from a couple who have been collecting for more years than most have had birthdays — a very long time! Alfred and Earlene Mitchell make up one of the nicest couples I've had the pleasure to meet and work with. When I hit a question that stumps me, I can always count on "Mr. Al" for help. And picking a favorite was understandably difficult for them. They've got some great pieces, as the following photos show. If any of you want to contact the Mitchells, send a letter to the address at the bottom of this page, and it will be forwarded to them.

Sadly between the time of this photo and the printing of this book, Mr. Alfred Mitchell passed away. He will be greatly missed by both his immediate family and his extended Coke family.

Al and Earlene Mitchell, in front of a portion of their calendars, agree that these would probably rate as their favorite collectible. It took a lot of thought, however, because as Earlene put it, "It's all my favorite!"

Here is Earlene holding another favorite item. Earlene's father worked for Coca-Cola, and her mother was a very good seamstress. Combine those qualities and you get a good Buddy Lee and a uniform that has extra touch and special meaning. Earlene is pictured here behind their soda fountain — a natural place for Coca-Cola.

Sharing your collection with others is one of the best parts of having a collection. Information can be gained here that would otherwise be lost. If you would like to contact the Mitchells, please use the address below, attention Earlene Mitchell. Let me hear from you at the following address:

Collector Books
ATTN: Earlene Mitchell
P.O. Box 3009
Paducah, KY 42002-3009

Aluminum die cut, "Drink Coca-Cola In Bottles" in script, truck radiator sign, 1920s, 17½" x 7½", EX, $375.00 D.
Courtesy of Muddy River Trading Co./Gary Metz.

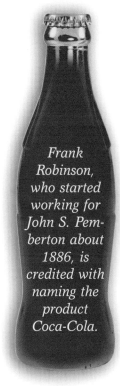

Frank Robinson, who started working for John S. Pemberton about 1886, is credited with naming the product Coca-Cola.

America's Fighting Planes, set of 20 scenes of planes in action, priced at $75.00 each if set is incomplete, 1940s, EX, $1,650.00 C.
Courtesy of Mitchell collection.

Bottle hanger, six pack in food basket, 1950s, 8" x 7," EX, $550.00 C.
Courtesy of Bill Mitchell.

Bottle hanger, "Ice Cold Coca-Cola King Size," red, white, and green, M, $12.00 C.
Courtesy of Mitchell collection.

Banner, "Be Really Refreshed ... Around the Clock," 1950s, EX .... $45.00 C

Banner, canvas, featuring a 24 bottle case with area at bottom for the price, 9' tall, EX ....$150.00 C

Banner, paper, "Home Refreshment," carton at left, 1941, 51" x 13", NM ....$85.00 C

Banner, paper, "King Size," 1958, 36" x 20", NM ....$110.00 C

Banner, "Take Coke Home," 108", EX...............$165.00 C

Banner, "Welcome to Super Bowl XXVIII," 102" x 34", EX..$75.00 D

Bottle hanger, "Ice Cold Coca-Cola King Size," red, white, and green, EX ....$10.00 C

Bottle topper, Bathing Girl, "Drink Coca-Cola Delicious and Refreshing," rare, 1929, VG, $1,800.00 B.
Courtesy of Gary Metz.

Bottle topper, Canadian, great graphics by Fred Mizen, "Refresh Yourself," 1926, 13" x 13", EX, $3,600.00 C.
Courtesy of Muddy River Trading Co./Gary Metz.

Bottle topper, plastic, "We let you see the bottle," 1950s, EX, $475.00 C.
Courtesy of Mitchell collection.

Bottle topper, woman with yellow scarf and parasol, 1927, 8" x 10", VG, $2,000.00 B.
Courtesy of Muddy River Trading Co./Gary Metz.

Bottle hanger, rectangular hanger with the message "Thank You for Visiting Us," 1960s, G ....$80.00 C

Bottle hanger, Santa Claus holding a bottle with information card about "Twas the Night Before Christmas," fold-out story inside, 1950s, M ....$20.00 C

Bottle hanger, Santa Claus in refrigerator full of bottles, being surprised by small child, 1950s, F ....$10.00 D

Bottle topper, Bathing Girl, "Drink Coca-Cola Delicious and Refreshing," rare, 1929, G ....$1,000.00 C

Bottle topper, plastic, "We let you see the bottle," 1950s, G..$350.00 D

Bottle topper, plastic, "We let you see the bottle," 1950s, VG ....$425.00 C

Canvas awning, Refreshment Center, red & white stripe, 1950s, 5' x 2', EX...$575.00 C

Canvas banner, "Take Coke Home," pricing information at bottom, 24 bottle case in center, 9' tall, EX ......$425.00 D

Cardboard advertisement for a deck of playing cards that can be purchased with six coupons taken from six pack cartons, Piqua Coca-Cola Bottling Company, 1938, 12" x 18"..$55.00 C

Canvas banner, advertising bottle sales and drinking through a straw, white, red, and black, 70" x 16", 1910, VG, $4,000.00 B. *Courtesy of Muddy River Trading Co./Gary Metz.*

Bumper sticker featuring Max Headroom pleading, "Don't Say the 'P' Word," 1980s, EX, $10.00 C. *Courtesy of Sam and Vivian Merryman.*

Cardboard, airplane hanger, one of set of 20, produced by Snyder & Black for Coca-Cola to show the winning war planes, started in 1941 and continued sets until the end of the war, EX, $50.00 C. *Courtesy of Mitchell collection.*

Cardboard, baseball scoreboard, made from very heavy stock material, very unusual, 1930s, 30" x 20", EX, $1,000.00 B. *Courtesy of Muddy River Trading Co./Gary Metz.*

Cardboard, bather in round blue background, framed and under glass, by Snyder & Black, rare, 1938, 22", NM, $2,700.00 C. *Courtesy of Mitchell collection.*

Cardboard, bather in diamond blue background pictured with a Coke button and a bottle, framed and under glass, 1940, 23" x 22", NM, $1,700.00 C. *Courtesy of Mitchell collection.*

Cardboard advertisement, horizontal, "Have a Coke," woman holding a bottle, 36" x 20", EX..............$250.00 B

Cardboard airplane hangers, complete set of 20 in original envelope, if sold separately price at $75.00 to $100.00 each, 1943, VG ....$1,500.00 C

Cardboard, an African-American family enjoying Coca-Cola, 1958, EX...$100.00 C

Cardboard and wood price board for 6½ oz. and 12 oz. sizes with original tin frame, 1950, 25" x 15", VG ....$150.00 D

Cardboard and wood right angle display featuring three 6-packs and carriers, "Easy to Carry," carriers have wooden handles, 1947, 42" x 33", EX ....$325.00 D

Cardboard, bather in diamond blue background pictured with a Coke button and a bottle, framed and under glass, 1940, 23" x 22", EX......................................$1,375.00 C

During WWII, Coca-Cola produced a few items used to promote aircraft identification...

...There were 2 decks of "Spotter" playing cards, a booklet titled "Know Your War Planes," and 4 series of large framed pictures showing war planes. Artist and aircraft professional William Heaslip painted all the aircraft.

Cardboard, airplane hangers, complete set of 20 in original envelope, if sold separately price at $35.00 to $50.00 each, 1943, EX, $2,000.00 C. *Courtesy of Mitchell collection.*

Cardboard, bather in round blue background, framed and under glass, by Snyder & Black, rare, 1938, 22", EX...$2,200.00 C

Cardboard bottle display, cut out, featuring a girl in a swimsuit, "So Refreshing," 1930, 9" x 17½", VG ....$475.00 D

Cardboard bottle display of girl holding tray, 1926, 11½" x 14", G ....$1,800.00 C

Cardboard bottle rack, "Enjoy Coca-Cola," 1970 – 80s, 18", red and white, EX ....$25.00 D

Cardboard, "Be Really Refreshed," sign in metal frame with scene of skiers, 36" x 20", 1955, EX, $325.00 C.

Cardboard, "Big Refreshment Value ... King Size Coke," horizontal poster with lady in straw sun hat, 36" x 20", 1960s, F, $225.00 C.

Cardboard cut-out bottle sign with message board under "Classic" label, NOS, NM, 14" x 45", C. *Courtesy of Sam & Vivian Merryman.*

Cardboard, boy and girl with bottles, "Coke for me too," 1946, 36" x 20", EX ....$750.00 C

Cardboard, Canadian poster featuring artwork of girl on ping pong table with a bottle of Coke, framed under glass, 14" x 28", G.....................................$600.00 D

Cardboard, Canadian trolley card, "Drink Coca-Cola, Made in Canada," 1920s, 21" x 11", F ....$200.00 C

Cardboard, carton insert, a lady's hand shown carrying a six pack, "Take Home This Handy 6 Bottle Carton," by Niagara Litho, 1936, G ....$75.00 D

Cardboard carton insert advertising Eddie Fisher's radio program, 20" x 12", 1954, EX............................$175.00 C

Cardboard carton insert, "Coke Is a Natural," EX..$15.00 C

Cardboard carton insert, "Easy to Serve," 1930s, EX...$175.00 C

Cardboard, carton insert, "Good with Food" in center, 1930s, EX ....$165.00 C

Cardboard, carton insert, "Good with Food," 1930s NM ....$175.00 D

Cardboard, carton insert, "Good with Food," 1930s, F ....$85.00 C

Cardboard, carton insert, "Refresh Your Guests," 1930, VG...$175.00 C

Cardboard, carton insert, "Six for 25¢ Plus Deposit," 1930s, NM ....$415.00 C

Cardboard, carton insert, slanted red billboard logo "Easy to Serve," 1930, G ....$135.00 C

Cardboard, carton insert, "Take Home This Handy Six Bottle Carton," 1936, EX...$95.00 C

Cardboard, carton stuffer celebrating Memorial Day, 1953, EX...$55.00 C

Cardboard, clown balancing on a bottle, 1950, G..$500.00 C

Cardboard bottle sign with graphics of boys playing around bottle, Canadian, 1930s, 11½" x 11½", NM, **$4,700.00 B.** *Courtesy Muddy River Trading Co./Gary Metz.*

Cardboard Christmas display for a holiday bell soda glass, NRFP, M, **$55.00 C.** *Courtesy Sam & Vivian Merryman.*

Cardboard, "Coke Float" sign, hot air balloons and message blank for "Today's Feature," 22" x 7", EX, **$65.00 C.** *Courtesy of Sam and Vivian Merryman.*

Cardboard Christmas tree string sign with dynamic wave "Drink...," 1970s, 14" x 24", G, **$32.00 D.**

Cardboard, Coca-Cola polar bear stand up, 6' tall, EX...$75.00 D

Cardboard, cut out, Athletic Games, 1932, EX....$75.00 C

Cardboard, cut out, "Buy Coca-Cola, Have for Picnic Fun," shows two couples having a picnic, 1950s, G...$95.00 C

Cardboard, cut out, "Buy Coca-Cola, Have for Picnic Fun," shows two couples having a picnic, 1950s, G...$95.00 C

Cardboard, cut out, cherub holding a tray with a glass in a glass holder, 14½", EX.....................................$3,800.00 B

Cardboard, cut out, couple at sundial, "It's Time to Drink Coca-Cola" on edge of dial, 1910s, 29" x 36", G ....$3,500.00 B

Cardboard, cut out, "Drink Coca-Cola, The Pause that Refreshes," used as a window display by Niagara Litho Co. N.Y, 1940s, 32½" x 42½", G ....$850.00 C

Cardboard, cut out, featuring glass in hand, has a 3-D effect, 1958, 19" x 21", G..................................$300.00 D

Cardboard, cut out, man and woman at sundial, both are holding flare glasses, 1910s, 30" x 36½", EX ....$6,000.00 B

Cardboard, cut out, model with a bottle and a colorful parasol, easel back, 1930s, 10" x 18½", G ......$1,100.00 D

Cardboard, cut, "Buy Coca-Cola Now For Picnic Fun," shows two couples having a picnic, 1950s, EX, $135.00 C. *Courtesy of Mitchell collection.*

Cardboard, "Buy the case Coke 10 oz. size," black, yellow, and white, EX, $95.00 C.

Cardboard, cut out, Coca-Cola policeman, waist up view with "Stop for pause, Go refreshed" ribbon in front, great graphics, hard to find, 1937, 45" x 32", G, $1,050.00 B. *Courtesy of Muddy River Trading Co./Gary Metz.*

Cardboard clown balancing on a bottle, 1950, EX, $875.00 B. *Courtesy of Muddy River Trading Co./Gary Metz.*

Cardboard, cut out, "Drink Coca-Cola, The Pause that Refreshes," used as a window display by Niagara Litho Co., N.Y., 1940s, 32½" x 42½", VG, $975.00 C. *Courtesy of Mitchell collection.*

Cardboard, cut out, sign with elves and a bottle on sled, 12" x 20", EX..$195.00 D

Cardboard, cut out stand up of Eddie Fisher, 1954, 19", EX..$225.00 D

Cardboard, cut out, Toonerville, 1930, EX ....$175.00 C

Cardboard, cut out, Toy Town, 1927, EX ....$90.00 D

Cardboard, die cast 3-D, featuring Claudette Colbert, 1933, 10" x 20", EX ....$5,500.00 C

Cardboard, die cut, embossed, easel back Victorian sign promoting Coca-Cola chewing gum, girl in woods, Kaufmann and Strauss Company, New York, framed and matted, 1903 – 1905, 4½" x 10½", NM ....$15,500.00 C

Cardboard, die cut, hand in bottle, "Take Enough Home," companion piece at top, 1952, 11" x 14", NM ....$185.00 C

Cardboard, cut out, woman with glass of Coke, similar to 1930 serving tray, 1930, 21" x 38", F, $600.00 C. *Courtesy of Muddy River Trading Co./Gary Metz.*

Cardboard cut out, model with a bottle and a colorful parasol, easel back, 1930s, 10" x 18½", EX, $1,650.00 C. *Courtesy of Mitchell collection.*

Cardboard, cut out, pretty young lady enjoying a bottle of Coke, matted and framed, unusual sign not seen very often, 1936, 15" x 21", F, $475.00 B. *Courtesy Muddy River Trading Co./Gary Metz.*

Cardboard, cut out, stand up Eddie Fisher holding a bottle of Coke with easel back, 1954, 5' tall, G, $375.00 B. *Courtesy Muddy River Trading Co./Gary Metz.*

Cardboard, cut out, waitress holding a tray full of Coke in glasses, "So Refreshing," can be used as stringer or counter with attached easel back, 17" x 20", G, $475.00 B. *Courtesy Muddy River Trading Co./Gary Metz.*

Cardboard, cut out, "The Pause That Refreshes Drink Coca-Cola," super piece and not seen very often, 1937, 34" x 14", VG, $200.00 B. *Courtesy of Muddy River Trading Co./Gary Metz.*

Cardboard, die cut, French Canadian string hanger with great graphics featuring woman with a Coke, 1939, 15" x 22", G..$1,600.00 B

Cardboard, die cut of couple with parasol reading sundial, 30" x 36½", 1910s, VG.....................................$5,600.00 C

Cardboard, die cut of Frances Dee and Gene Raymond on beach, "The Pause That Refreshes," 1932, EX.....$1,800.00 C

Cardboard, die cut of lady's face with actual scarf, EX...$150.00 D

Cardboard, die cut sailor girl, 1952, 11" x 7", VG..$225.00 C

Cardboard, die cut sailor girl, framed under glass, 1952, 11" x 7", EX...$325.00 C

Cardboard, die cut, "Serve Coca-Cola" button with candles, EX..$115.00 C

Cardboard, die cut six-pack, 1954, VG..................$650.00 B

Cardboard, die cut six-pack, 1954, 12", NM..........$700.00 C

Cardboard, die cut, "Take Enough Home," bottle in hand, 1952, EX..$175.00 B

Cardboard, die cut, two sided, girl and a glass, 1960s, 13" x 17", EX..$425.00 B

Cardboard, die cut, bottle in hand, framed, 1950s, NM, $650.00 B.
Courtesy of Muddy River Trading Co./Gary Metz.

Cardboard, cut out, woman shopping with a carton of Coke in her basket, 1944, 17½" tall, near mint, $1,900.00 B.
Courtesy Muddy River Trading Co./Gary Metz.

Cardboard, die cut, Coke cherub holding a tray with a glass of Coke, framed under glass, extremely rare, 1908, VG, $4,000.00 B.
Courtesy of Muddy River Trading Co./Gary Metz.

Cardboard, die cut bottle topper, girl with tray, three dimensional, rare item, 1920s, 11½" x 14", NM, $2,600.00 B.
Courtesy of Muddy River Trading Co./Gary Metz.

Cardboard, die cut, "Drink Coca-Cola, Delicious and Refreshing, Ours is Ice Cold," 1900s, 9" x 19", F, $495.00 C.
Courtesy of Bill Mitchell.

Cardboard, die cut six pack with "6 for 25¢" on carton, 1950, 12", NM ....$575.00 C

Cardboard, die cut window display, 15 piece Toonerville, F ....$450.00 D

Cardboard die cut with an ice bucket scene and a glass and bottle in front, 1926, EX ....$575.00 C

Cardboard die cut with easel back poster of airman drinking from a bottle of Coke, French Canadian, 12½" x 17", 1941, EX.................................$1,550.00 B

Cardboard, die cut, woman 5' tall, holding six pack, VG ....$125.00 C

Cardboard display, "Pick Up The Fixins, Enjoy Coke," 1957, 20" x 14", NM ....$55.00 D

Cardboard, double sided, Canadian, horizontal poster, featuring woman serving Coca-Cola on one side and a bottle in snow bank on reverse, 1950s, 36" x 20", G ....$195.00 C

Cardboard, double sided, Canadian poster featuring woman with bottle on both sides, different backgrounds, 1950s, 56" x 27", G ....$225.00 C

Cardboard, "Drink Coca-Cola," couple on a beach with a large towel, 1932, 29" x 50", Hayden-Hayden, VG ....$1,800.00 C

The Coca-Cola trademark was registered January 31, 1893, but had been in the market since 1886.

Cardboard, die cut easel back of boy on bike, 29" x 20", 1950s, F, $260.00 B.

Cardboard, die cut easel back sign of a bell glass in ice, 17" x 27", 1930s, EX, $500.00 B.
Courtesy of Muddy River Trading Co./Gary Metz.

Cardboard, die cut easel back sign of snowman with a glass of Coke, 19" x 32", 1953, EX, $800.00 B.
Courtesy of Muddy River Trading Co./Gary Metz.

Cardboard, die cut with easel back featuring Lionel Hampton, 12" x 15", 1953, EX, $975.00 B.
Courtesy of Muddy River Trading Co./Gary Metz.

Cardboard, "Drink Coca-Cola Delicious and Refreshing," sign with tin frame featuring 1915 bottle on each side, 1910s, 60" x 21", NM ....$1,450.00 C

Cardboard, easel back, boy and girl under mistletoe, "Things Go Better With Coke," 1960s, 16" x 27", EX ....$75.00 D

Cardboard, easel back French Canadian sign, "Coke Convient," 1948, 18" x 24", NM ....$225.00 D

Cardboard, easel back, girls on a bicycle built for two, "Extra Fun Takes More than One," 1960s, F ......$55.00 D

Cardboard, easel back, Kit Carson advertising bottle sales and Rodeo Tie promotion, 1953, 16" x 24", G...$285.00 C

Cardboard, easel back Kit Carson promotional sign, promoting kerchief, 1950s, 16" x 24", G ....$135.00 C

Cardboard, easel back or hanging sign featuring a glass of Coke, Canadian, 1949, 12' x 12", EX ....$125.00 D

Cardboard, easel back, Shopping Girl, 1956, 2½' x 5', EX..$900.00 C

Cardboard, easel back sign advertising Tab with the contoured Tab glass featured, 10" x 10", EX ....$15.00 D

Cardboard, easel back sign, "thirst asks nothing more," featuring bottle in hand, 1939, 12" x 16",NM ....$1,800.00 D

Cardboard, die cut, "Every Bottle Sterilized," framed and matted, 1930s, 14" x 12", EX, $1,100.00 C. *Courtesy of Bill Mitchell.*

Cardboard, die cut, embossed, WWII battleship, framed under glass, 26" x 14", NM, $1,300.00 B. *Courtesy of Muddy River Trading Co./Gary Metz.*

Cardboard, die cut, French Canadian featuring bottle in hand, 12" x 16", 1939, NM, $600.00 B. *Courtesy of Muddy River Trading Co./Gary Metz.*

Cardboard, die cut, fishing boy and dog with original pond, unusual find, 1935, 36" tall, G, $2,650.00 B. *Courtesy of Muddy River Trading Co./Gary Metz.*

Cardboard, die cut, girls on a bicycle for two, part of a larger sign, without the background, 1960s, EX, $275.00 C.

Cardboard, featuring Eddie Fisher on radio, 1954, 12" x 20", VG ....$125.00 C

Cardboard, French Canadian, girl in front of box cooler with bottle in hand, original easel back stand, 1940s, 12" x 17", EX ....$250.00 C

Cardboard, French Canadian poster, woman shopper, 1950s, EX ....$160.00 C

Cardboard, French Canadian sign featuring bottle in snow bank, 1950s, 22" x 50", EX ....$150.00 D

Cardboard, horizontal, "Accepted Home Refreshment," couple with popcorn and Coca-Cola in front of fireplace, "Drink..." button lower right, 1942, 56" x 27", EX..$250.00 C

Cardboard, horizontal, "Accepted Home Refreshment," couple with popcorn and Coca-Cola at fireplace, "Drink..." button lower right, 1942, 56" x 27", G..$225.00 C

Cardboard, horizontal, "Be Really Refreshed," scene of couple in boat on pond, 1960s, 36" x 20", EX...$175.00 C

Cardboard, die cut, service girl in uniform with bottle of Coke, 1944, 25" x 64", EX, $600.00 B.
Courtesy of Gene Harris Antique Auction Center, Inc.

Cardboard, die cut sign with Coke snowman that folds out from back to produce a three-dimensional effect, probably part of a larger sign, VG, $900.00 B. *Courtesy of Collectors Auction Services.*

Cardboard, die cut, sailor girl with "Take Home" flags, matted and framed, 1952, 11" x 7", NM, $375.00 B. *Courtesy of Muddy River Trading Co./ Gary Metz.*

Cardboard, die cut, poster, "Old Man North" with six pack, "Serve Ice Cold," 16" x 21", 1953, NM, $275.00 B. *Courtesy of Muddy River Trading Co./ Gary Metz.*

Cardboard, die cut sign of girl and boy, 20" x 13", 1950s, G, $160.00 B. *Courtesy of Muddy River Trading Co./Gary Metz.*

Cardboard, die cut sign, featuring winter girl with Coke glasses, framed and matted, 32" x 19", 1930 – 1940s, EX, $675.00 B.

Cardboard, die cut sign of three ladies at table, 24" x 18", 1951, G, $450.00 B. *Courtesy of Muddy River Trading Co./Gary Metz.*

Cardboard, horizontal, "Be Really Refreshed," scene of couple in boat on pond, 1960s, 36" x 20", G ......$50.00 B

Cardboard, horizontal, "Drink Royal Palm Beverages Made from Pure Cane Sugar by the Coca-Cola Bottling Company," 1930s, 17" x 11½", F ....$60.00 B

Cardboard, horizontal, "Enjoy the quality taste," girl in swimsuit at beach, 1956, 36" x 20", EX ....$275.00 C

Cardboard, horizontal, "For the taste you never get tired of," beside "Drink..." button, couple in pool, 1960s, 36" x 20", EX ....$180.00 C

Cardboard, horizontal, "Have a Coke," young cheerleader with megaphone and a bottle, "Coca-Cola" button on right, 1946, 36" x 20", G ....$230.00 B

Cardboard, horizontal, "Have a Coke," young cheerleader with megaphone and a bottle, "Coca-Cola" button on right, 1946, 36" x 20", VG..$250.00 D

Cardboard, horizontal, "Here's Something Good!," woman with crown, man in clown suit with bottle, 1950s, 56" x 27", G ....$215.00 B

Cardboard, horizontal, "Here's Something Good!," woman with crown, man in clown suit with bottle, 1950s, 56" x 27", VG ....$280.00 C

Cardboard, horizontal, "Home Refreshment," woman holding a bottle with flowers in the background, 1950s, 50" x 29", G ....$200.00 C

Cardboard, horizontal, in original wooden frame, "Coke is Coca-Cola," 1949, 36" x 20", EX ....$675.00 C

Cardboard, horizontal, "Inviting you to refreshment," VG...$500.00 C

Cardboard, die cut six pack, 1954, EX, $750.00. *Courtesy of Gary Metz.*

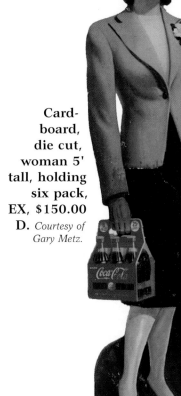

Cardboard, die cut, woman 5' tall, holding six pack, EX, $150.00 D. *Courtesy of Gary Metz.*

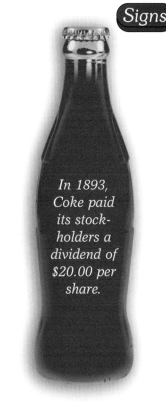

In 1893, Coke paid its stockholders a dividend of $20.00 per share.

Cardboard, die cut with attached hangers for wall or window display, Bathing Girl, 1910, F, $1,450.00 B. *Courtesy of Muddy River Trading Co./Gary Metz.*

Cardboard, die cut of lady with parasol and a straight-sided bottle of Coke, rare, 1900s, 24" x 27", G, $5,200.00 B. *Courtesy of Muddy River Trading Co./Gary Metz.*

Cardboard, die cut, "Take Enough Home," bottle in hand, 1952, VG, $160.00 B. *Courtesy of Muddy River Trading Co./Gary Metz.*

Cardboard, horizontal, lettered, button right side, "Fountain Service," 1950, 30" x 12", G ....$300.00 C

Cardboard, horizontal poster "Coke is Coca-Cola" in original gold frame, 1949, VG ....$500.00 B

Cardboard, horizontal poster "Coke time" featuring three women at table, 1943, EX ....$475.00 B

Cardboard, horizontal poster featuring artwork of woman at microphone with a bottle of Coke, "Entertain your thirst," 1941, 36" x 20", EX ....$500.00 B

Cardboard, horizontal poster featuring bottle in ice "Have a Coke," 1944, 36" x 20", NM ....$325.00 B

Cardboard, horizontal poster featuring Coke crossing guard, "Let's watch for 'em," 1950s, 66" x 32", NM ....$800.00 B

Cardboard, horizontal poster, featuring a lunch counter scene, "A great drink with food," Canadian, 1942, 36" x 20", G ....$550.00 B

Cardboard, horizontal poster, featuring people in a picnic scene with a cooler, 1954, 36" x 24", EX ....$400.00 B

Cardboard, horizontal poster, "How about a Coke" featuring artwork of three girls at counter, 1939, G ....$475.00 B

Cardboard, dimensional arrow sign, heavy brown cardboard, hard to find, 1944, 20" x 12", G, $150.00 B.
Courtesy of Muddy River Trading Co./Gary Metz.

Cardboard, die cut, woman sitting on bench with bottle, "Delicious and Refreshing, Coca-Cola in bottles," 1900s, 18" x 28½", G, $8,000.00 B. *Courtesy of Bill Mitchell.*

Cardboard, double-sided hanging mobile, 32" tall, 1957, NM, $425.00 B.
Courtesy of Muddy River Trading Co./ Gary Metz.

Cardboard, display unit for the "Beverage Dept.," 26" x 36", 1954, EX, $700.00 B.
Courtesy of Muddy River Trading Co./Gary Metz.

Cardboard, horizontal poster in original Kay Displays frame featuring two couples by fire, 1954, 36" x 24", G..$425.00 B

Cardboard, horizontal poster, "Play Refreshed" girl in cowboy hat, 1951, G ....$375.00 B

Cardboard, horizontal poster with circus scene "Here's Something Good" in original repainted frame without applied detail, 1951, EX ....$400.00 B

Cardboard, horizontal, "Refreshing," woman in white dress at counter with a bottle, 1949, 56" x 27", VG ....$375.00 B

Cardboard, horizontal, "Refreshing," woman in white dress at counter with a bottle, 1949, 56" x 27", EX ....$425.00 D

Cardboard, horizontal sign featuring girl with bottle and menu, 1960s, 66" x 32", NM ....$650.00 B

Cardboard, horizontal, "Sparkling" bottle in Q of quality in yellow background, original frame, 1957, 36" x 20", EX ....$475.00 D

Cardboard, horizontal, "That taste-good feeling," man drinking from bottle, "Drink Coca-Cola Delicious and Refreshing" button left, 1939, 56" x 27", VG ....$1,000.00 B

Cardboard, horizontal, "The best of taste," "Drink..." button on right, woman in green suit, 1957, 36" x 20", G ....$350.00 D

Cardboard, horizontal, "12 oz. ice cold," head shot of woman with a bottle, promoting sale of king size products, 1959, 36" x 20", EX...$235.00 D

Cardboard, horizontal, "Welcome aboard," shore scene with "Drink..." button upper right, 1957, 36" x 20", EX ....$300.00 D

Cardboard, horizontal, "Welcome," man in uniform and woman in yellow dress seated on couch with a bottle, 1943, 56" x 27", EX...$500.00 C

Cardboard, "I'm heading for Coca-Cola," woman in uniform getting off airplane, in original wood frame, 1942, 16" x 27", VG ....$650.00 D

Cardboard, Italian, horizontal poster with a woman and a Coke bottle, 1940s, 36" x 20", NM ....$450.00 B

Cardboard, "it's Twice Time, Twice the value," 1960s, 66" x 32", NM ....$800.00 D

Cardboard, large horizontal poster, cowgirl with bottle, 1951, F ....$75.00 C

Cardboard, "Drink Coca-Cola," couple on a beach with a large towel, 1932, 29" x 50", Hayden-Hayden, F, $625.00 C. *Courtesy of Mitchell collection.*

Cardboard, easel back die cut of woman, "Off to a fresh start," 12" x 27", 1931, EX, $875.00 B. *Courtesy of Muddy River Trading Co./Gary Metz.*

Cardboard, easel back poster promoting the Kit Carson Kerchief with advertising six pack information, 16" x 24", 1950s, EX, $225.00 B. *Courtesy of Muddy River Trading Co./Gary Metz.*

Cardboard, "Enjoy Tab" display sign, 1960s, EX, $65.00 C.

Cardboard, easel back die cut window display, 41" x 32", 1939, EX, $775.00 B. *Courtesy of Muddy River Trading Co./Gary Metz.*

Cardboard, large horizontal poster, double sided with a young couple on one side and a fishing girl on the other, 1950s, F..$235.00 C

Cardboard, large horizontal poster featuring hot dog roast, "Coca-Cola belongs," 1942, EX.........................$410.00 C

Cardboard, large horizontal poster featuring sailor girl in original frame, 1940, F......................................$400.00 C

Cardboard, large horizontal truck side poster featuring mod couple on a motor scooter, 1960s, 67" x 32", VG..$125.00 C

Cardboard, large vertical poster featuring girl on diving board, 1939, G..$450.00 C

Cardboard, large vertical poster featuring girl with horse, 1938, EX...$1,000.00 B

Cardboard, large vertical poster featuring ice skater, 1940s, F..$80.00 D

Cardboard, "Let's watch for 'em," silhouette of running girl, 1950s, 66" x 32", VG................................$500.00 C

Cardboard, light pulls with original strings advertising King Size Coca-Cola, two sided, 1950 – 1960s, M, $35.00; in six pack, "puts you at your sparkling best," round, M ....$55.00 D

Cardboard litho of circus performers, framed, 1936, 18" x 27", EX ....$275.00 D

Cardboard, embossed die cut, easel back sign featuring girl in woods illustrated in a beveled mirror with advertising at bottom marked "Kaufmann and Strauss Company, New York," 1903, 4½" x 10½", EX, $15,500.00 B. *Courtesy of Muddy River Trading Co./Gary Metz.*

Cardboard, Enjoy Coke, price blank with the dynamic wave in the center, NM, $8.00 C. *Courtesy of Sam and Vivian Merryman.*

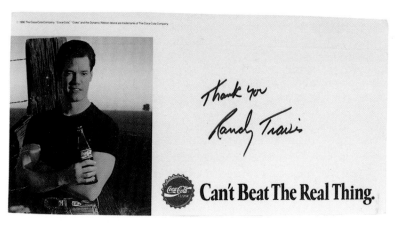

Cardboard, endorsement featuring Randy Travis with a bottle of Coke, 1990, 12" x 16", NM, $25.00 C. *Courtesy of Sam & Vivian Merryman.*

Cardboard, embossed die cut sign showing children sitting watching a show by a magic rabbit, extremely rare, 1890 – 1900s, 6½" x 7", NM, $16,000.00 B. *Courtesy of Muddy River Trading Co./Gary Metz.*

Cardboard, oval, string hung, denoting price, German, 1930s, EX ....$125.00 C

Cardboard, oval, string hung, denoting price, German, 1930s, F ....$75.00 D

Cardboard, panoramic view poster of couple in front of touring car, 1924, 32½" x 18", EX ....$800.00 D

Cardboard, "Party Pause," woman in clown suit, 1940s, 36" x 20", EX.......................................$400.00 C

Cardboard, "Party Pause," woman in clown suit, 1940s, 36" x 20", VG.......................................$395.00 C

Cardboard, "Popcorn Delicious with Ice Cold Coca-Cola," open box of popcorn on its side with Coca-Cola bull's-eye at right, 1950s, 15" x 12", EX............................$235.00 D

Cardboard poster, "At Ease ... for refreshment," military nurse in uniform holding a bottle, in original wooden frame, 1942, NM...$1,100.00 B

Cardboard poster, Bathing Girl on rocks at beach, 1938, 30" x 50", G ....$2,300.00 B

Cardboard poster, "Big Refreshment," girl with bowling ball, 1960s, 66" x 32", NM ....$725.00 B

Cardboard poster, "Big Refreshment," girl with bowling ball, 1960s, 66" x 32", EX ....$500.00 C

Cardboard, "Enjoy frosty, refreshing sugar free Fresca," with artwork of Fresca bottle and icy glass, 1960s, VG, $200.00 C.
Courtesy of Riverside Antique Mall.

Cardboard, horizontal, featuring silhouette girl running, "Let's watch for 'em," 1950s, 66" x 32", NM, $850.00 D.
Courtesy of Muddy River Trading Co./Gary Metz.

Cardboard, "Enjoy that refreshing new feeling!" with scene of scuba diving couple, 19" x 27", 1960s, G, $155.00 C.

Cardboard, horizontal, "Coke Party," with three girls around a table enjoying a Coke and sandwich, 1943, EX, $475.00 B. *Courtesy of Muddy River Trading Co./Gary Metz.*

Cardboard, girl with a bottle, 1940s, EX, $650.00 D. *Courtesy of Muddy River Trading Co./Gary Metz.*

Cardboard poster, bird on bell and bottle, in aluminum frame, 1954, EX ....$250.00 D

Cardboard poster, cameo, Lillian Nordica, 1905, VG ....$12,500.00 C

Cardboard poster, "Coke has the taste you never get tired of," with artwork of young girl with 45rpm record and bottle of Coke, 1960s, 36" x 20", EX ....$125.00 C

Cardboard poster, "Coke Time," cover girl with original frame, 1950s, 16" x 27", G ....$550.00 C

Cardboard poster, "Coke Time," cover girl with original frame, 1950s, 16" x 27", NM ....$800.00 B

Cardboard poster, "Coke Time," woman in cowboy hat and western neck scarf with bottle in hand framed by brands, 1955, EX ....$375.00 C

Cardboard poster, couple advertising six pack, framed and matted, 1940s, 16" x 27", F ....$350.00 C

Cardboard poster, die cut with food scene and bottles, 1939, 31" x 42", VG...$350.00 D

Cardboard poster, double sided, "Have A Coke" and Skater Girl on one side with "Refresh Yourself" with horses and riders, 1955, 16" x 27", EX...............................$235.00 C

Cardboard poster, double sided, "Have A Coke" and Skater Girl on one side with "Refresh Yourself" with horses and riders, 1955, 16" x 27", VG ....$250.00 C

Cardboard poster, double sided, one side "the Best of Taste," the other side "Enjoy the Quality Taste," 1956, 56" x 27", VG..$295.00 C

Cardboard, horizontal lettered, button right side, "Fountain Service," 1950, 30" x 12", EX, $450.00 B. *Courtesy of Muddy River Trading Co./Gary Metz.*

Cardboard, horizontal, "Home Refreshment," woman holding a bottle with flowers in the background, 1950s, 50" x 29", EX, $325.00 C. *Courtesy of Bill Mitchell.*

Cardboard, horizontal, "Drink Royal Palm Beverages Made from Pure Cane Sugar by the Coca-Cola Bottling Company," 1930s, 17" x 11¼", G, $135.00 C.

Cardboard, horizontal, "Inviting you to refreshment," EX, $650.00 B. *Courtesy of Muddy River Trading Co./Gary Metz.*

Cardboard, horizontal poster, "Planning hospitality," with artwork of hand taking bottle from six pack, 27" x 16", EX, $375.00 C. *Courtesy of Mitchell collection.*

Cardboard, horizontal, "Play Refreshed," with cowgirl enjoying a bottle of Coke, still in original gold frame, 1951, EX, $700.00 B. *Courtesy of Muddy River Trading Co./Gary Metz.*

Cardboard, horizontal poster, "Coke ... For Hospitality" featuring artwork of people at cookout, framed under glass, 1948, 36" x 24", NM, $425.00 B. *Courtesy of Muddy River Trading Co./Gary Metz.*

Cardboard poster, easel back, "Refresh Yourself," girl on chair with glass, 1926, 16" x 29½", EX ....$1,600.00 C

Cardboard poster, "Easy To Take Home," 1941, F ....$375.00 B

Cardboard poster, "Easy To Take Home," 1941, NM ....$450.00 C

Cardboard poster, Elaine with glass, same artwork that was used on the calendar of this year, 1915, EX ....$3,200.00 C

Cardboard, horizontal poster, "It's Twice Time...Twice the convenience," large truck sign, 67" x 32", 1960s, NM, $225.00 C. *Courtesy of Muddy River Trading Co./Gary Metz.*

Cardboard in wooden frame, "Betty," 1914, 30" x 38", VG, $2,750.00 D. *Courtesy of Mitchell collection.*

Cardboard, large horizontal "Mind reader!", woman on chaise being offered a bottle of Coke, EX, $625.00 C. *Courtesy of Muddy River Trading Co./Gary Metz.*

Cardboard, Hostess Girl, 1935, F, $200.00 C. *Courtesy of Muddy River Trading Co./Gary Metz.*

Cardboard, horizontal poster, "You taste its quality," featuring artwork of woman with flowers and a bottle of Coke, framed under glass, 1942, 36" x 20", NM, $1,150.00 B. *Courtesy of Muddy River Trading Co./Gary Metz.*

Cardboard, horizontal poster, "Here's Something Good," featuring party scene, 1951, EX, $350.00 B. *Courtesy of Muddy River Trading Co./Gary Metz.*

Cardboard poster featuring ballerinas, "Entertain your thirst," 1942, 16" x 27", F..................................$150.00 C

Cardboard poster featuring cartoon spaceman, 1960s, NM ....$195.00 C

Cardboard poster featuring cheerleader "Refresh yourself," 1944, 16" x 27", NM ....$1,250.00 C

Cardboard poster featuring elves with a carton on wagon, "Take enough Home," 1953, 16" x 27", G ....$195.00 C

Cardboard poster featuring girl at refrigerator, 1940, 16" x 27", EX ....$750.00 C

Cardboard poster featuring Hostess Girl, artwork by Hayden, 1935, 29" x 50", NM,............................$2,200.00 C

Cardboard poster, 5¢, framed under glass, 1930, 15" x 12", EX..$235.00 D

Cardboard poster, girl against a rock wall, resting from bicycle riding, from Niagara Litho, 1939, VG..$400.00 C

Cardboard poster, girl with a menu and a bottle, 1960s, 66" x 32", NM ....$675.00 B

Cardboard poster, "Have A Coke," a bottle against an iceberg, 1944, 36" x 20", EX ....$250.00 D

Cardboard poster, "Have A Coke," a bottle against an iceberg, 1944, 36" x 20", G....................................$195.00 C

29

Cardboard light pulls with original strings advertising King Size Coca-Cola, two sided, 1950 – 1960s, EX, $45.00 C.

Cardboard, large horizontal poster, featuring party scene with Coke iced down in a tub, hard to find item, 1952, F, $300.00 B. *Courtesy of Muddy River Trading Co./Gary Metz.*

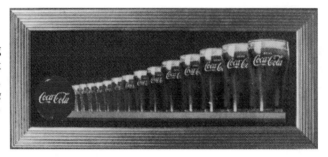

Cardboard, marching glasses, framed, 34" x 11", 1948, EX, $725.00 B. *Courtesy of Muddy River Trading Co./ Gary Metz.*

Cardboard, lobby poster featuring Clark Gable and Joan Crawford, "Dancing Lady," 1930s, EX, $1,900.00 B. *Courtesy of Muddy River Trading Co./Gary Metz.*

Cardboard, large vertical poster, "Mom knows her groceries," featuring woman at refrigerator, 1946, VG, $450.00 C. *Courtesy of Muddy River Trading Co./Gary Metz.*

Cardboard, lithograph, single side counter sign advertising a Coke and grilled cheese for 35¢, 11" x 16", 1952, G, $180.00 B. *Courtesy of Collectors Auction Services.*

Cardboard Merry Christmas price blank sign, 1992, EX, $6.00 C. *Courtesy Sam & Vivian Merryman.*

Cardboard poster, horizontal, "All set at our house," with boy holding cardboard six pack carrier, 1943, P ....$100.00 C

Cardboard poster, horizontal, "All set at our house," with boy holding cardboard six pack carrier, 1943, G ....$175.00 D

Cardboard poster, horizontal, "Be Really Refreshed," 1950s, G ....$95.00 C

Cardboard poster, horizontal, "Coca-Cola belongs," featuring couple with a picnic basket and a bucket of iced Coca-Cola, 1942, G ....$300.00 C

Cardboard poster, horizontal, "Coke belongs," 1940s, 36" x 20", F ....$225.00 C

Cardboard poster, horizontal, "Coke for me, too," couple with bottles and a hot dog, 1946, 36" x 20", G...$195.00 B

Cardboard poster, horizontal, "Coke knows no season," snow scene with a bottle in foreground and a couple of skiers in the background, framed, 1946, 62" x 33", F ....$250.00 C

Cardboard poster, horizontal, "Face your job refreshed," woman wearing visor beside a drill press, 59" x 30", F ....$375.00 C

Cardboard, "Party Pause," woman in clown suit, 1940s, 36" x 20", G, $350.00 C. *Courtesy of Mitchell collection.*

Cardboard poster, cameo, Lillian Nordica, 1905, F, $9,000.00 C.

Cardboard, "Pause," clown and an ice skater, in original wooden frame, 1930s, EX, $850.00 D. *Courtesy of Muddy River Trading Co./Gary Metz.*

Cardboard, "Play Refreshed," woman on a carousel horse, in original wooden frame, 1940s, EX, $1,200.00 B. *Courtesy of Muddy River Trading Co./Gary Metz.*

Cardboard poster, "Accepted home refreshment" with graphics of young couple sitting in front of a fireplace enjoying popcorn and bottled Cokes, 1942, VG, $425.00 B. *Courtesy of Muddy River Trading Co./Gary Metz.*

Cardboard poster advertising Coke Classic with an inviting message "This pizza calls for a Coke", with fold back to allow for counter top display, 11½" X 14½", NM, $25.00 C. *Courtesy of Sam and Vivian Merryman.*

Cardboard poster, horizontal, "Got enough Coke on ice?," three girls on sofa, one with phone receiver, framed, Canadian, 1945, VG.....................................$400.00 C

Cardboard poster, horizontal, "Got enough Coke on ice?" three girls on sofa, one with phone receiver, framed, Canadian, 1945, F ....$295.00 C

Cardboard poster, horizontal, "Have a Coke," 1944, 36" x 20", EX ....$195.00 C

Cardboard poster, horizontal, "Have a Coke," a bottle in snow, 1945, 36" x 20", G ....$175.00 C

Cardboard poster showing a bottle of Coke in a snow bank, 1946, NM, $550.00 B.
Courtesy of Muddy River Trading Co./Gary Metz.

Cardboard poster advertising the Red Hot Summer promotion and a chance to win "A Red Hot Summer Picnic Pack" with graphics of a picnic table complete with various Coke products, 18" x 25", NM, $35.00 C. *Courtesy of Sam and Vivian Merryman.*

Cardboard poster "Coke is Coca-Cola ... Coca-Cola is Coke," in original frame, 1949, EX, $600.00 C.
Courtesy of Muddy River Trading Co./Gary Metz.

Cardboard, poster "Coke Time," in original frame, 36" x 20", 1954, EX, $1,200.00 B.
Courtesy of Muddy River Trading Co./Gary Metz.

Cardboard poster, horizontal, "Have a Coke," cheerleader and a bottle, 1946, VG ....$425.00 C

Cardboard poster, horizontal, "Hello – Coke," couple with bottles, 1944, 36" x 20", EX ....$375.00 D

Cardboard poster, horizontal, "Hello Refreshment," woman in swimsuit coming out of swimming pool, 1940s, 36" x 20", VG ....$1,400.00 C

Cardboard poster, horizontal, "Here's to our G.I. Joes," 1944, F ....$150.00 C

Cardboard poster, horizontal, "He's Coming Home Tomorrow," woman in head scarf and coat with a picnic basket and a bottle, 1944, NM ....$1,300.00 C

Cardboard poster, horizontal, "Hospitality Coca-Cola," girl lighting a candle with a bottle in foreground, 1950, 59" x 30", VG ....$750.00 C

Cardboard poster, horizontal, "Hospitality in your hands," woman serving four bottles from tray, 1948, 36" x 20", VG..$275.00 C

Cardboard poster, horizontal, "Hospitality in your hands," woman serving four bottles from tray, 1948, 36" x 20", F ....$115.00 C

Cardboard poster, horizontal, "I'll bring the Coke," girl on phone at the foot of stairs, 1946, 36" x 20", EX..$350.00 C

Cardboard poster, horizontal, Italian, woman with a bottle, 1940s, 36" x 20", EX ....$425.00 C

Cardboard poster, horizontal, "Lunch Refreshed," 1943, G...$775.00 C

Cardboard poster, horizontal, majorette, "Refresh," 1952, 36" x 20", F ....$150.00 C

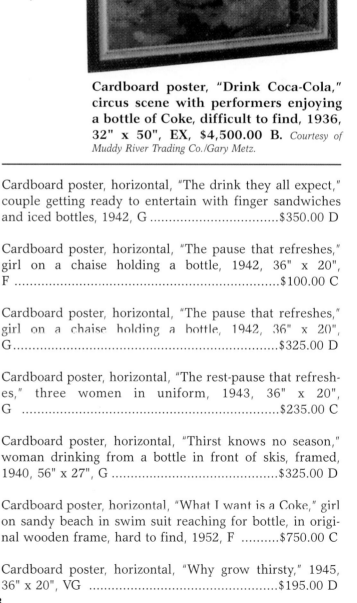

Cardboard poster, "Coke Time," woman in cowboy hat and western neck scarf, with bottle in hand, framed by brands, 1955, G, $300.00 C. *Courtesy of Mitchell collection.*

Cardboard poster, "Coke Convient," showing people enjoying a Coke and a six pack, 18" x 24", 1948, NM, $200.00 B. *Courtesy of Muddy River Trading Co./Gary Metz.*

Cardboard poster, "Come over for Coke," with hostess at serving table with food and bottles of Coke, 1947, 36" x 20", F, $255.00 D. *Courtesy of Collector's Auction Services.*

Cardboard poster, "Drink Coca-Cola," circus scene with performers enjoying a bottle of Coke, difficult to find, 1936, 32" x 50", EX, $4,500.00 B. *Courtesy of Muddy River Trading Co./Gary Metz.*

Cardboard poster, horizontal, majorette, "Refresh," 1952, 36" x 20", VG...$475.00 C

Cardboard poster, horizontal, "Now! for Coke," trapeze artist reaching for bottle, framed, 1959, 27" x 21", P ....$85.00 C

Cardboard poster, horizontal, "Now! for Coke," trapeze artist reaching for a bottle, framed, 1959, 27" x 21", VG...$325.00 C

Cardboard poster, horizontal, "Play refreshed," woman in cap with fishing rig and a bottle, 1950s, 36" x 20", G..$250.00 C

Cardboard poster, horizontal, "Refreshing," pretty girl holding sunglasses and a bottle, in a reproduction frame, 1948, EX ....$695.00 C

Cardboard poster, horizontal, "Shop refreshed," 1948, NM ....$1,400.00 B

Cardboard poster, horizontal, "The answer to thirst," 1945, 36" x 20", G..$135.00 D

Cardboard poster, horizontal, "The drink they all expect," couple getting ready to entertain with finger sandwiches and iced bottles, 1942, G ....$350.00 D

Cardboard poster, horizontal, "The pause that refreshes," girl on a chaise holding a bottle, 1942, 36" x 20", F ....$100.00 C

Cardboard poster, horizontal, "The pause that refreshes," girl on a chaise holding a bottle, 1942, 36" x 20", G...$325.00 D

Cardboard poster, horizontal, "The rest-pause that refreshes," three women in uniform, 1943, 36" x 20", G ....$235.00 C

Cardboard poster, horizontal, "Thirst knows no season," woman drinking from a bottle in front of skis, framed, 1940, 56" x 27", G ....$325.00 D

Cardboard poster, horizontal, "What I want is a Coke," girl on sandy beach in swim suit reaching for bottle, in original wooden frame, hard to find, 1952, F ....$750.00 C

Cardboard poster, horizontal, "Why grow thirsty," 1945, 36" x 20", VG ....$195.00 D

Cardboard poster, "Drink Coke in Bottles" in original wood gold frame featuring three boxers, the best known being Floyd Patterson, all three shown drinking bottled Coke, 1954, F, $375.00 B. *Courtesy of Muddy River Trading Co./Gary Metz.*

Cardboard poster, "for good eating," with staggered bottles, 1950s, 36" x 20", G, $250.00 C. *Courtesy of Mitchell collection.*

"Just a drink ... but what a drink!" introduced in 1928.

Cardboard poster, girl on lifeguard stand, 1929, 17" x 29¾", VG, $1,000.00 B. *Courtesy of Muddy River Trading Co./Gary Metz.*

Cardboard poster, girl coming out of swimming pool, 1942, EX, $600.00 B. *Courtesy of Muddy River Trading Co./Gary Metz.*

Cardboard poster, horizontal, "Why grow thirsty," 1945, 36" x 20", G .... $125.00 C

Cardboard poster, horizontal, with Coke cap, 66" x 32", EX .... $800.00 B

Cardboard poster, horizontal, "Zing together with Coke," party scene and cooler on table, 1962, 37" x 21", G .... $215.00 C

Cardboard poster, horizontal, "Zing together with Coke," party scene, cooler on table, 1962, 37" x 21", P .... $110.00 D

Cardboard poster, "Hospitality," artwork of woman and girl, both in sun bonnets, add $250.00 if in original wooden frame, 1950s, 36" x 20", EX.......................... $300.00 C

Cardboard poster, "It's a Family Affair," family holding Coca-Cola, 1941, 36" x 20", G .... $100.00 C

Cardboard poster, "It's Twice the Time, Twice the Value," 1960, 66" x 32", NM .... $800.00 D

Cardboard poster, Jeff Gordon Coca-Cola 600, 23" x 33", M .... $20.00 C

Cardboard poster, "Good taste for all," 1955, 16" x 27", NM, $250.00 D.
Courtesy of Muddy River Trading Co./ Gary Metz.

Cardboard poster, "Have a Coke," with skater, 1955, F, $500.00 B.
Courtesy of Muddy River Trading Co./Gary Metz.

Cardboard poster with the message "Home refreshment" featuring a young lady and a military man, in the original wood frame by Kay Displays, 1944, EX, $1,300.00 B.
Courtesy of Muddy River Trading Co./Gary Metz.

Cardboard poster, horizontal, "All set at our house," with boy holding cardboard six pack carrier, 1943, EX, $650.00 B. *Courtesy of Muddy River Trading Co./Gary Metz.*

Cardboard poster, horizontal, "Be really refreshed... Enjoy Coke"/"Take Home Plenty of Coke," with scene at swimming pool, 1959, 21½" x 37½", G, $295.00 C.

Cardboard poster, horizontal, "Coca-Cola belongs," featuring couple with a picnic basket and a bucket of iced Coca-Cola, 1942, EX, $750.00 B. *Courtesy of Muddy River Trading Co./Gary Metz.*

Cardboard poster, "Just a Drink But What a Drink," girl in bathing attire on lifeguard stand, 1929, 17" x 29¾", F ....$325.00 D

Cardboard poster, large horizontal, "A Coke belongs," young boy and girl with a bottle, in original Coke frame, 1944, EX ....$950.00 C

Cardboard poster, large horizontal, "Accepted Home Refreshment," couple in front of warm fireplace, 1942, G...$750.00 D

Cardboard poster, large horizontal, couple at open refrigerator with bottles, "Welcome Home," 1944, EX...$475.00 D

Cardboard poster, large horizontal, girl on beach, in original Coke frame, 1953, EX ....$1,250.00 D

Cardboard poster, large horizontal, "Good Pause Drink Coca-Cola in Bottles," 1954, 36" x 20", EX ....$675.00 C

Cardboard poster, large horizontal, "The pause that refreshes at home," framed, 1940s, 56" x 27", G...$275.00 C

Cardboard poster, large vertical, a soldier and a girl with bicycles and bottles, in original wooden frame, 1943, G ....$525.00 C

Cardboard poster, horizontal, "Coke belongs," young couple with a bottle, 1944, EX, $700.00 B.
Courtesy of Muddy River Trading Co./Gary Metz.

"Coke belongs" introduced in 1941.

Cardboard poster, horizontal, "Coke for me, too," couple with bottles and a hot dog, 1946, 36" x 20", EX, $375.00 C.

Cardboard poster, horizontal, "Coke Time ... Join the friendly circle," people in pool around cooler on float, 1955, 36" x 20", EX, $375.00 B. *Courtesy of Muddy River Trading Co./Gary Metz.*

Cardboard poster, horizontal, "Coke knows no season," snow scene with a bottle in foreground and a couple of skiers in the background, framed, 1946, 62" x 33", G, $350.00 C.

Cardboard poster, large vertical, couple and man in navy uniform, 1943, G ....$800.00 C

Cardboard poster of woman with straw hat in water, 1960s, 36" x 20", F..$95.00 C

Cardboard poster, "On The Refreshing Side," 1941, 30" x 50", G ....$425.00 D

Cardboard poster, one part of a series, "Through the years" with Victorian era advertising, 1939, 16" x 27", NM ....$950.00 C

Cardboard poster, part of "Through the Years," Victorian advertising series, 1939, 16" x 27", G.................$750.00 D

Cardboard poster, "Play Refreshed," tennis girl sitting on drink box holding a bottle, in reproduction frame, 1949, 16" x 27", G..$500.00 D

Cardboard poster, Reece Tatum of the Harlem Globetrotters holding a basketball with a bottle on top of the ball, 1952, 16" x 27", EX ....$700.00 C

Cardboard poster, "Refreshing," girl in water, 1960, 36" x 20", EX ....$150.00 C

Cardboard poster, seated Chinese girl, 1936, 14½" x 22", NM..$1,300.00 D

Cardboard poster, "Serve Coke At Home," 1949, EX ....$375.00 C

Cardboard poster, horizontal, "Face your job refreshed," woman wearing visor beside a drill press, 59" x 30", VG, $800.00 C.

Cardboard poster, horizontal, "Hello Refreshment," woman in swim suit coming out of swimming pool, 1940s, 36" x 20", EX, $1,700.00 B.
Courtesy of Muddy River Trading Co./Gary Metz.

Cardboard poster, horizontal, "Got enough Coke on ice?," three girls on sofa, one with phone receiver, framed, Canadian, 1945, G, $350.00 C.

Cardboard poster, "So Delicious," snow ski scene, 1954, 36" x 20", NM ....$600.00 C

Cardboard poster, "So Refreshing," boy and girl by pool, 1946, 30" x 50", EX ....$700.00 D

Cardboard poster, "The Best of Taste," girl being offered a bottle, 1956, G ....$250.00 C

Cardboard poster, "Things go better with Coke" in original frame, 1960s, 16" x 27", G ....$275.00 D

Cardboard poster, "Tingling Refreshment," girl with a glass waving, 1931, 21" x 38", VG ....$350.00 D

Cardboard poster, vertical, "And Coke Too," 1946, 16" x 27", EX ....$350.00 D

Cardboard poster, vertical, "Coke headquarters," 1947, G ....$175.00 C

Cardboard poster, vertical, "Coke Time," in original wooden frame, 1943, G ....$650.00 C

Cardboard poster, vertical, couple, woman in swim suit with large brim hat, 1934, 29" x 50", EX ....$2,700.00 C

Cardboard poster, vertical, "Extra-Bright Refreshment," couple at party holding bottles, 33" x 53", G ....$125.00 D

Cardboard poster, vertical, "Face the sun refreshed," pretty girl in white dress shielding her eyes from the sun with one hand while holding a bottle with the other, 1941, 30" x 53½", G...$500.00 C

Cardboard poster, horizontal, "Hospitality Coca-Cola," girl lighting a candle with a bottle in foreground, 1950, 59" x 30", EX, $900.00 D.

Cardboard poster, horizontal, "Play refreshed," woman in cap with fishing rig and a bottle, 1950s, 36" x 20", VG, $375.00 C. *Courtesy of Mitchell collection.*

Cardboard poster, horizontal, "The drink they all expect," couple getting ready to entertain with finger sandwiches and iced bottles, 1942, NM, $600.00 B. *Courtesy of Muddy River Trading Co./Gary Metz.*

Cardboard poster, horizontal, "Me too," young boy looking up at large bottle, two sided, 62" x 33", G, $500.00 C.

Cardboard poster, vertical, "For People on the Go," 1944, 16" x 27", G..............................$275.00 D

Cardboard poster, vertical, "For the party," soldier and woman on bicycle for two, 29" x 50½", VG ......$300.00 C

Cardboard poster, vertical, French Canadian, 1947, 16" x 27", VG ....$250.00 D

Cardboard poster, vertical, "Happy Ending to Thirst," 1940s, 16" x 27", EX ....$400.00 D

Cardboard poster, vertical, "Happy Ending to Thirst," 1940s, 16" x 27", VG ....$350.00 D

Cardboard poster, vertical, "Have a Coke, Coca-Cola," couple at masquerade ball, framed under glass, rare item, EX ....$775.00 C

Cardboard poster, vertical, "Have a Coke, Coca-Cola," couple at masquerade ball, framed under glass, rare item, VG ....$550.00 C

Cardboard poster, vertical, "Home Refreshment," framed under glass, EX................................$1,800.00 C

Cardboard poster, vertical, "Just Like Old Times," 1945, 16" x 27", EX ....$400.00 C

Cardboard poster, vertical, "Let's have a Coke," cooler and majorette, 1946, 16" x 27", G ....$125.00 C

Cardboard poster, vertical, man and woman advertising bottle sales, 1930 – 40s, 18" x 36", VG ....$675.00 C

Cardboard poster, vertical, man in uniform and girl walking, each with a bottle, 1944, NM.................$1,250.00 D

Cardboard poster, vertical, mother and daughter at table opening bottle, French Canadian, 1946, 16" x 27, VG..$300.00 C

Cardboard poster, vertical, "Play Refreshed," 1949, VG..$850.00 D

Cardboard poster, vertical, "Refreshment," pretty girl in fancy dress at a pool setting with bottles on table, 1949, 33½" x 54", EX ....$550.00 D

Cardboard poster, vertical, "Right off the ice," girl at ice skating rink, 1946, 16" x 27", G ....$235.00 D

Cardboard poster, horizontal, "The rest-pause that refreshes," three women in uniform, 1943, 36" x 20", EX, $425.00 B. *Courtesy of Muddy River Trading Co./Gary Metz.*

Cardboard poster, horizontal, "The pause that refreshes," girl in yellow dress propped against table holding a bottle, in a reproduction frame, 36" x 20", EX, $925.00 B. *Courtesy of Muddy River Trading Co./Gary Metz.*

"The pause that refreshes" introduced in 1929.

Cardboard poster, horizontal, "They all want Coca-Cola," girl delivering a tray with four hamburgers, framed under glass, 36" x 20", EX, $425.00 C. *Courtesy of Muddy River Trading Co./Gary Metz.*

Cardboard poster, horizontal, "To be refreshed," girl holding a bottle in each hand, in reproduction frame, 1948, EX, $450.00 C. *Courtesy of Muddy River Trading Co./Gary Metz.*

Cardboard poster, vertical, same scene that appears on the 1936 serving tray, the Hostess, framed and under glass, 1935, Hayden, VG .... $750.00 C

Cardboard poster, vertical, "Start Refreshed," couple at roller skating rink, 1943, 16" x 27", VG .... $325.00 C

Cardboard poster, vertical, "Talk about refreshing," girl in rain with umbrella in front of cooler holding a bottle, 1942, 16" x 27", NM .... $750.00 D

Cardboard poster, vertical, "The drink they all expect," similar to horizontal poster of this year but showing full length artwork of couple preparing for entertaining, 1942, F .... $150.00 C

Cardboard poster, vertical, "Thirst knows no season," couple building a snowman, graphics are great, 1942, 30" x 50", G .... $375.00 D

Cardboard poster, vertical, two sided, bottle on one side and target and bottle on the other side, French Canadian, 1951, EX .... $250.00 D

Cardboard poster, vertical, two sided, bottle on one side and target and bottle on the other side, French Canadian, 1951, G .... $125.00 C

Cardboard poster, vertical, with large bottle in foreground and places and events in background, "58 Million a Day," 1957, 17½" x 28½", P .... $75.00 D

Cardboard poster, horizontal, "Thirst knows no season," woman drinking from a bottle in front of skis, framed, 1940, 56" x 27", EX, $500.00 C.
Courtesy of Muddy River Trading Co./Gary Metz.

Cardboard poster, horizontal, "Welcome Home," 1944, 36" x 20", VG, $375.00 C. *Courtesy of Muddy River Trading Co./Gary Metz.*

Cardboard poster, horizontal, "What I want is a Coke," girl on sandy beach in swimsuit reaching for a bottle, in original wooden frame, hard to find, 1952, VG, $1,100.00 D.

Cardboard poster, large horizontal, "Good Pause Drink Coca-Cola in Bottles," 1954, 36" x 20", G, $500.00 C. *Courtesy of Mitchell collection.*

Cardboard poster, in frame, featuring girl in swim suit with a bottle of Coke, "Yes," 1947, 15" x 25", F, $375.00 B. *Courtesy of Muddy River Trading Co./Gary Metz.*

Cardboard poster, "Welcome Aboard," nautical theme, 1958, 36" x 20", NM ....$400.00 C

Cardboard poster, "Wherever thirst goes," great graphics of girl in row boat with a bucket of iced Coca-Cola, 1942, G ....$475.00 C

Cardboard poster, "Wherever you go," travel scenes in background, 1950s, G ....$175.00 D

Cardboard poster, woman sitting wearing a broad brimmed hat with flowers, holding a Coca-Cola 5¢ bamboo fan and a glass, framed, 1912, F ....$2,200.00 D

Cardboard poster, "Yes," girl on beach with bottle, 1946, 56" x 27", VG ....$350.00 D

Cardboard rack display, vertical, "Take more than one," 1960s, 16" x 27", EX ....$115.00 D

Cardboard, red-haired woman in yellow scarf with cup of Coca-Cola, in original aluminum frame, 1951, 13" x 11", NM ....$675.00 D

Cardboard, "Serve Yourself," hand in cup, in original aluminum frame, 1951, 13" x 11", VG ....$95.00 C

Cardboard, sign advertising a hamburger and a bottle of Coke, 17" x 12", 1950s, EX.................................$65.00 C

Cardboard, poster, in original gold frame, "Hospitality in your hands," featuring hostess with tray of Cokes, 1948, EX, $425.00 B. *Courtesy of Muddy River Trading Co./Gary Metz.*

Cardboard poster, large horizontal, "America's Favorite Moment," a couple in a diner booth, each with a bottle, 1940s, 36" x 20", EX, $295.00 C. *Courtesy of Muddy River Trading Co./Gary Metz.*

Cardboard poster, "Join the friendly circle," double sided in original wood gold frame, young people gathered around a Coke cooler on the grass, 1954, G, $500.00 B. *Courtesy of Muddy River Trading Co./Gary Metz.*

Cardboard poster, horizontal, "Lunch Refreshed," 1943, EX, $1,000.00 B. *Courtesy of Muddy River Trading Co./Gary Metz.*

Cardboard poster, Lunch Refreshed" with great graphics of waitress serving bottled Coca-Cola and sandwiches from a tray, difficult to locate, 1948, 16" x 27", NM, $1,600.00 B. *Courtesy of Muddy River Trading Co./Gary Metz.*

Cardboard, poster, large vertical, "Drink Coca-Cola 50th Anniversary," two women in period dress of 1886 and 1936 sitting together, 1936, 27" x 47", VG, $1,250.00 B. *Courtesy of Muddy River Trading Co./Gary Metz.*

Cardboard, sign featuring girl with bowling ball, 1960s, 66" x 32", NM ....$650.00 D

Cardboard six pack bottle display with motorized hand in bottle that moves up and down, "Take Enough Home," 1950s, EX ....$425.00 D

Cardboard, small vertical, "So refreshing" with woman in white spotlight, 1941, EX................................$750.00 C

Cardboard, sports favorite, hanging, complete set consists of 10 signs; individual signs go in the $85.00 – $110.00 range, 1947, G ....$1,200.00 C

Cardboard poster, lady about to enjoy a Coke from the bottle, 1957, NM, $400.00 B. *Courtesy of Muddy River Trading Co./Gary Metz.*

Cardboard poster, MGM actress Florine McKinney sitting on patio table, 1935, 13½" x 30", F, $425.00 B. *Courtesy of Muddy River Trading Co./Gary Metz.*

Cardboard, poster, Lillian Nordica, "Coca-Cola Delicious and Refreshing 5¢," standing beside Coca-Cola table with her hand resting on screen at rear of room, rare, 1904, 26" x 40", EX, $9,000.00 C.

Cardboard poster, majorette with a bottle of Coke and the message "Refresh," 1952, G, $250.00 B. *Courtesy of Muddy River Trading Co./Gary Metz.*

Cardboard poster, "Pause and Refresh," great graphics of girl drinking a glass of Coke at soda fountain, counter and dispenser shown, 1948, 41" x 23½", NM, $2,300.00 B. *Courtesy of Muddy River Trading Co./Gary Metz.*

Cardboard poster, "Play refreshed," young lady in tennis attire sitting on a Coke lift top floor cooler, enjoying a bottle of Coke, 1949, NM, $2,700.00 B. *Courtesy of Muddy River Trading Co./Gary Metz.*

Cardboard poster, "Now for a Coke", 36" x 20", 1951, NM, $1250.00 B. *Courtesy of Muddy River Trading Co./Gary Metz.*

Cardboard, St. Louis Fair, woman sitting at table with a flare glass that has a syrup line, 1909, G ....$4,700.00 C

Cardboard, stand up, Jeff Gordon & Coke, 1995, NM ....$150.00 D

Cardboard store display, inside, featuring girl in roses, 1937, 52" x 34", Hayden Hayden, EX ....$5,000.00 C

Cardboard, "Things go better with Coke" sign with gold frame, 1950s – 60s, 24" x 20", VG ....$250.00 D

Cardboard, three piece panel "The Dahlias," with Coca-Cola logo at top, extremely rare, EX ....$25,000.00 D

Cardboard, 3-D, "Boy oh Boy," pictures boy in front of cooler with a bottle in hand, 1937, 36" x 34", EX ....$1,700.00 C

Cardboard, 3-D cut-out sign featuring a sandwich and a glass, 1958, 17" x 20", EX ....$95.00 D

Cardboard, 3-D, "On Your Break," self-framing, 1950s, G..$95.00 D

Cardboard poster, pretty girl cheerleader with a megaphone and a bottle of Coke, and the message "Have a Coke," 1946, EX, $750.00 B. *Courtesy of Muddy River Trading Co./Gary Metz.*

Cardboard poster, pretty lady enjoying a bottle of Coke and the message 'Refreshing," in original gold frame, 1949, G, $375.00 B. *Courtesy of Muddy River Trading Co./Gary Metz.*

Cardboard poster, pretty red headed young lady at pool's edge with a bottle of Coke, message reads "Cooling Lift," 1958, EX, $500.00 B. *Courtesy of Muddy River Trading Co./Gary Metz.*

Cardboard poster, pretty young lady being offered a bottle of Coke and the message "The best of taste," 1956, VG, $350.00 B. *Courtesy of Muddy River Trading Co./Gary Metz.*

Cardboard poster promoting a free trip to the NFL Pro Bowl in Hawaii with message and price board at right of graphics, NM, $12.00 C. *Courtesy of Sam and Vivian Merryman.*

Cardboard, 3-D, "On Your Break," self-framing, 1950s, VG ....$135.00 C

Cardboard, trifold display of movie star Madge Evans holding a glass of Coke, 42" x 31", 1935, EX ....$1,550.00 C

Cardboard, trolley car sign, "Delicious and Refreshing Drink Coca-Cola At Fountains Everywhere 5¢", 1905, 20½" x 10¾", VG ....$2,500.00 B

Cardboard, trolley car sign featuring a woman sitting off the side of a hammock holding a glass, 1912, EX ....$3,600.00 C

Cardboard, trolley car sign featuring a woman sitting off the side of hammock holding glass, 1912, F ..$2,100.00 C

Cardboard, trolley car sign, "Tired? Coca-Cola Relieves Fatigue," young man at dispensers, 1907, VG ..$2,000.00 C

Cardboard, trolley sign, double long, "Yes," 1946, 28" x 11", NM..$825.00 C

Cardboard, trolley sign, "Anytime Everywhere ... The Favorite Beverage," 21" x 11", 1910s, EX ....$1,900.00 C

Cardboard, trolley sign, "Drink Coca-Cola Delicious and Refreshing," 21" x 11", VG ....$975.00 C

Cardboard, truck poster, hard to find, girl in water, 1960s, 67" x 32", NM ....$125.00 C

Cardboard, truck poster, "Refreshing new feeling," 1960s, 67" x 32", EX ....$135.00 C

Cardboard, truck poster, "Yield to the Children," hard to find, NM ....$400.00 C

Cardboard, vertical, "Be Really Refreshed...Enjoy Coke!," woman at beach picnic with a bottle, 1959, 16" x 27", EX..$225.00 D

Cardboard, vertical, "Be Really Refreshed," girl in party dress, "Drink..." button in lower left, 1960s, 16" x 27", EX..$205.00 D

Cardboard, vertical, "Coke Time," bottle in hand with woman's face, "Drink..." button in lower center, 1954, 16" x 27", EX..$325.00 D

Cardboard, vertical, "Come and get it," farm bell and a bottle, "Drink..." button in lower right, in original wooden frame, 1954, 16" x 27", EX..............................$375.00 C

Cardboard, vertical, "Come and get it," western dinner gong behind a bottle, "Drink..." button in lower right, 1952, 16" x 27", EX ....$300.00 C

Cardboard poster, "Shop Refreshed," young girl in front of a countain dispenser enjoying her Coke from a glass, 1948, 41" x 23½", NM, $2,000.00 B. *Courtesy of Muddy River Trading Co./Gary Metz.*

Cardboard poster, "So Delicious" with ski scene in background and a pretty young lady in the foreground with a bottle of Coke, 1950s, VG, $475.00 B. *Courtesy of Muddy River Trading Co./Gary Metz.*

Cardboard poster featuring sports stars Jesse Owens and Alice Coachman with bottles of Coke and the message "Quality you can trust," 1952, EX, $925.00 B. *Courtesy of Muddy River Trading Co./Gary Metz.*

Cardboard poster string hanger, "Familiar refreshment," bottle of Coke and plate with sandwich, 1940, 14" x 31", F, $250.00 B. *Courtesy of Muddy River Trading Co./Gary Metz.*

Cardboard poster with graphics of snowman with his arm around an oversized bottle of Coke, Canadian and difficult to find, 1941, 16" x 27", NM, $225.00 B. *Courtesy Muddy River Trading Co./Gary Metz.*

Cardboard poster, "Talk about refreshing," two young ladies on a blanket at the beach enjoying a bottle of Coke, 1943, VG, $800.00 B. *Courtesy of Muddy River Trading Co./Gary Metz.*

Cardboard, vertical double sided sign, "The best of taste" on one side, "Enjoy the quality taste" on the other, 1956, 56" x 27", VG ....$250.00 D

Cardboard, vertical, "For Holiday Entertaining," six bottle carton 36¢, featuring Christmas decor, Canadian, 1950, 12½" x 18½", EX ....$115.00 C

Cardboard, vertical, "For Holiday Entertaining," six bottle carton 36¢, featuring Christmas decor, Canadian, 1950, 12½" x 18½", VG ....$95.00 D

Cardboard, vertical, "Now Coke in handy Plastic Cartons," eight pack, easel back, 1960s, 16" x 27", EX ....$100.00 D

Cardboard, vertical poster featuring bathing beauty, great graphics, 1934, 29" x 50", EX ....$2,700.00 B

Cardboard, vertical poster featuring fishing girl, 1953, 16" x 27", EX ....$600.00 C

Cardboard, vertical poster featuring girl at beach, framed under glass, 1930s, G ....$1,150.00 C

Cardboard, vertical poster featuring girl on sidewalk, "So easy to carry home," 1942, 16" x 27", EX..........$800.00 C

Cardboard, vertical poster featuring girl standing beside a cooler with an umbrella, 1942, F ....$125.00 C

Cardboard, vertical poster featuring girl with a tennis racquet, 1945, EX .... $525.00 D

Cardboard, vertical poster featuring girl with umbrella in front of cooler, "Talk about refreshing," 1942, 16" x 27", VG ....$375.00 C

The pause that refreshes

Cardboard poster, "The pause that refreshes," girl on beach in swim suit, add $250.00 if in original aluminum frame, 1950s, 36" x 20", F, $300.00 C. *Courtesy of Mitchell collection.*

Cardboard poster, "The best is always the better buy," girl with grocery sack and six pack, framed under glass, 1943, EX, $975.00 B. *Courtesy of Muddy River Trading Co./Gary Metz.*

Cardboard poster, "Things go better with Coke," part of a larger unit, 24" x 20", 1950 – 1960s, VG, $160.00 B. *Courtesy of Muddy River Trading Co./Gary Metz.*

Cardboard poster, "Take Coke along," 16" x 27", 1951, EX, $700.00 B. *Courtesy of Muddy River Trading Co./Gary Metz.*

Cardboard poster, three women, "Friendly pause," 1948, 16" x 27", NM, $1,500.00 B. *Courtesy of Muddy River Trading Co./Gary Metz.*

Cardboard poster, two couples enjoying themselves, Coke in bottles shown, in original gold frame that has been restored, 1954, NM, $600.00 B. *Courtesy of Muddy RiverTrading Co./Gary Metz.*

Cardboard, vertical poster featuring woman in yellow dress, walking in rain with an umbrella, 1942, VG ....$475.00 C

Cardboard, vertical poster with a couple at "Coke Time" and a six pack in spotlight at bottom, 1943, G ....$275.00 C

Cardboard, vertical poster, with girl on ping pong table, framed under glass, Canadian, 14" x 28", EX ....$675.00 C

Cardboard, vertical poster with girl on ping pong table, framed under glass, Canadian, 14" x 28", VG....$600.00 D

Cardboard, vertical, "So Refreshing," Autumn Girl in art work, 1940, 16" x 27", EX ....$575.00 C

Cardboard, vertical, "So Refreshing," Autumn Girl in art-work, 1940, 16" x 27", VG ....$500.00 D

Cardboard, vertical, "The pause that refreshes," couple with bottles, "Drink..." button over woman's head, original wooden frame, 1959, 16" x 27", VG ....$400.00 D

Cardboard, "Welcome friend," red and white lettering on simulated oak background, 1957, 14" x 12", VG ....$250.00 C

Cardboard, window display, cameo fold out, 1913, G ....$3,500.00 D

45

Cardboard poster, "Time out for food and drink," showing pretty young lady enjoying a bottle of Coke, 1938, G, $625.00 B. *Courtesy of Muddy River Trading Co./Gary Metz.*

Cardboard poster, two young ladies with a globe and a bottle of Coke, and the message "Here's to our G.I. Joes," 1944, G, $600.00 B. *Courtesy of Muddy River Trading Co./Gary Metz.*

Cardboard poster, vertical, "Coke headquarters," 1947, EX, $395.00 C. *Courtesy of Gary Metz.*

Cardboard poster, vertical, "Coke Time," head shot of woman, bottle in hand, and various sports activities, 1950s, F, $225.00 C. *Courtesy of Mitchell collection.*

Cardboard poster, vertical, "Coke Time," in original wooden frame, EX, $950.00 B. *Courtesy of Muddy River Trading Co./Gary Metz.*

Cardboard poster, vertical, "Drink Coca-Cola Delicious and Refreshing," cowboy holding a bottle, 1941, 16" x 27", G, $550.00 C. *Courtesy of Mitchell collection.*

Cardboard, window display, die cut, depicting a circus, large center piece is 4' x 3', a separate girl and ring master are approx. 30" tall, three scenes, clown at big top, vendors and tents, ringmaster and girl, 1932, VG ....$4,500.00 D

Cardboard window display, die cut, depicting a circus, large center piece is 4' x 3', a separate girl and ring master is approx. 30" tall, three scenes, clown at big top, vendors and tents, ringmaster and girl, 1932, EX ....$5,500.00 D

Cardboard, window display, trifold, Wallace Beery and Jackie Cooper sitting in director's chairs with a bottle in between them, 1934, 43" x 31½", G ....$1,800.00 D

Cardboard window display, tri-fold, Wallace Berry and Jackie Cooper sitting in director's chairs with a bottle in between them, 1934, 43" x 31½", VG ....$2,750.00 B

Celluloid bottle, "Drink Coca-Cola Delicious and Refreshing," 1900, 6" x 13¼", F.................................$1,800.00 C

Celluloid disc, foreign, Spanish, rare, yellow and white on red, 1940s, 9", NM ....$350.00 D

Celluloid, hand in bottle, foreign, 6½" x 16", G ....$135.00 C

46

Cardboard poster, vertical, "Drink Coca-Cola" upper left hand corner, girl on towel at beach, bottle, framed under glass, rare, hard to find, 1930s, 30" x 50", EX, $1,700.00 B. *Courtesy of Muddy River Trading Co./Gary Metz.*

Cardboard poster, vertical, "Entertain your thirst," two ballerinas at a green bench, framed under glass, 1942, 16" x 27", VG, $600.00 C. *Courtesy of Muddy River Trading Co./Gary Metz.*

Cardboard poster, vertical, "Drink Coca-Cola" on button, girl at stadium in the fall holding a program and a bottle, framed under glass, 1940, 30" x 50", EX, $1,400.00 B. *Courtesy of Muddy River Trading Co./Gary Metz.*

Actress Pauline Moore was the model for this piece of art.

Cardboard poster, vertical, double sided, Old Man North on one side and bottles on the other, French Canadian, 16" x 27", $200.00 C. *Courtesy of Muddy River Trading Co./Gary Metz.*

Cardboard poster, vertical, "Drink Coca-Cola," Hostess Girl, 1935, 30" x 50", G, $375.00 C. *Courtesy of Muddy River Trading Co./Gary Metz.*

Celluloid over tin, "Refresh Yourself Drink Coca-Cola," probably manufactured in the U.S.A. for use in Canada, yellow & white on red with green frame, 1930s, 11¾" x 6", EX .... $1,800.00 C

Celluloid, round, "Coca-Cola," white lettering on top of a bottle in center with red background, 1950s, 9" diameter, G .... $165.00 C

Celluloid, round, hanging on easel back, "Delicious Coca-Cola Refreshing," white and black lettering on red background, 1940, VG .... $180.00 D

Celluloid sign, "Delicious and Refreshing," red, 1940s, 9" diameter, NM .... $275.00 D

Coca-Cola fashion girl, one of four fashion girls, framed and under glass, 1932, VG .... $5,000.00 C

Decal, bottle in hand, EX .... $35.00 D

"Face the sun refreshed" introduced in 1941.

Cardboard poster, vertical, "Face the sun refreshed," pretty girl in white dress shielding her eyes from the sun with one hand while holding a bottle with the other, 1941, 30" x 53½", VG, $625.00 C.

Cardboard poster, vertical, "Extra-Bright Refreshment," couple at party holding bottles, 33" x 53", EX, $295.00 C.

Decal, "Drink Coca-Cola In Bottles," mounted on glass, 1950s, 15" x 9", NM...$85.00 C

Decal, "Drink Coca-Cola in Bottles," on glass, framed, 1950s, 15" x 18", EX ....$95.00 C

Decal, "Drink Coca-Cola In Bottles," red background with white and yellow lettering, 1950s, 16" x 8", EX .. $85.00 C

Decal, "Drink" emblem on triangle, "Ice and Cold" by bottle, 1934, 15" x 18", NM ....$165.00 D

Decal, "Drink," fishtail logo, foil, NM ....$35.00 D

Decal, "Enjoy That Refreshing New Feeling," fishtail logo, M ....$40.00 D

Decal, fishtail logo with sprig of leaves, EX ....$45.00 C

Decal for Fanta root beer, "Enjoy Fanta Root Beer," 8" x 4", 1960s, EX ....$5.00 C

Decal for window, featuring bottle on blue background with original envelope, 1940s, 8" x 13½", EX...$35.00 D

Decal promoting Fanta orange featuring a glass of the product, 1960s, EX ....$10.00 C

Decal, "Thank You Come Again," on bow tie emblem, foil, 1950s, NM...$35.00 D

Decal, "Things Go Better With Coke," 1960, NM ....$35.00 D

Decal, white background, has been sanded down and reworked, 1950s, 24", NM ....$300.00 B

Die cut bottle sign, 1953, 3' tall, EX ....$350.00 D

Cardboard poster, vertical, "For the party," soldier and woman on bicycle for two, 29" x 50½", EX, $475.00 C. *Courtesy of Muddy River Trading Co./Gary Metz.*

Cardboard poster, vertical framed, "Home Refreshment on the way," 24½" x 50", VG, $650.00 C. *Courtesy of Muddy River Trading Co./Gary Metz.*

Decal, "Drink Coca-Cola Ice Cold," 1960, EX...$40.00 D

Decal, "Drink Coca-Cola Ice Cold," 1960, G ......$30.00 D

Cardboard poster, vertical, "Have a Coke, Coca-Cola," couple at masquerade ball, framed under glass, rare item, F, $250.00 C.

Cardboard poster, vertical, "Have a Coke," girl with bottle in each hand in front of drink machine, 1940s, 16" x 27", EX, $350.00 C. *Courtesy of Muddy River Trading Co./Gary Metz.*

Cardboard poster, vertical, "Home refreshment," woman holding a bottle with the refrigerator door ajar, 1950s, 16" x 27", NM, $550.00 B. *Courtesy of Muddy River Trading Co./Gary Metz.*

Die cut original artwork of boy with Coke glass, framed under glass, 1940s, 8" x 14", EX ....$1,375.00 C

Dispenser sign featuring stainless band around border, red on white, 1950s, 27" x 28", EX..........................$900.00 B

"Drink Coca-Cola, Cures Headache ... Relieves Exhaustion at Soda Fountains 5¢," framed under glass, 1890 – 1900s, EX ....$1,250.00 C

Fountain service sign, two sided, features early dispenser, red on yellow background, 1941, 25" x 26", NM..$2,200.00 B

Glass and metal frame menu board with fishtail logo at top center, 1960s, 37" x 20", VG ....$475.00 D

Glass and metal light-up, "work safely, work refreshed," 1950s, 16" x 16", VG ....$475.00 C

Glass framed sign featuring a bell-shaped glass with diminishing logo at top, hard-to-find piece, 1930s, 6" x 9½", M ....$2,000.00 C

Glass front light-up, "Have a Coke" with cup at right, 1950s, 17" x 10", EX ....$1,425.00 C

Glass front light-up, metal frame, "Lunch With Us," 1950s, 18" x 8", EX...$750.00 C

Glass front light-up, "Please Pay When Served," located on top of courtesy panel, 1950s, 18" x 8", EX ....$650.00 C

Glass front light-up, "Please Pay When Served," located on top of courtesy panel, 1950s, 18" x 8", VG........$600.00 D

Glass light-up, hand and bottle, probably an independent sign made by a bottler, unusual, 14" x 10½", EX ....$1,200.00 D

Glass light-up, hanging, "Have A Coca-Cola," 1948, 20" x 12", EX ....$550.00 D

Glass light-up, "Have A Coke, Refresh Yourself" with red arrow, 1950s, 10" x 17", EX..........................$1,200.00 C

Glass light-up, "Have A Coke, Refresh Yourself" with red arrow, 1950s, 10" x 17", NM ....$1,300.00 C

Glass light-up, NOS, Coca-Cola Beverage Department, fishtail, 1960s, 50" x 14", M ....$375.00 C

Glass light-up, 20 oz. bottle, 1994, EX ....$175.00 C

Glass, round mirror, "Drink Carbonated Coca-Cola 5¢ in Bottles," EX ....$600.00 C

Cardboard poster, vertical, "Nothing refreshes like a Coke," couple on bicycles, 1943, EX, $1,700.00 B. *Courtesy of Muddy River Trading Co./Gary Metz.*

Cardboard poster, vertical, mother and daughter at table opening bottle, French Canadian, 1946, 16" x 27", $235.00 B. *Courtesy of Muddy River Trading Co./ Gary Metz.*

Cardboard poster, vertical, "Let's have a Coke," cooler and majorette, 1946, 16" x 27", EX, $350.00 C.

Cardboard poster, vertical, "On the refreshing side," couple with bottles, 1941, 30" x 50", VG, $600.00 B. *Courtesy of Muddy River Trading Co./Gary Metz.*

Cardboard poster, vertical, "Join me," fencer resting against a chest cooler with a bottle, in reproduction frame, 1947, 16" x 27", EX, $775.00 B. *Courtesy of Muddy River Trading Co./Gary Metz.*

Cardboard poster, vertical, "Refreshment," pretty girl in party dress at a pool setting with bottles on table, 1949, 33½" x 54", VG, $525.00 C.

Kay Displays sign "Quick Service" with die cut metal filigree, 1930s, 36" x 10", EX..............................$2,400.00 C

Light-up, "Beverage Department" with fishtail logo, 1960s, 50" x 14", EX ....$300.00 C

Cardboard poster, vertical, "Refreshment right out of the bottle," girl with skates drinking from a bottle, 1941, EX, $750.00 B. *Courtesy of Muddy River Trading Co./Gary Metz.*

Cardboard poster, vertical, "Right off the ice," girl at ice skating rink, 1946, 16" x 27", EX, $400.00 C. *Courtesy of Muddy River Trading Co./Gary Metz.*

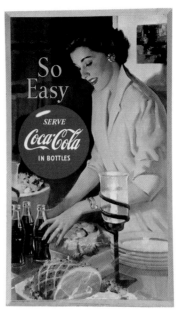

Cardboard poster, vertical, "So Easy," woman illuminated by candle getting ready for small gathering, 1950s, VG, $450.00 C. *Courtesy of Mitchell collection.*

Cardboard poster, vertical, "Start Refreshed," couple at roller skating rink, 1943, 16" x 27", EX, $375.00 C. *Courtesy of Muddy River Trading Co./ Gary Metz.*

Cardboard poster, vertical, "Take some home today," in original wooden frame, 1950s, 16" x 27", VG, $650.00 C.

Cardboard poster, vertical, "The drink they all expect," similar to horizontal poster of this year but showing full length artwork of couple preparing for entertaining, 1942, EX, $700.00 B. *Courtesy of Muddy River Trading Co./Gary Metz.*

Light-up, "Beverage Department" with fishtail logo, 1960s, 50" x 14", VG .... $250.00 D

Light-up, cash register top, "Drink Coca-Cola, Lunch With Us," 1940 – 1950s, 11" x 6", NM .... $425.00 D

Light-up counter sign featuring 20 oz. bottle, NOS in original box, 1990s, 12" x 13", EX .... $225.00 C

Light-up counter sign with dispenser, 1959, 12"w x 27"t x 15"d, G .... $950.00 B

"Thirst knows no season" introduced in 1922.

"Thirst knows no season"

Cardboard poster, vertical, "Thirst knows no season," couple building a snowman, graphics are great, 1942, 30" x 50", NM, $725.00 C.

Cardboard poster, vertical, "Welcome Pause," girl in yellow with tennis racquet at chest vending machine, 1940s, 16" x 27", $350.00 C. *Courtesy of Muddy River Trading Co./Gary Metz.*

Cardboard, poster, vertical, with large bottle in foreground and places and events in background, "58 Million a Day," 1957, 17½" x 28½", F, $125.00 D.

Cardboard poster, vertical, woman sitting on a dock with a parasol behind her, holding a glass, "7 million drinks a day," 1926, 18" x 31", VG, $1,500.00 B. *Courtesy of Muddy River Trading Co./Gary Metz.*

Cardboard poster with graphics of young lady being offered a bottle of Coke, 1956, EX, $750.00 B. *Courtesy of Muddy River Trading Co./Gary Metz.*

Cardboard poster, "Wherever thirst goes," great graphics of girl in rowboat with a bucket of iced Coca-Cola, 1942, EX, $550.00 B. *Courtesy of Muddy River Trading Co./Gary Metz.*

Cardboard poster with entertainer singing in front of microphone with bottle, "Entertain your thirst," 1940s, 36" x 20", EX, $600.00 B. *Courtesy of Gene Harris Antique Auction Center, Inc.*

Cardboard poster with Johnny Weissmuller and Maureen O'Sullivan sitting on springboard, "Drink Coca-Cola, Come up smiling," 1934, 13½" x 29½", EX, $2,900.00 C. *Courtesy of Mitchell collection.*

Cardboard poster, "Wherever you go," travel scenes in background, 1950s, EX, $250.00 C. *Courtesy of Mitchell collection.*

Cardboard poster, with girl and horse, 30" x 50", 1938, G, $950.00 B. *Courtesy of Muddy River Trading Co./Gary Metz.*

Cardboard poster, "Yes," girl on beach with bottle, if found in original frame add $400.00 to this price, 1946, 56" x 27", EX, $500.00 C. *Courtesy of Mitchell collection.*

Cardboard poster, woman with different size cartons, and the message "Get Both sizes in Cartons," 1956, NM, $500.00 B. *Courtesy of Muddy River Trading Co./Gary Metz.*

Light-up counter top, motion wheel behind "Pause" at left of "Drink Coca-Cola" with "Please Pay Cashier" at bottom, 1950s, M ....$975.00 C

Light-up counter top sign, "Please Pay When Served," red and white, 1948, 20" x 12", EX ....$2,800.00 B

Cardboard, rack sign featuring Eddie Fisher on radio, 1954, 12" x 20", EX, $135.00 C. *Courtesy of Muddy River Trading Co./Gary Metz.*

Cardboard, rack sign for 12 oz. cans with large diamond cans, 1960s, NM, $75.00 D. *Courtesy of Farmers Daughter.*

Cardboard poster, woman sitting wearing a broad brimmed hat with flowers, holding a Coca-Cola 5¢ bamboo fan and glass, framed, 1912, EX, $4,750.00 D.

Cardboard, Red Hot Summer game cup display poster, 1994, 20" x 12", NM, $35.00 C. *Courtesy of Sam and Vivian Merryman.*

Light-up, lantern on stand with four panels, "Have a Coke Here" on two panels and fishtail "Drink Coca-Cola" on other panels, 1960s, NM .... $195.00 C

Light-up, plastic and glass, "Pause and Refresh," "Quality carries on" on right side with bottle in hand, same art work as appears on fans of this vintage, 1940s, 19" x 15½", G .... $600.00 C

Light-up, plastic and metal display, "Always a Party, Always Coca-Cola," for Super Bowl XXVII, EX .... $65.00 D

Light-up, plastic and metal display, "Always a Party, Always Coca-Cola," for Super Bowl XXVII, NM .... $75.00 C

Cardboard, Red Hot Summer poster advertising a contest to win a new Ford Mustang convertible and the Fox network, along with the summer game cup promotion, 1994, 12" x 20", NM, $35.00 C. *Courtesy of Sam and Vivian Merryman.*

Cardboard poster, "Zing for your supper with ice cold Coke," young cartoon man in early version space suit with food and a bottle, 1960s, EX, $135.00 C. *Courtesy of Mitchell collection.*

Light-up, plastic, double sided, hanging, 1950s, 16" diameter, EX .... $500.00 D

Light-up, plastic with metal base, "Shop Refreshed," "Drink Coca-Cola," 1950s, VG .... $400.00 D

Cardboard, set of 14 Toonerville cutouts designed to be standups, 14 pieces, G, $1,900.00 B. *Courtesy of Muddy River Trading Co./ Gary Metz.*

Toonerville Trolley was first used as a window display in January 1930.

Cardboard, ringmaster and assistant, two separate pieces combined, matted, framed under glass, 32" T, 1920 – 1930s, EX, $550.00 C. *Courtesy of Muddy River Trading Co./Gary Metz.*

Cardboard, "Refresh Yourself," sign with scene of horses, 16" x 27", 1957, VG, $375.00 C.

Cardboard sign with graphics of bottle opening and Coke emerging, message "drive with real refreshment," 1999, 8" x 8", NM, $10.00 C. *Courtesy of Sam and Vivian Merryman.*

Light-up, plastic with metal base, "Shop Refreshed," "Drink Coca-Cola," 1950s, EX ....$475.00 D

Light-up, red two-sided globe hanger, 1950 – 1960, 16" diameter, EX ....$425.00 D

Masonite, "Delicious & Refreshing," girl with bottle, 1940s, EX...$150.00 D

Masonite, "Delicious & Refreshing," girl with bottle, 1940s, F ....$70.00 D

Cardboard, sign featuring straight sided bottle "Demand the Genuine by Full Name, Nicknames Encourage Substitution," 1914, 30" x 18", F, $500.00 B. *Courtesy of Muddy River Trading Co./Gary Metz.*

Cardboard sign with girl at a refrigerator holding a bottle of Coke and proclaiming "Home Refreshment" on one side and kids at a picnic cooler with bottled Cokes on the reverse side, 1950, NM, $675.00 B. *Courtesy of Muddy River Trading Co./Gary Metz.*

Cardboard sign, family enjoying Coke, "It's a Family Affair," probably Canadian, 1941, EX, $400.00 B. *Courtesy of Muddy River Trading Co./Gary Metz.*

Cardboard sign insert, "Serve yourself," with hand holding glass of Coke, 1949, 13" x 11", NM, $170.00 B. *Courtesy of Muddy River Trading Co./Gary Metz.*

Cardboard sign, "Shop refreshed," young lady at a box vending machine with a bottle of Coke, framed and under glass, 1948, EX, $600.00 B. *Courtesy of Muddy River Trading Co./ Gary Metz.*

Cardboard sign, woman with six pack with the message "Take home a carton ... Easy to carry," string hanger, 1937, 14" x 32", EX, $1,600.00 B. *Courtesy of Muddy River Trading Co./Gary Metz.*

Cardboard sign showing woman picking up a carton of Coke from store rack, with the message "Easy To Take Home," 1941, EX, $800.00 B. *Courtesy of Muddy River Trading Co./Gary Metz.*

Cardboard sign with original string hanger and graphics of bottle, probably Canadian, 13" x 33," EX, $475.00 B. *Courtesy of Muddy River Trading Co./Gary Metz.*

Cardboard sign with young woman in the moonlight with the message "The pause that refreshes," 1939, G, $550.00 B. *Courtesy of Muddy River Trading Co./Gary Metz.*

Masonite, diamond-shaped "Drink Coca-Cola" sign with bottle in spotlight at bottom, yellow and white on red background, 1946, 42" square, EX .... $900.00 D

Masonite, "Drink," featuring bottle, 1940s, 54" x 19", EX...$500.00 C

Masonite, horizontal, "Drink Coca-Cola Fountain Service," fountain heads on outside of lettering, 1930 – 1940s, 27" x 14", NM ....$1,800.00 D

Masonite, Kay Displays sign featuring the silhouette girl, white on red, 1939, 17" diameter, F.................$225.00 D

Cardboard, single sided poster with "The Pause That Refreshes," three women workers gathered around cooler for break, 1940s, G, $325.00 C. *Courtesy of Collectors Auction Services.*

Cardboard, St. Louis Fair, woman sitting at table with a flare glass that has a syrup line, 1909, F, $6,000.00 D.

Cardboard, stand up, "For the emergency shelf," folds in middle, EX, $285.00 B. *Courtesy of Muddy River Trading Co./Gary Metz.*

Cardboard, string hung die cut "Float with Coke," 1960s, 10" diameter, EX, $85.00 C. *Courtesy of Mitchell collection.*

Cardboard, "Stop ... Go refreshed" poster, framed under glass, 16" x 27", 1950s, VG, $185.00 C. *Courtesy of Muddy River Trading Co./Gary Metz.*

Cardboard, 3-D, "Boy oh Boy," pictures boy in front of cooler with a bottle in hand, 1937, 36" x 34", VG, $850.00 C. *Courtesy of Mitchell collection.*

Cardboard, "The pause that refreshes at home," large horizontal poster, featuring woman with bottle, and 6 for 25¢ carrier, add $375.00 for original frame, $500.00 C. *Courtesy of Mitchell collection.*

Masonite, oval, "Drink Coca-Cola," white lettering on red, 1940, 13" x 5½", EX..$275.00 C

Masonite with metal arrow, 1940s, 17", EX ......$800.00 D

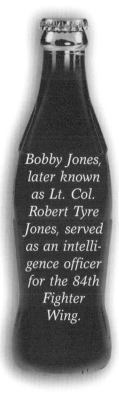

Bobby Jones, later known as Lt. Col. Robert Tyre Jones, served as an intelligence officer for the 84th Fighter Wing.

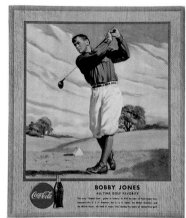

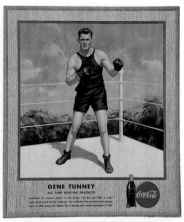

Cardboard, sports favorites, hanging, complete set consists of 10 signs; individual signs go in the $100.00 – 200.00 range, 1947, EX, complete set, $2,000.00 – 2,400.00 C.
Courtesy of Mitchell collection.

Cardboard, trolley car sign, "Drink Coca-Cola Delicious and Refreshing," matted and framed, 21" x 11", 1910s, EX, $675.00 B.
Courtesy of Muddy River Trading Co./Gary Metz.

Metal and glass light-up, motion, red "Drink Coca-Cola" button in center with motion appearance between button and gold case, 1960s, 11¼" diameter, EX   ....$525.00 C

Metal, building sign, "Drink Coca-Cola," 1950 – 1960s, 48" diameter, EX ....$250.00 D

Cardboard, trolley car sign, matted and framed, "Around the corner from anywhere," 1927, EX, $2,600.00 B. *Courtesy of Muddy River Trading Co./Gary Metz.*

"Around the corner from anywhere" debuted in 1927.

Cardboard, trolley car sign, matted and framed, "Four Seasons," 1923, 20¼" x 10¼", NM, $4,000.00 B. *Courtesy of Muddy River Trading Co./Gary Metz.*

Cardboard, trolley car sign, "Relieves fatigue, Sold everywhere," good graphics, 1907, 20" x 10¼", F, $3,400.00 B. *Courtesy of Muddy River Trading Co./Gary Metz.*

Cardboard, trolley car sign, "Tired?, Coca-Cola relieves fatigue," 1907, 20½" x 10¼", F, $2,300.00 B. *Courtesy of Muddy River Trading Co./Gary Metz.*

Cardboard, trolley sign, "Drink Coca-Cola Delicious and Refreshing," if mint the value would increase to the $3,500.00 range, 1914, F, $800.00 C. *Courtesy of Mitchell collection.*

Metal, Canadian carton rack, features sign at top advertising "Take home a carton 30¢," 1930s, 5' tall, EX...$450.00 D

Metal, die-cut radiator script sign "Drink Coca-Cola In Bottles," 1920s, 17", NM.......................................$450.00 D

Metal, double-sided, "In any weather Drink Coca-Cola," thermometer on one side fits on outside of screen door, while the "Thanks, Call Again" fits on the inside of the door, rare, 1930s, NM....................................$3,500.00 D

Metal double-sided sidewalk sign, 30" x 60", EX...$850.00 D

Metal, double-sided sidewalk sign featuring an early dispenser, difficult to find, 1940s, 25" x 26", NM...$2,500.00 B

Metal, "Drink Coca-Cola, Delicious and Refreshing," bottle on left side, "The Icy-O Company Inc., Charlotte, N.C.," F...$475.00 D

Metal, "Drink Coca-Cola Ice Cold," original four type bracket, 1930s, NM.......................................$500.00 D

Cardboard, trolley sign, "Coca-Cola 5¢ at fountains," 20½" x 10¾", 1905, G, $1,850.00 B. *Courtesy of Muddy River Trading Co./Gary Metz.*

Cardboard, truck poster, "Refreshing new feeling," woman in pool with straw hat, 67" x 32", 1960s, NM, $135.00 C. *Courtesy of Muddy River Trading Co./Gary Metz.*

Cardboard, truck poster, "Refreshing new feeling," 67" x 32", 1960s, NM, $125.00 C. *Courtesy of Muddy River Trading Co./ Gary Metz.*

Cardboard, truck poster, "Yield to the children," 67" x 32", 1960s, NM, $95.00 C. *Courtesy of Muddy River Trading Co./Gary Metz.*

Cardboard, two sided die cut foldout sign featuring girl with glass "Be Really Refreshed," 1960s, 13" x 17", EX, $425.00 D. *Courtesy of Muddy River Trading Co./Gary Metz.*

Cardboard, two piece set, display sign and a paper window banner, "We sell Coca-Cola part of every day — Served ice cold," printed by Snyder & Black, 1942, EX, $525.00 C. *Courtesy of Mitchell collection.*

Cardboard, vertical poster featuring girl at water, 1938, 30" x 50", EX, $4,000.00 B. *Courtesy of Muddy River Trading Co./Gary Metz.*

Metal, "Drink Coca-Cola in Bottles," original bent wire frame and stand, white lettering on red background wire is painted white, 1950s, G ....$175.00 C

Metal, fishtail, painted "Drink Coca-Cola," white lettering on red, 1960s, 14" x 8", VG ....$140.00 D

Metal fountain service sign, 1936, 27" x 14", EX ....$500.00 C

Metal, French Canadian carton rack, advertising 25¢ cartons, sign has French on one side and English on the reverse side, 1930s, 5' tall, EX ....$475.00 D

Cardboard, vertical poster, "Refresh your taste," girl in sailing scene, in original wooden frame, 16" x 27", 1950s, EX, $725.00 C. *Courtesy of Mitchell collection.*

Cardboard, vertical poster, "So easy to carry home," with woman in rain with umbrella, 1942, EX, $400.00 C. *Courtesy of Muddy River Trading Co./Gary Metz.*

Cardboard, vertical poster, "So Refreshing ... Drink Coca-Cola," 1941, EX, $750.00 B. *Courtesy of Muddy River Trading Co./Gary Metz.*

Cardboard, vertical poster, "Talk about refreshing," featuring woman with umbrella by cooler, 1942, EX, $450.00 B. *Courtesy of Muddy River Trading Co./Gary Metz.*

Cardboard, vertical poster, "The pause that refreshes," featuring the tennis girl, 1943, EX, $500.00 B. *Courtesy of Muddy River Trading Co./Gary Metz.*

Cardboard, vertical poster, "Things go better with Coke," scene of food and Coke, 1960s, F, $125.00 C.

Cardboard, vertical sign featuring a burger plate and a bottle of Coke, "A great combination," EX, $110.00 C. *Courtesy of Mitchell collection.*

Metal, French Canadian sidewalk sign, "Buvez Coca-Cola," 1949, 58" x 28", EX ....$375.00 D

Metal, horizontal, painted, "Enjoy Coca-Cola," red background with white lettering, white background block on right side with bottle centered in box, 1960, 32" x 11¾" ....$150.00 C

Metal light-up sign, "Drink Coca-Cola" on disc, wall basket, 1950s, EX ....$300.00 C

Cardboard, window display, cameo fold-out, 1913, VG, $5,200.00 B. *Courtesy of Muddy River Trading Co./Gary Metz.*

Cardboard, "Welcome friend," red and white lettering on simulated oak background, 1957, 14" x 12", EX, $300.00 C. *Courtesy of Mitchell collection.*

Cast iron curb sign, base with embossed lettering, beware of reproductions, 21" diameter, G, $175.00 C. *Courtesy of Collectors Auction Services.*

Celluloid, hand and bottle, foreign, 6½" x 16", VG, $225.00 B. *Courtesy of Muddy River Trading Co./Gary Metz.*

Celluloid, hanging "Highballs" sign, with original hanging chain, gold lettering on black background, 1921, 11¼" x 6", EX, $6,200.00 D.

Metal pilaster, bottle under a 16" "Drink Coca-Cola" button, 1950, VG ....$625.00 D

Metal pilaster, six pack being sold with a 16" "Sign of good taste" button on top, 1947, NM ....$750.00 D

Metal policeman, unusual paint on shield that reads "Stop Emergency Vehicles Only," 1957, 5" tall, EX..$1,500.00 D

Metal rack, round, "Take home a Carton," 1930 – 1940s, NM ....$250.00 D

Metal sidewalk, "Coca-Cola Ice Cold Sold Here," for curb service, 1931, 20" x 28", VG..............................$275.00 C

Metal sidewalk fishtail, "Ice Cold," 1960s, NM ....$225.00 D

Metal sidewalk with case of drinks, 1957, EX ..$250.00 D

Metal sign with wood frame on back, large version of the "Betty — Drink Coca-Cola" sign, rolled edge creates self frame, 59" x 24", 1940s, EX ....$595.00 C

Celluloid, round, "Coca-Cola," white lettering on top of a bottle in center with red background, 1950s, 9" diameter, EX, $250.00 C.

Countertop light-up sign, "Drink Coca-Cola" with glass in spotlight at bottom center, back lit with red and white bulbs, manufactured by Brunhoff Mfg. Co., red and white, 1930s, 12" x 14", EX, $6,200.00 B. *Courtesy of Muddy River Trading Co./Gary Metz.*

Celluloid bottle, "Drink Coca-Cola Delicious and Refreshing," 1900s, 6" x 13¼", VG, $2,300.00 C.

"Delicious and Refreshing" introduced in 1904.

Celluoid disc sign, string hanger, similar to white version below but in hard-to-find red, 1942, 9" diameter, G, $3,700.00 B. *Courtesy of Muddy River Trading Co./Gary Metz.*

Celluloid round sign with graphics of bell glass, scarce item, "Pause Go Refreshed," 1942, 9" diameter, EX, $4,700.00 B. *Courtesy of Muddy River Trading Co./ Gary Metz.*

Decal, "King Size ... Ice Cold" with bottle, 8" x 17", 1950s, EX, $35.00 B. *Courtesy of Muddy River Trading Co./Gary Metz.*

Composition round sign, "Pause ... go refreshed," heavily embossed with wings showing bottle in hand at the center, 1941, 9½" diameter, NM, $2,100.00 B. *Courtesy of Muddy River Trading Co./Gary Metz.*

Coca-Cola fashion girl, one of four fashion girls, framed and under glass, 1932, EX, $5,800.00 C. *Courtesy of Mitchell collection.*

Decal, "Drink Coca-Cola in Bottles," framed, 1950s, 15" x 9", EX, $50.00 D. *Courtesy of Muddy River Trading Co./Gary Metz.*

Metal two-sided rack sign, "Serve Coca-Cola Sign of Good Taste," 1960s, 17" x 10", G.................................$100.00 D

Original cost of this item was a whopping 17¢.

Decal, paper, unused, "Drink Coca-Cola Ice Cold," bottle in shield, 1934, 18" x 15", EX, $130.00 C. *Courtesy of Muddy River Trading Co./Gary Metz.*

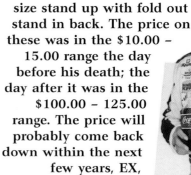

Dale Earnhardt die-cut life-size stand up with fold out stand in back. The price on these was in the $10.00 – 15.00 range the day before his death; the day after it was in the $100.00 – 125.00 range. The price will probably come back down within the next few years, EX, $100.00 C. *Courtesy of Sam & Vivian Merryman.*

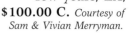

Die cut Coca-Cola bottle sign, 1951, 6' tall, G, $550.00 D. *Courtesy of Muddy River Trading Co./Gary Metz.*

Mileage and driving time chart from Rand McNally with Coke message information around map, 1950s, 24" x 18", EX..$275.00 C

Mobile, red disc, double sided, 1950s, 19", EX...$625.00 D

Neon, "Coca-Cola in bottles," great colors, metal base, 1950s, VG....................................$2,000.00 D

Neon, "Coke with Ice," three colors, 1980s, G ..$325.00 C

Neon, "Coke with Ice," three colors, 1980s, VG...$400.00 C

Neon, "Coca-Cola," dynamic wave logo, M ......$650.00 D

Neon, "Coca-Cola In Bottles," on original base, rare, 1930 – 1940, EX ....$4,500.00 C

Neon counter top, "Drink Coca-Cola in Bottles" on a wrinkle paint base with rubber feet on bottom, 1939, 17" x 13½", VG ....$2,000.00 C

Neon disc, "Drink...Sign of Good Taste," 1950s, 16" diameter, EX..$550.00 C

Neon disc, "Drink...Sign of Good Taste," 1950s, 16" diameter, G ....$400.00 D

Neon, "Enjoy Coca-Cola," two-color red and white, NOS, M ....$450.00 D

Neon, girl drinking from a can, pink, red, and yellow, in original box, new, 20" x 20", EX ....$350.00 D

Neon, girl drinking from a can, yellow, red and pink, recent, 20" x 20", NM ....$400.00 D

Neon, "The Official Soft Drink of Summer," 1989, G...$500.00 C

Neon, "The Official Soft Drink of Summer," 1989, VG...$750.00 B

Neon script sign on two glass rods with the transformer hooked up in a separate location, red, 1930s, 27" x 12", EX ....$1,350.00 D

"Drink Coca-Cola, Cures Headache...Relieves Exhaustion at Soda Fountains 5¢," framed under glass, 1890 – 1900s, VG, $1,500.00 B.

Probably the earliest script logo was used around June 1887.

Glass and metal light-up, "work safely work refreshed," cardboard insert, with original packing box, 1950s, 16" x 16", EX, $675.00 B.
Courtesy of Muddy River Trading Co./Gary Metz.

Glass and metal, light up counter sign, "Please Pay When Served," red and white, 20" x 12", 1948, VG, $2,000.00 B. *Courtesy of Muddy River Trading Co./Gary Metz.*

Glass and metal, reverse painted message, "Drink Coca-Cola," original chrome frame and chain, white on red, 20" x 12", 1932, EX, $3,500.00 B. *Courtesy of Muddy River Trading Co./Gary Metz.*

Neon window unit, "Drink Coca-Cola," two colors, 1940s, 28" x 18", EX ....$600.00 D

Oil cloth, Lillian Nordica, "Coca-Cola at Soda Fountain 5¢," "Delicious Refreshing," rare, 1904, 25" x 47", G ....$7,500.00 B

Oil painting by Hayden Hayden, original, rosy cheeked woman holding a glass, framed, 1940s, 24" x 28", EX ....$4,700.00 C

Oil painting, girl with mittens holding a glass, 1940, 24" x 28", Hayden, NM ....$4,500.00 C

Original artwork depicting actors taking a break from work on a western movie, signed by Verne Tossey, 1950s, 22" x 14", EX..$750.00 C

Oval, string hung, "Drink Coca-Cola Evegerkuhlt," German, 1930s, 12½" x 8¼", G ....$75.00 D

65

Glass and plastic, motion light, 11½" diameter, 1950s, NM, $675.00 B. *Courtesy of Muddy River Trading Co./Gary Metz.*

Glass and wire, sign, 14" diameter, 1965, EX, $400.00 B. *Courtesy of Muddy River Trading Co./Gary Metz.*

Glass front light-up sign that has an illusion of movement, featuring "Have a Coke," arrow and a cup of Coke, hard-to-find item, 1950s, 17" x 10" x 3", NM, $1,400.00 B. *Courtesy of MuddyRiver Trading Co./Gary Metz.*

Glass, round, "Drink Coca-Cola 5¢," gold trademark with blue background, 1900s, 8" diameter, F, $2,200.00 D.

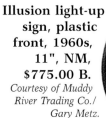

Glass, oval, "Drink Coca-Cola 5¢," silver lettering on maroon colored background, 1906, 9" x 6¾", VG, $2,400.00 C.

Illusion light-up sign, plastic front, 1960s, 11", NM, $775.00 B. *Courtesy of Muddy River Trading Co./ Gary Metz.*

Glass, round mirror, "Drink Carbonated Coca-Cola 5¢ in Bottles," G, $550.00 C. *Courtesy of Mitchell collection.*

Heavy paper die cut of woman in heavy cold weather coat with hood, advertising Coke in a glass, framed and matted, "Round the world, 1944," Litho in USA, 1944, EX, $295.00 D. *Courtesy of Riverside Antique Mall.*

Kay Displays, metal and wood soda glass sign, 9" x 11½", 1930s, NM, $825.00 B. *Courtesy of Muddy River Trading Co./Gary Metz.*

Paper advertising, "See adventures of Kit Carson," 1953, 24" x 16", VG .... $100.00 D

Paper advertising, "See adventures of Kit Carson," 1953, 24" x 16", G .... $85.00 C

Kay Displays, wood and wire sign with badminton theme, 1930 – 1940s, EX, $400.00 C.
Courtesy of Riverside Antique Mall.

Kay Displays, wood and wire sign with golfing theme, 1930 – 1940s, EX, $400.00 C.

Kay Displays, wood and wire sign with scene of girl fishing, 1930 – 1940s, EX, $400.00 C.

Kay Displays, wooden die-cut sign with a glass logo in lower center on metal ring, 16" diameter, 1930s, EX, $1,200.00 B. *Courtesy of Muddy River Trading Co./Gary Metz.*

Kay Displays, "Work Refreshed" with "Education" center medallion, 23" x 11½", 1940s, EX, $375.00 B.
Courtesy of Muddy River Trading Co./Gary Metz.

Kay Displays, wood and wire sign with scene of girl in lake, 1930 – 1940s, EX, $400.00 C.

Kay Displays, wood sign with airplane, 27" x 7", 1940s, EX, $650.00 B.
Courtesy of Muddy River Trading Co./Gary Metz.

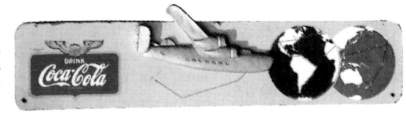

Paper, Autumn Girl, in original wooden frame, 1941, 16" x 27", VG ....$875.00 C

Paper banner, "Celebration Of The Century," 72" x 26", 1986, EX ....$25.00 C

Paper banner with 3-D letters and button logo, 60" x 18", 1950s, EX ....$350.00 C

Paper banner with iceberg and COLD carved in ice, 57" x 19", 1941, EX ....$375.00 C

Paper banner with Santa, 56" x 35", 1972, EX ....$25.00 C

Paper, bell-shaped glass with logo at top, in original black frame, 1930, 6″ x 9½", EX.............................$2,300.00 C

Light-up counter-top sign, featuring bottle with message "Always feels right Always Coca-Cola," NOS, 12" x 13", 1990s, NM, $250.00 C.
Courtesy of Muddy River Trading Co./Gary Metz.

Light-up double-sided sign, with fishtail logo, 38" x 20" x 9", 1960s, EX, $350.00 B.
Courtesy of Muddy River Trading Co./Gary Metz.

Light-up glass and plastic counter-top sign, with logo at each end, 18½" x 8", 1950s, NM, $2,600.00 B. *Courtesy of Muddy River Trading Co./Gary Metz.*

Light-up, plastic and glass, "Pause and Refresh," "Quality carries on" on right side with bottle in hand, same artwork as appears on fans of this vintage, 1940s, 19" x 15½", EX, $675.00 B. *Courtesy of Muddy River Trading Co./Gary Metz.*

Light-up halo type sign, double sided with "Have a Coke Here" on one side and "In Bottles" on the other side, plastic and metal, 1950s, 16" diameter, near-mint, $1,400.00 B. *Courtesy of Muddy River Trading Co./Gary Metz.*

Light-up double-sided halo type sign with cup insert, "Same quality as bottled Coca-Cola now in cups," 1950s, 16" diameter, EX, $2,400.00 B.
Courtesy of Muddy River Trading Co./Gary Metz.

Light-up, plastic and metal, round, double sided, "Drink Coca-Cola Sign of Good Taste," 1950, 16" diameter, EX, $475.00 C. *Courtesy of Mitchell collection.*

Paper, bottler's calendar advance print, Garden Girl on a golf course, rare, 1919, G ....$5,200.00 C

Paper, China girl sitting with a glass of Coke, matted and framed, 1936, 14¼" x 22", NM ....$1,900.00 C

Light-up, plastic, rotating, "Shop Refreshed Drink Coca-Cola," 1950s, 21" tall, G, $525.00 B. *Courtesy of Muddy River Trading Co./Gary Metz.*

Light-up metal and plastic sign with flourescent double-sided message board that carries the message on one side "Baby Needs / Drink Coca-Cola / Toys – Gifts" and on the reverse side "cosmetics & prescriptions" with arrow pointing the way, 1950s, 28" x 23", EX, $1,900.00 B. *Courtesy of Muddy River Trading Co./Gary Metz.*

Light-up metal and plastic sign with flourescent double-sided message board that carries the message on one side "Thank You / Drink Coca-Cola / Call Again" and on the reverse side "fountain and prescriptions," 1950s, 28" x 23", NM, $1,800.00 B. *Courtesy of Muddy River Trading Co./Gary Metz.*

Light-up sign, "Have a Coke" with beveled edge, 18" x 12", 1940 – 1950s, EX, $775.00 B. *Courtesy of Muddy River Trading Co./Gary Metz.*

Light-up sign featuring a young lady enjoying a bottle of Coke in a witch's costume with a jack-o-lantern on the table, unusual item, 1940s, 10" x 8", NM, $2,000.00 B. *Courtesy of Muddy River Trading Co./Gary Metz*

Light-up starburst behind Coke cup, 14" x 16", 1960s, EX, $500.00 C.

Light-up, "Work Safely" sign, 15½" square, 1950s, EX, $775.00 B. *Courtesy of Muddy River Trading Co./Gary Metz.*

Light-up "Work Safely" plastic with cardboard insert and Coca-Cola paper cup on left of lower panel, 1950s, 15½" square, G, $725.00 B. *Courtesy of Muddy River Trading Co./Gary Metz.*

Paper, "Cold" with bottle and button logo on iceberg, 1930s, VG ....$75.00 C

Paper, calendar top, girl sitting on slat back bench wearing a large white hat with a red ribbon and drinking from a bottle with a straw, 1913, 16" x 24", F ....$4,000.00 C

Paper, "Drink Coca-Cola Delicious and Refreshing," bottle on front of hot dog, framed and under glass, VG...$155.00 C

Lillian Nordica, hanging celluloid and metal frame sign, 1900s, EX, $9,000.00 B. *Courtesy of Muddy River Trading Co./Gary Metz.*

Masonite and aluminum cooler sign with arrow through outside circle, 1940s, M, $550.00 C. *Courtesy of Mitchell collection.*

Masonite, die cut, pretty blond girl holding a glass and a bouquet of flowers, 1940s, 42" x 40", VG, $550.00 B. *Courtesy of Muddy River Trading Co./Gary Metz.*

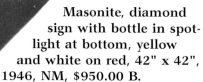

Masonite, diamond sign with bottle in spotlight at bottom, yellow and white on red, 42" x 42", 1946, NM, $950.00 B. *Courtesy of Muddy River Trading Co./Gary Metz.*

Masonite, horizontal, "Drink Coca-Cola Fountain Service," fountain heads on outside of lettering, 1930 – 40s, 27" x 14", EX, $1,200.00 B. *Courtesy of Muddy River Trading Co./Gary Metz.*

Masonite, die-cut sign with teenagers on records, hard to find, 1950s, 12", EX, $2,200.00 B. *Courtesy of Muddy River Trading Co./Gary Metz.*

Paper, "Drink Coca-Cola Delicious and Refreshing," bottle in front of hot dog, G ....$90.00 C

Paper, "Drink Coca-Cola, Quick Refreshment," bottle in front of hot dog, framed under glass, VG ....$155.00 C

Paper, "Drink Coca-Cola, Quick Refreshment," bottle in front of hot dog, G .... $100.00 C

Paper, Edgar Bergen and Charlie McCarthy, CBS Sunday Evenings, 1949, 22" x 11", G ....$175.00 C

Paper, Gibson Girl, matted and framed, 1910, 20" x 30", VG ....$2,500.00 D

Paper, girl in white dress with large red bow in back with a bottle and a straw, matted and framed under glass, 1910s, VG ....$4,000.00 D

Masonite sign, with waitress serving four glasses of Coke, 37" x 39", 1940s, EX, $250.00 C. *Courtesy of Muddy River Trading Co./Gary Metz.*

Metal and glass, light-up cash register topper, 1940 – 1950s, EX, $950.00 B. *Courtesy of Muddy River Trading Co./Gary Metz.*

Metal, cooler panel insert, "Serve Yourself, Please Pay the Clerk," yellow & white on red, 1931, 31" x 11", G, $140.00 B. *Courtesy of Muddy River Trading Co./Gary Metz.*

Metal and glass light-up counter sign, waterfall motion, "Pause and Refresh," 1950s, EX, $1,150.00 B. *Courtesy of Muddy River Trading Co./Gary Metz.*

Metal, "Coca-Cola Sold Here," store sign, red and white, 1920s, G, $850.00 B. *Courtesy of Muddy River Trading Co./Gary Metz.*

Metal and glass light-up counter top "Pause" motion sign, with original box, 1950s, EX, $875.00 C.

Metal curb sign, double-sided metal sign in sidewalk sign, with fishtail sign over bottle, 22½" x 33" x 24", VG, $425.00 C. *Courtesy of Collectors Auction Services.*

Paper, heavy stock poster "out of this world CORN DOG with Coke," featuring a '60s cup of Coke and a corn dog, seen in theater concession stands, 14" x 20", 1960s, EX ....$45.00 B

Paper, "Home Refreshment," three pieces of products, 1940s, NM...$215.00 D

Paper, horizontal, "Cold Drink Coca-Cola," framed under glass, 1939, 58" x 20", VG ....$600.00 C

Paper, instruction for hand in bottle outdoor painted signs, matted and framed, VG ....$100.00 B

Paper, "Let Us Put A Case In Your Car," with red carpet, 36" x 20", EX..$250.00 C

Paper, Lupe Valez in swim suit holding a bottle, framed and under glass, 1932, 11" x 21½", VG ....$900.00 C

Metal curb sign insert advertising the eight bottle carton with the message "Take Home 8 Bottle Carton" and graphics of eight bottle pack, eight bottle advertisements are difficult to find, 1960s, 20" x 28", EX, $4,000.00 B. *Courtesy of Muddy River Trading Co./Gary Metz.*

Metal curb sign insert with fishtail logo at top and the message "Take home a carton" and graphics of a regular size six pack at bottom, 1959, 20" x 28", EX, $1,300.00 B. *Courtesy of Muddy River Trading Co./Gary Metz.*

Metal curb sign insert advertising the King Size carton, message reads "Take home a carton...Big King Size," 1961, 20" x 28", NM, $1,500.00 B. *Courtesy of Muddy River Trading Co./Gary Metz.*

Metal, flange with filigree at top of piece, 1936, 20" x 13", EX, $700.00 B. *Courtesy of Muddy River Trading Co./Gary Metz.*

Metal double-sided flange sign with the message "Hart Cafe," 1950s, EX, $1,800.00 B. *Courtesy of Muddy River Trading Co./Gary Metz.*

Metal double-sided flange sign featuring graphics of a Coke bottle and the message "Enjoy Coca-Cola in Bottles," difficult sign to locate, 1954, EX, $4,500.00 B. *Courtesy of Muddy River Trading Co./Gary Metz.*

Metal double-sided flange sign with the message "Ice Cold" at the bottom next to a glass of Coke, 1954, EX, $2,500.00 B. *Courtesy of Muddy River Trading Co./Gary Metz.*

Metal double-sided flange sign with the message "Soda," 1950s, EX, $3,300.00 B. *Courtesy of Muddy River Trading Co./Gary Metz.*

Paper, "Plastic Cooler For Picnics & Parties," 1950s, NM ....$125.00 D

Paper poster featuring flapper girl with a bottle of Coke, 1920s, 12" x 2", G ....$475.00 C

Paper poster, flapper girl holding a bottle, 1927 – 1928, 12" x 20", VG...$550.00 C

Metal, double-sided fountain service sign, 1934, 23" x 26", NM, $1,600.00 D.

Metal, double-sided rack sign, "Serve Coca-Cola Sign of Good Taste," 17" x 10", 1960s, G, $110.00 C. *Courtesy of Muddy River Trading Co./Gary Metz.*

Metal, double-sided, "In any weather Drink Coca-Cola," thermometer on one side fits on outside of screen door, while the "Thanks Call Again" fits on the inside of the door, rare, 1930s, EX, $2,100.00 B. *Courtesy of Muddy River Trading Co./Gary Metz.*

Metal, double-sided sidewalk sign, Canadian, 1949, 58" x 28", NM, $1,200.00 D.

Metal double-sided triangle sign hung from overhead wrought iron holder with great filigree at top, 1937, EX, $4,000.00 B. *Courtesy of Muddy River Trading Co./Gary Metz.*

Metal, "Drink Coca-Cola, Delicious and Refreshing," bottle on left side, "The Icy-O Company Inc., Charlotte, N.C.," EX, $850.00 B. *Courtesy of Muddy River Trading Co./Gary Metz.*

Paper poster, man and woman with flared glasses and the globe motif, very rare, under glass, 1912, 38" x 49", VG ....$19,500.00 C

Paper poster, "Ritz Boy," first time Ritz Boy was used, framed under glass, 1920s, EX ....$975.00 C

Paper poster, "The Taste You're Thirsty For," featuring a large cup of Coke, Diet Coke, and, of course, Sprite, 24" x 18", 1985, NM..$25.00 C

Paper poster, vertical, "Drink Coca-Cola Delicious and Refreshing," 1927 – 1928, 12" x 20", G ....$325.00 C

Paper "That taste-good feeling," boy with Coca-Cola and hot dog, 1920s, F..$200.00 D

Paper, two women drinking from bottles sitting in front of an ocean scene with clouds in the sky, 1912, 16" x 22", F ....$1,875.00 D

Paper, "Take Along Coke In 12 oz. Cans, Buy A Case," men beside boat, 1960s, 35" x 19", EX ....$150.00 D

Paper, textured, travel exhibition promoting travel in France, matted and framed, 1970 – 80s, 24" x 32", NM ....$175.00 D

Paper, "That Taste-Good Feeling," 1920s, 14" x 20", VG ....$300.00 D

Paper, "Treat Yourself Right, Drink Coca-Cola," 1920s, 12" x 20", VG...$675.00 B

Metal, "Drink Coca-Cola," with bottle at right of message, 1950s, 54" x 18", EX, $300.00 C. *Courtesy of Eric Reinfeld.*

Metal, "Drink Coca-Cola in Bottles," original bent wire frame and stand, white lettering on red background wire is painted white, 1950s, EX, $300.00 C. *Courtesy of Gary Metz.*

Metal, fishtail, painted, "Coca-Cola Sign of Good Taste," bottle on right side of sign, 31¾" x 11¾", G, $235.00 C.

Metal, fishtail, painted horizontal, "Coca-Cola, Sign of Good Taste," white lettering on red background on white frame with green stripes, 1960s, 46" x 16", EX, $245.00 C.

Metal, flange, Italian, American-made sign, white & yellow on red, 1920s, 16" x 12", NM, $1,500.00 B. *Courtesy of Muddy River Trading Co./Gary Metz.*

Metal footed revolving four panel light up sign in likeness of lantern, 1960s, 20" tall, NM, $1,600.00 B.
Courtesy of Muddy River Trading Co./Gary Metz.

Metal, golf hole, 1950s, EX, $25.00 C.

Paper, "which" Coca-Cola or Goldelle Ginger Ale, 1905, VG ....$5,000.00 D

Paper window set for bottle sales, three piece, "Home Refreshment," 1941, 31" tall, EX ....$350.00 D

Paper window set for bottle sales, three piece, "Home Refreshment," 1941, 31" tall, VG ....$325.00 C

Paper window sign, "Let Us Put A Case In Your Car," case of Coca-Cola, 36" x 20", EX..............................$300.00 D

Paper window sign, "Let Us Put A Case In Your Car," case of Coca-Cola, 36" x 20", G...............................$225.00 D

Plastic and metal light-up die-cut sign, shaped like a paper serving cup, 1950 – 60s, 16" x 17", G ....$1,300.00 D

Plastic, curved barrel, "Be really refreshed Coca-Cola," 1960, 17" x 8", EX..$40.00 D

Plastic, "Delicious With Ice Cold Coca-Cola," popcorn box overflowing with popcorn, 24" x 7", EX ....$65.00 D

Metal "Have a Coke" with spotlight bottle in a metal frame, 1940s, 18" x 54", EX, $325.00 D. *Courtesy of Patrick's Collectibles.*

Metal, "Ice Cold" with cup in center, 1960s, 20" x 28", NM, $300.00 B. *Courtesy of Muddy River Trading Co./Gary Metz.*

Metal lollipop, "Drink Coca-Cola Refresh!," not on proper base, 1950s, $495.00 D. *Courtesy of Riverside Antique Mall.*

Metal lollipop sign "Drink Coca-Cola refresh!," 1940 – 1950s, fair, $595.00 D. *Courtesy of Ginger's Antique Mall.*

Metal, painted "Drink Coca-Cola ... Sold Here Ice Cold," rolled self frame, has Christmas bottle in center, 1932, EX, $695.00 D. *Courtesy of Riverside Antique Mall.*

Metal, painted sign with rolled edge, "Enjoy Coke ... Have a Coke and a smile ... Coke adds life," white, red, and black, 1960 – 1970s, EX, $125.00 D.

Metal, painted "Drink ..." sign with bottle in spotlight, 1948, 54" x 18", G, $350.00 D. *Courtesy of Patrick's Collectibles.*

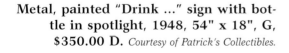

Plastic, "Delicious With Ice Cold Coca-Cola," popcorn box overflowing with popcorn, 24" x 7", G ....$50.00 D

Plastic, "Drink Coca-Cola" on red oval, Canadian, 1940 – 1950s, 11" x 9", NM ....$275.00 D

Plastic front light up sign that gives an illusion of movement when lit, "Drink Coca-Cola In Bottles" in red center, 1960s, 11" diameter, EX ....$725.00 D

Plastic hanging light-up sign, "Leo's Fountain," 1950s, 24" x 28", EX..$500.00 D

Metal, "Pause Refresh yourself," various scenes in yellow border, lettering, 1950s, 28" x 10", VG, $235.00 C. *Courtesy of Mitchell collection.*

"Pause and refresh yourself" introduced in 1924.

Metal, pilaster sign, "Serve Coke at Home," featuring bottle with 16" button at top of unit, 1948, 16" x 54", NM, $675.00 D.

Metal pilaster sign with graphics of 12 pack and the message "pick up 12" with original connecting material and button at top, 1954, 16" x 55", NM, $3,300.00 B. *Courtesy of Muddy River Trading Co./Gary Metz.*

Metal rack, round, "Take home a Carton," 1930 – 1940s, EX, $200.00. *Courtesy of Gary Metz.*

Metal rolled frame edge, "Coke adds life to everything nice" with dynamic wave, 1960s, EX, $275.00 D. *Courtesy of Rare Bird Antique Mall/Jon & Joan Wright.*

Metal rack sign with rolled edges, painted message "Please Place Empties Here," 1960s, 14½" x 5", VG, $125.00 C. *Courtesy of Sam and Vivian Merryman.*

Plastic, "Here's the real thing. Coke," wave logo, 1970s, 51" x 7", M ....$30.00 D

Plastic light-up, "Work Safely," "Safety is a job" cardboard insert, shows a Coca-Cola paper cup in lower left, 1950s, 15½" square, EX ....$725.00 D

Metal rolled frame edge with message "Pick up 6," graphics of six pack, 1956, 50" x 16", NM, $1,450.00 B. *Courtesy of Muddy River Trading Co./Gary Metz.*

Metal rolled frame edge with "Pick up 12... Refreshment for All," with artwork of 12 pack carton, 1960s, 50" x 16", EX, $550.00 D. *Courtesy of Rare Bird Antique Mall/Jon & Joan Wright.*

The crossing guard was the idea of Atlanta's police chief in 1952.

Metal policeman crossing guard with original base. This is a very volatile piece. I've seen them sell for as little as $600.00 or as high as $3,500.00. 1950s, G, $1,300.00 D.

Metal sign with rolled framing edge, "Things go better with Coke," bottle at right of message, 35¼" x 35¼", G, $275.00 D. *Courtesy of Patrick's Collectibles.*

Metal string holder with double-sided panels, "Take Home Coca-Cola in Cartons," featured with six pack for 25¢, 1930s, EX, $1,100.00 B. *Courtesy of Muddy River Trading Co./Gary Metz.*

Plywood and metal, Kay Displays sign, black lettering on yellow background, 1930s, 37" x 10", G ....$1,550.00 D

Plywood, double sided, "Slow School Zone Enjoy Coca-Cola, Drive Safely," 1950 – 1960s, VG ....$750.00 C

Porcelain bottle button, 3' dia., EX ....$495.00 C

Porcelain bottle button, 3' dia., M ....$550.00 D

Porcelain, bottle button with "Coca-Cola" across bottle front, 24", EX ....$475.00 D

Porcelain bottle, die cut, 16" tall, NM ....$325.00 D

Porcelain bottle, die cut, 1940s, 12", G ....$175.00 D

Porcelain bottle, die cut, 1940s, 12", VG ....$200.00 C

Porcelain bottle, die cut, 1950s, 16", EX ....$300.00 D

Porcelain button, candy, film with Coke in center, 1950, 18" x 30", NM ....$325.00 D

Early Coca-Cola contained as much as ¹/₁₀ grain of cocaine per drink, and 3 to 4 times the caffeine used today.

Metal, sidewalk, "For Headache and Exhaustion Drink Coca-Cola," with 4" legs, manufactured by Ronemers & Co, Baltimore, Md., 1895 – 90, G, $7,500.00 B. *Courtesy of Muddy River Trading Co./Gary Metz.*

Metal whirly top with original base with four wings and eight sides for advertisement, NOS, 1950, NM, $750.00 C.

Porcelain button, "Drink Coca-Cola" considered to be the plain version of this piece, white on red, 1950s, 24", EX.................................$325.00 C

Porcelain button, "Drink Coca-Cola in Bottles," white on red, 1950s, 24", EX ....$350.00 C

Porcelain button, NOS, 1940s, 24", M ....$875.00 C

Porcelain button with bottle, "Coca-Cola," red, 24", EX...$575.00 C

Porcelain button with bottle only, white, 1950s, 24", NM ....$775.00 D

Porcelain button with bottle, white on red, 1950s, 48" diameter, VG ....$275.00 C

Porcelain, "Buvez Coca-Cola," French Canadian sign, 1956, 29" x 12", EX...$175.00 C

Porcelain, Canadian button with flat edge, "Drink Coca-Cola Ice Cold," 1940s, 3' diameter, G ....$175.00 D

Porcelain, Canadian "Coca-Cola Sold Here Ice Cold," white & yellow on red, 1947, 29" x 12", G ....$275.00 D

Porcelain, Canadian "Drink Coca-Cola," 1946, 28" x 20", EX...$220.00 D

Porcelain, Canadian "Drink Coca-Cola" button, 1954, 4' diameter, NM ....$550.00 D

Porcelain, Canadian "Drink Coca-Cola" sign, red, yellow, and white, 1955, 29" x 12", EX ....$275.00 B

Porcelain, Canadian flange "Iced Coca-Cola Here," 1952, 18" x 20", NM ....$575.00 C

Porcelain, Canadian fountain service sign, 1937, 8' x 4', NM...$1,800.00 B

Porcelain, "Come In! Have A Coca-Cola," yellow and white, 1940s, 54", NM ....$1,200.00 D

Porcelain cooler, die cut, white with black trim, 1930s, 18", EX...$700.00 D

Porcelain, "Delicious & Refreshing," white background, 1950s, 24" x 24", EX ....$325.00 D

Porcelain, delivery truck cab, "Ice Cold," red, white, and yellow, arched top, 1930s, NM.......................$750.00 C

Porcelain delivery truck cab, "Ice Cold," red, white, and yellow, arched top, 1930s, VG ....$500.00 D

Porcelain, die-cut bottle sign, 1950s, 16" tall, EX...$275.00 C

Porcelain, die-cut bottle sign, 12' tall, G ....$200.00 D

Porcelain, die-cut script "Drink Coca-Cola" sign, white, 18" x 5½", M ....$775.00 B

Metal Tab self-framing sign with the message "flavor in — calories out", 31½" x 12", VG, $265.00 C. *Courtesy of Sam and Vivian Merryman.*

Neon, "Coca-Cola in bottles," great colors with metal base, 1950s, EX, $3,000.00 D. *Courtesy of Muddy River Trading Co./Gary Metz.*

Tab was released to bottlers in May 1963.

Neon sign with original wrinkle paint, 1939, 17" x 13½", G, $1,700.00 B. *Courtesy of Muddy River Trading Co./Gary Metz.*

Neon, "The Official Soft Drink of Summer," 1989, EX, $1,100.00 B. *Courtesy of Gary Metz.*

Oil on canvas that has been dry mounted on board, featuring soda jerk with glasses of Coke, back is marked Forbes Litho, 1940s, 22" x 17", F, $2,300.00 B. *Courtesy of Muddy River Trading Co./Gary Metz.*

Neon, "Coke with Ice," three colors, 1980s, EX, $425.00 D. *Courtesy of Gary Metz.*

Porcelain, double-sided "Drink.." sign, Made in Canada P & M 49, 1940s, 58" x 27½", G ....$450.00 B

Porcelain, double sided, "Drink Coca-Cola" on one side, "Isenhower Cigar Store" on other side, 1930, 30" x 40", EX..$450.00 C

Porcelain, double sided, "Drink Coca-Cola" on one side, "Isenhower Cigar Store" on other side, 1930, 30" x 40", VG ....$300.00 D

Original artwork of outdoor retail location, 1970s, 30" x 20", EX, $150.00 C. *Courtesy of Muddy River Trading Co./Gary Metz.*

Oil cloth, Lillian Nordica, "Coca-Cola at Soda Fountain 5¢ Delicious Refreshing," rare, 1904, 25" x 47", EX, $13,000.00 C.

Original artwork of gouache on board, showing actors on western set enjoying a Coke break, 22" x 14", 1950 – 1960s, NM, $1,000.00 B. *Courtesy of Muddy River Trading Co./Gary Metz.*

Paper advertising, "See adventures of Kit Carson," 1953, 24" x 16", EX, $135.00 C. *Courtesy of Mitchell collection.*

Paper, bottler's calendar advance print, Garden Girl on a golf course, framed under glass, rare, 1919, NM, $8,200.00 C. *Courtesy of Mitchell collection.*

Paper, calendar print sent to bottlers in advance of calendar, two models on a beach outing, framed under glass, rare, 1917, NM, $8,200.00 C. *Courtesy of Mitchell collection.*

Paper, calendar print sent to Coca-Cola bottlers a year in advance of the calendar, Autumn Girl, rare, framed under glass, 1921, NM, $8,200.00 C. *Courtesy of Mitchell collection.*

Porcelain, double sided, "Drink Coca-Cola" with bottle in yellow circle at bottom of sign, 1939, 5'x4', G ..$375.00 C

Porcelain, "Drink Coca-Cola Delicious & Refreshing," 1930s, EX ....$500.00 D

Paper, die cut, "Home Refreshment," with six for 25¢ carton, 22" x 16", 1941, NM, $45.00 B. *Courtesy of Muddy River Trading Co./Gary Metz.*

Paper, calendar top, girl sitting on slat back bench wearing a large white hat with a red ribbon and drinking from a bottle with a straw, framed, 1913, 16" x 24", G, $4,500.00 C.

Paper, "Drink Coca-Cola Delicious and Refreshing," bottle in front of hot dog, framed and under glass, EX, $175.00 C. *Courtesy of Mitchell collection.*

Paper, "Drink Coca-Cola, Quick Refreshment," bottle in front of hot dog, framed under glass, EX, $175.00 C. *Courtesy of Mitchell collection.*

Paper, girl in white dress with large red bow in back with a bottle and a straw, matted and framed under glass. There are two versions of this, the other one is identical except the waist bow is pink. 1910s, F, $3,800.00 C. *Courtesy of Mitchell collection.*

Paper, Gibson Girl, matted and framed, if in mint condition price would go to about $5,000.00, 1910, 20" x 30", EX, $4,500.00 C. *Courtesy of Mitchell collection.*

Paper, Hilda Clark, oval "Drink Coca-Cola 5¢" sign on table, framed under glass, 1901, EX, $7,500.00 C.

Porcelain, "Drink Coca-Cola Delicious & Refreshing," self framing, 1930s, 4'x8', NM ....$775.00 C

Porcelain, "Drink Coca-Cola, Ice Cold," fountain dispenser, 1950s, 28" x 28", EX ....$775.00 D

Porcelain, "Drink Coca-Cola, Ice Cold," fountain dispenser, 1950s, 28" x 28", F..$550.00 C

In 1950, Edgar Bergen and Charlie McCarthy appeared in the first live TV program sponsored by Coca-Cola.

Paper, Edgar Bergen and Charlie McCarthy, CBS Sunday Evenings, 1949, 22" x 11", EX, $200.00 C. *Courtesy of Mitchell collection.*

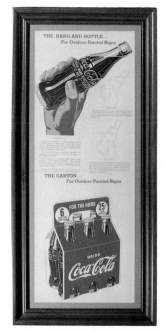

Paper poster featuring man and woman with flared glasses and the globe motif, 1912, 38" x 49", F, $16,500.00 B. *Courtesy of Muddy River Trading Co./Gary Metz.*

Paper, Lupe Velez in swim suit holding a bottle, framed and under glass, 1932, 11" x 21½", NM, $1,250.00 C. *Courtesy of Mitchell collection.*

Paper, instruction for hand-and-bottle outdoor painted signs, framed and matted, EX, $135.00 C. *Courtesy of Gary Metz.*

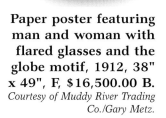

Paper poster featuring a bottle of Coke on snow, printed on heavy outdoor paper, 1942, 57" x 18", EX, $130.00 B. *Courtesy of Muddy River Trading Co./Gary Metz.*

Paper poster featuring bottle and icicles with the message "refreshing," 1957, 57" x 19", NM, $400.00 B. *Courtesy of Muddy River Trading Co./Gary Metz.*

Paper poster "Refresh," on heavy outdoor paper, 1940s, 57" x 18", EX, $300.00 D. *Courtesy of Muddy River Trading Co./Gary Metz.*

Porcelain, "Drink Coca-Cola in bottles" sign with curved ends, white lettering on red, 1950s, 44" x 16", EX ....$225.00 C

Porcelain, "Drink Coca-Cola" on button over bottle, 1950s, 18" x 28", NM ....$550.00 C

Porcelain, "Drink Coca-Cola" on fishtail, 1950 – 1960s, 44" x 16", VG ....$275.00 D

Porcelain, "Drink Coca-Cola" on fishtail, 1950 – 1960s, 44" x 16", EX..$375.00 C

Paper poster, horizontal, "Such a friendly custom," two women in uniform at soda fountain, 1930s, G, $375.00 C. *Courtesy of Muddy River Trading Co./Gary Metz.*

Paper poster, horizontal, "Let's have a Coke," couple in uniform, 1930s, 57" x 20", G, $850.00 B. *Courtesy of Muddy River Trading Co./Gary Metz.*

Paper poster, "Ritz Boy," first time Ritz Boy was used, framed under glass, 1920s, F, $700.00 C. *Courtesy of Mitchell collection.*

Paper poster, "Sold Everywhere 5¢," has been trimmed, but is a rare piece, 1908, 14" x 22", M, $10,000.00 – 11,000.00; F, $1,050.00 B. *Courtesy of Muddy River Trading Co./Gary Metz.*

Paper poster, "Treat yourself right" featuring man with a sandwich opening a bottle of Coke, 1920s, 12" x 20", F, $550.00 B. *Courtesy of Muddy River Trading Co./ Gary Metz.*

Paper poster, vertical, "Drink Coca-Cola Delicious and Refreshing," matted, framed under glass, 1927 – 28, 12" x 20", VG, $675.00 B. *Courtesy of Muddy River Trading Co./Gary Metz.*

Paper poster, vertical, "Pause a minute Refresh yourself," roll down with top and bottom metal strips, 1927 – 1928, 12" x 20", EX, $1,800.00 B. *Courtesy of Muddy River Trading Co./Gary Metz.*

Porcelain, "Drink Coca-Cola" sign, 1910s, 45" x 18", EX ....$1,000.00 B

Porcelain, "Drink Coca-Cola," trademark in C tail, white lettering on red background, 1910 – 20s, 30" x 12", VG ....$695.00 D

Porcelain, double-sided flange, "Coca-Cola Here," colorful in yellow, red, and white, Canadian, 1952, 18" x 20", VG..$275.00 C

Porcelain, "Drug Store" over "Drink Coca-Cola Delicious & Refreshing," red, white, and green, 1930s, 90" x 60", EX...$795.00 C

Porcelain, "Drug Store" over "Drink Coca-Cola Delicious & Refreshing," red, white, and green, 1930s, 90" x 60", F ....$375.00 D

Porcelain, "Drugs, Soda," 1950s, 18" x 30", NM ..$950.00 D

Paper, printer's proof of 1923 card-board poster, found in the estate of Mrs. Diana Allen who posed for this in 1922, 15¾" x 25", 1922, EX, $8,000.00 B. *Courtesy of Collectors Auction Services.*

Paper, "which" Coca-Cola or Goldelle Ginger Ale, this one has been trimmed with lettering eliminated, framed and under glass, if mint value would increase to $8,500.00, 1905, G, $4,750.00 C. *Courtesy of Mitchell collection.*

Paper, two women drinking from bottles sitting in front of an ocean scene with clouds in the sky, 1912, 16" x 22", VG, $4,750.00 C.

Paper, "That taste-good feeling," boy with Coca-Cola and hot dog, 1920s, EX, $650.00 B. *Courtesy of Muddy River Trading Co./Gary Metz.*

Paper, "Sun-worship" center magazine ad, 1960s, EX, $75.00 C. *Courtesy of Mitchell collection.*

Porcelain, featuring hand pulling dispenser top, 1930, 24" x 26", EX.................................$500.00 D

Porcelain flange, die cut, "Rafraichissez vous Coca-Cola," foreign, G ....$400.00 D

Porcelain flange, double sided, "Refresh yourself! Coca-Cola Sold Here, Ice Cold," 1930s, EX................$825.00 C

Porcelain, flange "Drink" sign, Canadian, yellow and white on red, 1930s, 17" x 20", EX ....$550.00 D

Pennant with the message "Enjoy Coke We're #1," EX, $15.00 C. *Courtesy of Sam and Vivian Merryman.*

Pennant with the message "Taste Diet Coke," EX, $15.00 C. *Courtesy of Sam and Vivian Merryman.*

Paper, window display, die cut, glass shaped, "Drink Coca-Cola," rare, 12" x 20", EX, $1,800.00 B. *Courtesy of Muddy River Trading Co./Gary Metz.*

Plywood, triangle die-cut sign with down arrow, "Ice Cold Drink Coca-Cola," Kay Displays, 1933, EX, $575.00 B. *Courtesy of Muddy River Trading Co./Gary Metz.*

Plywood, double sided, "Slow School Zone Enjoy Coca-Cola, Drive Safely," 1950 – 1960s, EX, $950.00 C.

Plywood and metal arrow and bottle sign "Drink Coca-Cola Ice Cold," 1939, 17" diameter, G, $425.00 C.

Plywood and metal Kay Displays, advertising "Pause Here," yellow, red, and black, 37" x 10", 1930s, G, $1,550.00 B.

Porcelain, flange, "Enjoy Coca-Cola In Bottles," very rare and hard to find, 1948, VG ....$850.00 B

Porcelain flange, "Enjoy Coca-Cola In Bottles," very rare, 1948, EX ....$950.00 D

Porcelain, flange French Canadian, "Prenez un Coca-Cola," 1950s, 17" x 19", EX ....$250.00 D

Porcelain, flange mount, "Iced Coca-Cola Here," yellow and white lettering on red background with yellow trim around outside of sign, 1950s, NM ....$650.00 C

Porcelain, fountain service, diagonal, "Drink Coca-Cola," 1933, 22" x 26", NM ....$1,100.00 C

Porcelain, fountain service, double sided, red and white fountain head and glass, 1950s, 28" x 28", NM ....$1,600.00 D

Porcelain, fountain service, "Drink Coca-Cola Fountain Service," white and yellow lettering on red and black background framed by fountain heads, 27" x 14", EX ....$1,200.00 D

Porcelain, "Fountain Service, Drink Coca-Cola" on button, 1950s, 34" x 12", G ....$300.00 D

Porcelain, "Fountain Service, Drink Coca-Cola" on button, 1950s, 34" x 12", NM......................................$450.00 C

Porcelain fountain service, green lettering on white background with red decoration and "Drink Coca-Cola" in red bull's-eye at right, 1950s, 30" x 12", EX ....$425.00 C

Porcelain, fountain service sign, "Fountain Service, Drink Coca-Cola," red, green, white, 1950s, 28" x 12", VG..$525.00 C

The year I was born — 1947 — a 24" painted button cost the bottler $1.14.

Porcelain button sign, "Drink Coca-Cola," 2' diameter, NM, $375.00 B. *Courtesy of Muddy River Trading Co./Gary Metz.*

Porcelain button sign with "Coca-Cola" over the center of a Coke bottle, 1950s, 3' diameter, EX, $475.00 B. *Courtesy of Muddy River Trading Co./Gary Metz.*

Porcelain button sign, "Drink Coca-Cola in Bottles," white on red, 2' diameter, NM, $425.00 B. *Courtesy of Muddy River Trading Co./Gary Metz.*

Porcelain button sign, "Drink Coca-Cola...Sign of Good Taste," white lettering on red, 2' diameter, EX, $400.00 B. *Courtesy of Muddy River Trading Co./Gary Metz.*

Porcelain, Canadian fountain service sign, 1935, 27" x 14", NM, $1,300.00 D. *Courtesy of Muddy River Trading Co./Gary Metz.*

Porcelain, "Delicious, Refreshing" with bottle in center, 1950s, 24" square, EX, $250.00 D. *Courtesy of Muddy River Trading Co./Gary Metz.*

Porcelain double-sided dispenser sign with metal frame, 28" x 27", G, $850.00 B. *Courtesy of Collectors Auction Services.*

Porcelain, double-sided, "Drink Coca-Cola," white lettering on red, 52½" x 35½", F, $130.00 B. *Courtesy of Collectors Auction Services.*

Porcelain, double sided, flange "Have A Coke," yellow and white lettering on red, 17½" x 19", EX, $425.00 B. *Courtesy of Collectors Auction Services.*

Porcelain, fountain service sign, 1935, 27" x 14", EX ....$950.00 C

Porcelain fountain service, two sided, dispenser with stainless steel banding around the edge of the sign, 1950s, 27" x 28", VG...$375.00 C

Porcelain, French Canadian door kick plate, 1939, 29" x 12", NM ....$250.00 C

Porcelain, French Canadian double-sided flange sign, 1940, EX ....$500.00 B

Porcelain, double-sided fountain sign, featuring an early dispenser, 25" x 26", 1941, EX, $2,200.00 B. *Courtesy of Muddy River Trading Co./Gary Metz.*

Porcelain, double sided flange, "Iced Coca-Cola Here," red, white, and yellow, 18" x 20", EX, $700.00 B. *Courtesy of Collectors Auction Services.*

Porcelain, double-sided flange sign, "Drink Coca-Cola Here," 1940s, NM, $850.00 B. *Courtesy of Muddy River Trading Co./Gary Metz.*

Porcelain, double-sided hanging sign, with additional bottle sign that gives a 3-D effect, designed to hang from store arm over sidewalk, white on red, 48" x 60", 1923, G, $625.00 B. *Courtesy of Collectors Auction Services.*

Porcelain, double-sided lunch sign, 1950s, 28" x 25", NM, $1,500.00 B. *Courtesy of Muddy River Trading Co./Gary Metz.*

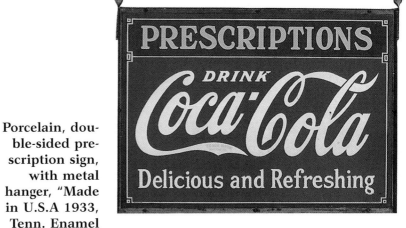

Porcelain, double-sided prescription sign, with metal hanger, "Made in U.S.A 1933, Tenn. Enamel Mfg. Co., Nash," designed to hang over sidewalk from building arm, white and yellow lettering on red and green, 60½" x 46½", 1933, EX, $1,200.00 B. *Courtesy of Collectors Auction Services.*

Porcelain double-sided sidewalk sign with bracket for hanging over sidewalk on arm, featuring a courtesy panel at top with Coke bottle at bottom in yellow spotlight, 5' x 5', VG, $850.00 B. *Courtesy of Muddy River Trading Co./Gary Metz.*

Porcelain, fishtail sign with turned ends, "Drink Coca-Cola," white on red, 1950s, 44" x 16", M, $325.00 B. *Courtesy of Muddy River Trading Co./Gary Metz.*

Porcelain, French Canadian sidewalk sign, both message and legs are porcelain, 1941, 27" x 46", F..........$350.00 B

Porcelain, French Canadian sign, because of its construction it resembles the smaller door push, 1930s, 18" x 54", G ....$400.00 B

Porcelain, double sided with mounting hanger advertising tourist stop and Coca-Cola, Coke sign is mounted to bottom which gives a 3-D effect, 40" x 58", VG, $1,400.00 B. *Courtesy of Collectors Auction Services.*

Porcelain, flange, "Refresh Yourself, Coca-Cola Sold Here Ice Cold" on shield shaped sign, 1930s, 17" x 20", G, $525.00 B. *Courtesy of Muddy River Trading Co./Gary Metz.*

Porcelain, "Drink Coke," "Ask for it either way," 1940s, 9" diameter, EX, $375.00 C. *Courtesy of Mitchell collection.*

Porcelain fountain service sign with the message "Fountain Service Drink Coca-Cola Delicious and Refreshing," double sided, 1930s, 5' x 3½', fair, $450.00 B. *Courtesy of Muddy River Trading Co./ Gary Metz.*

Porcelain flange, die cut, "Rafraichissez vous Coca-Cola," foreign, VG, $425.00 C.

Porcelain, French Canadian flange sign, "Buvez Coca-Cola Glace," 1950s, 18" x 19", NM, $225.00 D. *Courtesy of Muddy River Trading Co./Gary Metz.*

Porcelain, fountain service sign, 28" x 12", EX, $800.00 B. *Courtesy of Muddy River Trading Co./Gary Metz.*

Porcelain fountain service sign with red stripes on white background and button at right of message, 1950s, 30" x 12", G, $325.00 B. *Courtesy of Muddy River Trading Co./Gary Metz.*

Porcelain foreign sign, 1950s – 60s, 18" x 24", EX, $225.00 B. *Courtesy of Muddy River Trading Co./Gary Metz*

Porcelain, horizontal, "Coca-Cola Sold Here Ice Cold," red background trimmed in yellow with white lettering, 1940s, 29" x 12", EX, $275.00 D.

Porcelain, French Canadian sign, "Buvez Coca-Cola," white, red, and yellow, 1955, 29" x 12", G ....$150.00 C

Porcelain, horizontal, "Coca-Cola Sold Here Ice Cold," red background trimmed in yellow with white lettering, 1940s, 29" x 12", NM ....$375.00 C

Porcelain, horizontal, "Drink Coca-Cola Fountain Service," yellow background, 1950s, 28" x 12", $700.00 B. *Courtesy of Muddy River Trading Co./Gary Metz.*

Porcelain, Italian sign with button inside square, NOS, white on red, 22" square, EX, $225.00 B. *Courtesy of Muddy River Trading Co./Gary Metz.*

Porcelain outdoor bottle, tall vertical, "Drink Coca-Cola," believed to be a foreign sign where English was the dominant language, 1950 – 1960s, 16" x 4', NM, $475.00 D. *Courtesy of Muddy River Trading Co./Gary Metz.*

Porcelain, self framing, single sided sign, "Tenn. Enamel Manufacturing Co. Nashville," advertising fountain service, yellow, red, white on green, 60" x 45½", EX, $2,200.00 B. *Courtesy of Collectors Auction Services.*

Porcelain, sidewalk sign and legs, double sided, "Stop Here Drink Coca-Cola," 1941, 27" x 46", VG, $850.00 C. *Courtesy of Muddy River Trading Co./Gary Metz.*

Porcelain, shield sign, "Drink Coca-Cola," white and yellow and red, 36" x 24", 1942, EX, $325.00 B. *Courtesy of Muddy River Trading Co./Gary Metz.*

Porcelain, kick plate for screen door "Drink Coca-Cola Sold Here Ice Cold," 1930s, 31" x 12", G ....$475.00 C

Porcelain, outdoor advertising sign, "Drug Store, Drink Coca-Cola, Delicious and Refreshing," red, white, and green, 1933, 5' x 3½', EX ....$1,500.00 D

Porcelain outdoor, "Drink Coca-Cola Delicious and Refreshing," white and yellow lettering on red background, 1938, 8' x 4', NM.............$1,300.00 D

Porcelain, outdoor, "Drink Coca-Cola Delicious and Refreshing," white and yellow lettering on red background, 1938, 8' x 4', P ....$300.00 B

Porcelain outdoor, "Drink Coca-Cola, Delicious and Refreshing," white lettering on red background, 1932, 5' x 3', G ....$575.00 D

Porcelain, round bottle unit, probably part of a larger sign, features the 1923 bottle, 18", NM ....$295.00 D

Reverse glass with original chain and frame, "Drink Coca-Cola," rare version in red, white lettering on red background, 1932, 20" x 12", EX, $3,500.00 B. *Courtesy of Muddy River Trading Co./Gary Metz.*

Porcelain one-sided neon, "Drug Store... Fountain Service", 86" x 58" x 8", G, $3,500.00 B. *Courtesy of Collectors Auction Services.*

Porcelain truck cab sign with the message "Drink Coca-Cola Ice Cold," 1950s, 50" x 10", EX, $350.00 B. *Courtesy of Muddy River Trading Co./Gary Metz.*

Porcelain, single-sided sign, French, yellow and white lettering on red, 30½" x 12", EX, $200.00 B. *Courtesy of Collectors Auction Services.*

Reverse glass, "Drink Coca-Cola," 1920s, 10" x 6", EX, $1,250.00 C.

Reverse glass, "Drink Coca-Cola," metal frame that could be illuminated from the back, 1930s, 13" x 9", G, $800.00 C. *Courtesy of Mitchell collection.*

Porcelain, sidewalk, double sided, courtesy panel over a 24" button, NOS, 1950s, 2' x 5', EX ....$3,200.00 B

Porcelain, sidewalk, double sided, "Drink Coca-Cola In Bottles," 1940 – 50s, 4' x 4½', VG ....$650.00 C

Porcelain sidewalk, double sided vertical, "Stop Here Drink Coca-Cola," Canadian, 1941, 26" x 36", EX..................................$375.00 C

Porcelain, sidewalk, double sided vertical, "Stop Here Drink Coca-Cola," Canadian, 1941, 26" x 36", G.................................$300.00 B

Porcelain, square sign featuring button in center, Italian, 22" square, NM ....$525.00 B

Porcelain, square sign with bottle, "Delicious Refreshing," green on white, 1950s, 24" square, NM ....$300.00 C

Porcelain truck cab, "Drink Coca-Cola Ice Cold," yellow and white lettering on red background trimmed in yellow, 1950s, G ....$400.00 D

Porcelain, truck sign, "Drink Coca-Cola Ice Cold," yellow and white lettering on red, 1940s, 50" x 10", G .... $200.00 C

Porcelain, truck cab, "Drink Coca-Cola in Bottles," red lettering on white background, 1950, EX..............$275.00 C

Porcelain, 24" button "Drink Coca-Cola, Sign of Good Taste," white lettering on red, 1950s, 24", NM ....$550.00 C

Porcelain wall, one sided, advertising fountain service, red and green background with yellow and white lettering, 1934, G ....$650.00 C

Sticker, "Please pay Cashier," 1960s, EX, $25.00 C.

Stainless steel from dispenser, "Drink Coca-Cola," horizontal lettering, 1930s, 6½" x 3¼", G, $95.00 D. *Courtesy of Gary Metz.*

Sticker, "Please Pay Cashier," 13" x 6", 1960s, EX, $5.00 C.

Tin, bottle, oval, "Drink A Bottle of Carbonated Coca-Cola," rare, 1900s, 8½" x 10½", G, $6,000.00 C.

Tin, "Beverages" with 12" buttons on each end, hard-to-find sign, 70" x 12", 1950s, EX, $950.00 B. *Courtesy of Muddy River Trading Co./Gary Metz.*

Tin bottle, embossed, 1931, 4½" x 12½", VG, $375.00 B. *Courtesy of Muddy River Trading Co./Gary Metz.*

Tin bottle rack sign with space for price for "Big King size," 1960s, 9" x 17", EX, $125.00 B. *Courtesy of Muddy River Trading Co./Gary Metz.*

Tin, bottle, Christmas, 1933, 3' tall, EX, $1,000.00 C.

Tin, bottle, die cut embossed, 3' tall, G, $350.00 C. *Courtesy of Muddy River Trading Co./Gary Metz.*

Poster celebrating the 100th anniversary of Coca-Cola, with message "Great Taste Is Timeless," EX ......$25.00 C

Reverse glass, "Drink Coca-Cola," for back bar mirror, 1930s, 11" diameter, EX ....$625.00 D

Reverse glass light-up, "Drink Coca-Cola In Bottles," by Cincinnati Advertising Products Co., rare, 1920s, 15" x 7" x 5", EX ....$2,000.00 D

Reverse glass mirror, "Please Pay when Served, Drink Coca-Cola, Thank You," 1920 – 1930, 11¼" diameter, EX...$350.00 C

Reverse glass, "Drink Coca-Cola," for back bar mirror, 1930s, 11" dia., VG, $625.00 C. *Courtesy of Mitchell collection.*

Reverse painted glass, "Refresh Yourself Drink Coca-Cola," Canadian, 1927, 11½" x 5½", G ....$350.00 B

Rice paper napkin with Oriental scene, EX ......$375.00 B

Rice paper napkin with Oriental scene, VG ......$350.00 C

Advertising button signs were available in 12", 16", 18", 24", 36", and 48" sizes, and were used into the 1960s.

Tin button featuring decal of six pack "Standard 6," 1950s, 16" diameter, NM, $425.00 **B.** *Courtesy of Muddy River Trading Co./Gary Metz.*

Tin button sign with bottle in hand decal, 1950s, 16" diameter, NM, $250.00 **B.** *Courtesy of Muddy River Trading Co./Gary Metz.*

Tin button sign, "Drink Coca-Cola in Bottles," white on red, 12", 1954, EX, $250.00 **B.** *Courtesy of Muddy River Trading Co./Gary Metz.*

Tin button sign with the original applied decal featuring two different size bottles and the price on each, 1950s, 16" diameter, NM, $450.00 **B.** *Courtesy of Muddy River Trading Co./ Gary Metz.*

Tin button with painted message "Drink Coca-Cola ... Sign of Good Taste," white and yellow lettering on red, 16", 1948, EX, $450.00 **C.**

Tin Canadian sign "Drink Coca-Cola" with bottle, 1959, G, $300.00 **B.** *Courtesy of Muddy River Trading Co./Gary Metz.*

Tin button sign with "Coca-Cola" over bottle center, 1953, 24" diameter, EX, $475.00 **B.** *Courtesy of Muddy River Trading Co./Gary Metz.*

Tin, Canadian sign featuring 6 oz. bottle on right, 1930s, 28" x 20", G, $350.00 **C.** *Courtesy of Muddy River Trading Co./Gary Metz.*

Tin, button, white painted with bottle in center, 1940s, 24" diameter, NM, rare and hard to find, $400.00 **B.** *Courtesy of Muddy River Trading Co./ Gary Metz.*

Rice paper napkin with girl and bottle with arrow, framed and matted under glass, EX.................................$95.00 D

Rice paper napkin with girl and bottle with arrow, framed and matted under glass, G.................................$75.00 D

"Sign of Good Taste," ribbon attachments on both streamers, 1957, 3' x 4', NM ....$225.00 C

Stainless steel from dispenser, "Drink Coca-Cola," horizontal lettering, 1930s, 6½" x 3¼", EX....................$115.00 C

Tin, Canadian, six pack in spotlight "Take home a carton," 1940, 36" x 60", G, $250.00 C.

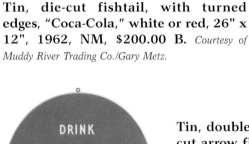

Tin, die-cut fishtail, with turned edges, "Coca-Cola," white or red, 26" x 12", 1962, NM, $200.00 B. *Courtesy of Muddy River Trading Co./Gary Metz.*

Tin, double-sided die cut arrow sign "Ice Cold Coca-Cola Sold Here," 1927, 30" x 8", VG, $400.00 C. Beware of reproductions.

Tin, double-sided die-cut arrow flange, "Drink Coca-Cola Ice Cold," with button at top and bottle in lower arrow point, EX, $550.00 D.

Tin, double-sided flange fishtail sign, red on white and green, 1960s, 18" x 15", VG, $325.00 C.

Tin, double-sided flange sign with arrow shape at bottom, carrying the message "lunch," 1950, 18" x 22", NM, $4,000.00 B. *Courtesy of Muddy River Trading Co./Gary Metz.*

Tin, arrow, "Ice Cold Coca-Cola Sold Here," white lettering on red and green background, 30", G ....$275.00 D

Tin arrow, "Ice Cold Coca-Cola Sold Here," white lettering on red and green background, 30", F ....$150.00 C

Tin, bottle, oval, "Drink A Bottle of Carbonated Coca-Cola," rare, 1900s, 8½" x 10½", F ....$2,000.00 B

Tin bottle, die cut, 1951, 3' tall, EX..................$295.00 D

Tin bottle, die cut, 1954, 20" x 6', NM.............$595.00 C

Tin bottle, die cut, 1956, 16", NM ....$425.00 D

Tin bottle, die cut embossed, from a larger sign, 38" tall, EX ....$375.00 C

Tin, bottle, embossed die cut, with original silver and black wooden frame, 2' x 4', NM.....................$625.00 C

Tin, bottle in original frame, on white background, 1950s, 36" x 18", EX..$275.00 C

Tin, bottle rack, double sided, round, "Take Home a Carton," yellow and white lettering on red background, 1930 – 1940, EX ....$255.00 D

Tin, bottle sign with original wooden frame, 1950s, 18" x 36", EX ....$205.00 C

Tin, bottle sign with original wooden frame, 1948, 18" x 36", F ....$125.00 D

Tin, double-sided rack sign, "Take Home a Carton ... Coca-Cola ... 6 bottles 25¢ plus deposit," yellow and white on red, 13" diameter, 1930s, G, $225.00 C.

Tin double-sided tire sign, "Enjoy Coca-Cola," 17" diameter, 1952, EX, $3,400.00 B.

Tin, "Drink Coca-Cola" button with silver metal arrow, 1950 – 1960s, 18" diameter, VG, $750.00 C. *Courtesy of Mitchell collection.*

Tin, "Drink Coca-Cola Enjoy that Refreshing New Feeling," painted fishtail with Coca-Cola bottle on right side, 1960s, 32" x 12", VG, $235.00 D.

Tin distributors, oval, from McRae Coca-Cola Bottling Co. in Helena, Georgia, featuring pretty long-haired girl, 1910, EX, $3,500.00 D.

Tin, "Drink Coca-Cola" sign with marching bottles, note shadow on bottles, 1937, 54" x 18", NM, $800.00 B. *Courtesy of Muddy River Trading Co./Gary Metz.*

Tin, bottle, vertical, in original silver wood frame, full-color bottle on white background, 1950s, 1½' x 3', EX ....$375.00 C

Tin button, "Drink Coca-Cola Sign of Good Taste," yellow and white lettering, 1950s, 16", NM ....$375.00 D

Tin button, showing bottle on white, 1940 – 1950, 24", EX...$400.00 D

Tin button with arrow, red lettering on white, all original hardware, 1950s, 16" diameter, EX ....$525.00 C

Tin, button with circle and earlier arrow, with framework on back, red & white, 1953, 12" diameter, EX ..$500.00 D

Tin, button with large arrow and original connecting hardware, red on white, 16" diameter, NM ....$550.00 + D

Tin, "Drink Coca-Cola," with couple at right of message holding bottle, 1940s, 35" x 11", EX, $575.00 D.
Courtesy of Patrick's Collectibles.

Tin, "Drink Coca-Cola Ice Cold," 1923 with embossed bottle at left, note shadow on bottle, 1937, 28" x 20", G, $525.00 B. *Courtesy of Muddy River Trading Co./Gary Metz.*

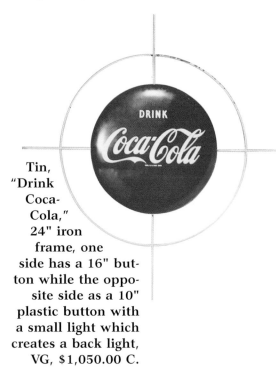

Tin, "Drink Coca-Cola," 24" iron frame, one side has a 16" button while the opposite side as a 10" plastic button with a small light which creates a back light, VG, $1,050.00 C.

Tin, "Drink Delicious Refreshing Coca-Cola," Hilda Clark, very rare, 1900, 20" x 28", EX, $15,000.00 C.

Tin, embossed, Buvez Coca-Cola, painted, foreign, 17¼" x 53", G, $125.00 C.

Tin, button, with mechanic on duty under the button, 1950 – 1960s, VG ....$465.00 D

Tin, Buvez Coca-Cola, embossed, painted, foreign, 17¼" x 53", VG ....$150.00 C

Tin, Canadian "Drink Coca-Cola Ice Cold," 1938, 5' x 3', G..$450.00 B

Tin, Canadian "Drink Coca-Cola" sign, bright colors, 1956, 28" x 20", EX ....$475.00 D

Tin, Canadian six pack in spotlight "Take home a carton," 1940, 36" x 60", EX ....$475.00 C

Tin, Canadian six pack in spotlight, "Take home a carton," 1942, 18" x 54", EX ....$525.00 B

Tin, Canadian vertical "Refresh yourself" sign with 6 oz. bottle, 1920s, 18" x 54", G ....$600.00 B

Tin, "Candy-Cigarettes" over fishtail logo, self-framed, 1960s, 28" x 20", VG ....$275.00 C

Tin, "Candy Cigarettes" over fishtail logo, self-framed, 1960s, 28" x 20", G ....$225.00 D

Tin, "Coca-Cola," red background with green and yellow border, bottle centered, 1930s, 45" diameter, EX...$375.00 D

Tin, "Cold Drinks," 1960s, 24" x 15", NM ....$200.00 D

Tin, "Cold Drinks" with "Drink" fishtail, "With Crushed Ice," 1960s, 24" x 15", NM................................$325.00 D

Tin, "Cold Drinks" with "Drink" fishtail, "With Crushed Ice," 1960s, 24" x 15", G ....$225.00 C

Tin, "Cold Drinks" with fishtail in center, 1960s, 24" x 15", NM ....$300.00 D

Tin dynamic wave sign, unusual variation, 1970s, 35" x 13", EX, $125.00 B. *Courtesy of Muddy River Trading Co./Gary Metz.*

Tin, embossed, "Drink Coca-Cola Delicious and Refreshing," 14" x 10", F, $225.00 C. *Courtesy of Gary Metz.*

Tin, embossed "Drink Coca-Cola Delicious and Refreshing" with bottle at left of message, with trademark in tail, 1930s, 36" x 12", EX, $550.00 C. *Courtesy of Mitchell collection.*

Tin, embossed over cardboard with string holder, "Drink Coca-Cola," 1922, 8" x 4", EX, $900.00 B. *Courtesy of Muddy River Trading Co./Gary Metz.*

Tin, embossed "Gas Today," with bottle in hand, red, white, and yellow, 23½" x 15", 1926, G, $775.00 B. *Courtesy of Muddy River Trading Co./Gary Metz.*

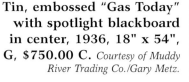

Tin, embossed "Gas Today" with spotlight blackboard in center, 1936, 18" x 54", G, $750.00 C. *Courtesy of Muddy River Trading Co./Gary Metz.*

Tin, Dasco bottle with 1923 bottle, 1931, 4½" x 12", M ....$625.00 C

Tin, "Deli" with "Drink Coca-Cola" on dot at right, 1950s, 50" x 15", NM ....$425.00 D

Tin, diamond shaped, with bottle spotlighted at bottom, in original black wooden frame, "Drink Coca-Cola" at top, 1940, 42" x 42", NM ....$500.00 C

Tin, diamond shaped, with bottle spotlighted at bottom, "Drink Coca-Cola" at top, 1940, 42" x 42", G....$400.00 D

Tin, die cut bottle sign, 1930s, 39" tall, G ....$575.00 C

Tin, die cut bottle sign, 1949, 20" x 72", NM....$625.00 D

Tin, die cut bottle sign, 1951, 16" tall, G ....$150.00 D

Tin, die cut, double sided, "Drink & Take Home A Carton," 1930s, 10" x 13", EX ....$250.00 D

Tin, die cut fishtail "Coca-Cola" sign, white on red, 1962, 24" x 12", VG ....$425.00 D

Tin, die cut fishtail sign "Coca-Cola," white on red, 1962, 26" x 12", M, NOS...$500.00 C

Tin, die cut six pack sign, 6 for 25¢, 1950s, 11" x 13", G ....$600.00 D

Tin, die cut triangle sign with the original bracket and mounting hardware, 1934, EX.......................$1,750.00 B

Tin, embossed painted kick plate, white and yellow lettering on red, 27" x 10", 1931, EX, $750.00 B. *Courtesy of Muddy River Trading Co./Gary Metz.*

Tin, embossed painted Spanish kick plate, message is in center between straight sided bottles, 36" x 12", 1908, EX, $2,300.00 B. *Courtesy of Muddy River Trading Co./Gary Metz.*

Tin, embossed painted kick plate featuring the 1923 bottle, white on red, 35" x 11", 1933, EX, $900.00 B. *Courtesy of Muddy River Trading Co./Gary Metz.*

Tin, die cut 12 pack sign, 1954, 20" x 14", G ....$875.00 D

Tin, die-cut, two-sided hanger, 1930s, 60" x 48", EX..$275.00 D

Tin, door kickplate sign, "Drink Coca-Cola" with bottle in spotlight, yellow & white on red, 1946, 34" x 11", EX...$200.00 D

Tin, double-sided arrow sign "Coca-Cola Sold Here Ice Cold," red, green & white, 1927, F....................$350.00 C

Tin, double-sided rack sign, "Take home a Carton," yellow and white on red, 1930s, 13", G........................$225.00 C

Tin, double-sided triangle "Ice Cold" with bottle at bottom, filigree work at top, 1936, 23" x 23", F..............$675.00 B

Tin, "Drink Coca-Cola Enjoy that Refreshing New Feeling," self-framed, painted, fishtail design, 1960s, 28" x 12", VG ....$225.00 D

Tin, embossed painted sign with border and straight line advertising, red, yellow, and white, 20" diameter, 1932, NM, $1,250.00 B. *Courtesy of Muddy River Trading Co./Gary Metz.*

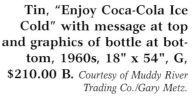

Tin embossed sign with 1923 bottle "Delicious and refreshing," 54" x 30", 1934, EX, $525.00 B. *Courtesy of Muddy River Trading Co./Gary Metz.*

Tin, "Enjoy Coca-Cola Ice Cold" with message at top and graphics of bottle at bottom, 1960s, 18" x 54", G, $210.00 B. *Courtesy of Muddy River Trading Co./Gary Metz.*

Tin, "Drink" button with '40s style arrow attachment at back of fixture with original hardware, 1948, 16", NM ....$900.00 C

Tin, "Drink..." button with wings, 1950s, 32" x 12", NM ....$350.00 C

Tin, "Drink Coca-Cola," American Artworks with scalloped top and filigree, 1936, EX ....$900.00 C

Tin, "Drink Coca-Cola," American Artworks with scalloped top and filigree, 1936, G ....$700.00 C

Tin, "Drink Coca-Cola," bottle at right, self framing, 1951, 28" x 10", EX...$225.00 C

Tin fishtail sign with message panel "Candy-Cigarettes," 1960s, EX, $300.00 B. *Courtesy of Muddy River Trading Co./Gary Metz.*

Tin, flange, "Drink Coca-Cola" with bottle in spotlight at lower corner, 1947, 24" x 20", G, $575.00 D. *Courtesy of Rare Bird Antique Mall.*

Tin, featuring Elaine holding a glass, 1916, 20" x 30", VG, $5,700.00 C.

Tin, flat "Refresh yourself," sign "Drink Coca-Cola Sold Here Ice Cold," yellow and white on red, 1927, 28" x 29", VG, $450.00 D. *Courtesy of Muddy River Trading Co./Gary Metz.*

Tin, Hilda Clark, considered rare due to the fact this artwork is rarely found in the tin version, 1903, 16¼" x 19½", EX, $3,700.00 B. *Courtesy of Muddy River Trading Co./Gary Metz.*

Tin, Hilda Clark, round, "Coca-Cola Drink Delicious and Refreshing," very rare and hard-to-find piece, 1903, 6" diameter, EX, $5,700.00 C.

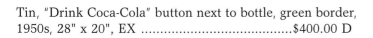

Tin, "Drink Coca-Cola" button next to bottle, green border, 1950s, 28" x 20", EX ....$400.00 D

Tin, "Drink Coca-Cola" button with small arrow and original hardware, white on red, 1950s, 12" diameter, EX ....$475.00 C

Tin, "Drink Coca-Cola" button with small arrow, 1950s, 12" diameter, VG ....$275.00 C

Tin, "Drink Coca-Cola Delicious & Refreshing," couple with a bottle, 1940s, 28" x 20", EX...................$575.00 C

Tin, Hilda Clark, showing her drinking from a glass while seated at a table with roses and stationery, very rare, 1899, VG, $15,500.00 C.

Tin, horizontal embossed, "Drink Coca-Cola Ice Cold," matted and framed, white and yellow lettering on red and black background, bottle in left part of sign, 1936, 28" x 20", EX, $850.00 C. *Courtesy of Muddy River Trading Co./Gary Metz.*

Tin, horizontal, "Drink Coca-Cola," self framing, white, VG, 32" x 10½", 1927, VG, $750.00 D. *Courtesy of Muddy River Trading Co./Gary Metz.*

Tin, horizontal, "Drink Coca-Cola," red background, silver border on self frame with bottle in spotlight in lower right-hand corner, 1946, 28" x 20", EX, $350.00 D. *Courtesy of Muddy River Trading Co./Gary Metz.*

Tin, "Ice Cold Coca-Cola Sold Here," yellow and white on red, 1933, 20" diameter, G, $225.00 B. *Courtesy of Muddy River Trading Co./Gary Metz.*

Tin, "Ice Cold ... Prepared by the bottler of Coca-Cola," sign with '60s cup, 28" x 20", 1960s, G, $325.00 C. *Courtesy of Muddy River Trading Co./Gary Metz.*

Tin, "Ice Cold" sign featuring artwork of '60s cup of Coke, white lettering on blue background, 28" x 20", 1960s, NM, $675.00 B. *Courtesy of Muddy River Trading Co./Gary Metz.*

Tin, "Drink Coca-Cola Delicious & Refreshing," couple with a bottle, 1940s, 28" x 20", G ....$550.00 D

Tin, "Drink Coca-Cola Delicious & Refreshing," couple with bottle, self-framing, 1940s, NM ....$800.00 D

Tin, "Drink..." button with wings, 1950s, 32" x 12", NM ....$350.00 D

Tin, "Drink Coca-Cola" fishtail, "Refreshes You Best," self-framing, 1960s, 28" x 20", EX ....$250.00 D

Tin, "Drink Coca-Cola" fishtail, white lettering on red fishtail against white sign background, 7½" x 3½", NM ....$65.00 D

Tin, "Drink Coca-Cola 5¢ Ice Cold," self framing, tilted bottle, 1930s, 54" x 18", EX ....$425.00 C

Tin, "Drink Coca-Cola 5¢ Ice Cold," self framing, tilted bottle, 1930s, 54" x 18", G ....$325.00 C

Tin "Ice Cold...Prepared by the bottler of Coca-Cola" sign in the vertical version with graphics of '60s cup, 1960s, 20" x 28", EX, $550.00 B. *Courtesy of Muddy River Trading Co./ Gary Metz.*

Tin, Lillian Nordica, oval framed, "Coca-Cola Delicious and Refreshing," featuring Coca-Cola table and oval "Drink Coca-Cola 5¢," rare, 1904, 8½" x 10¼", EX, $8,000.00 D.

Tin, Lillian Nordica, oval framed with framed backdrop showing "Delicious and Refreshing 5¢," 1905, 8¼" x 10¼", VG, $7,000.00 C.

Tin, outdoor sign, courtesy panel blank, 72" x 36", 1950 – 1960s, F, $95.00 C. *Courtesy of Muddy River Trading Co./Gary Metz.*

Tin, Lillian Nordica, self framed, embossed, promoting both fountain and bottle sales, 1904 – 1905, EX, $8,500.00 C.

Tin, "Now! Enjoy Coca-Cola at home," featuring hand carrying cardboard six pack, rare and hard to find, Canadian sign, 1930s, 18" x 54", F, $1,050.00 B. *Courtesy of Muddy River Trading Co./Gary Metz.*

Tin over cardboard, "Drink Coca-Cola," with bottle graphics, 1920s, 6" x 13", VG, $1,200.00 B. *Courtesy of Muddy River Trading Co./Gary Metz.*

Tin, "Drink Coca-Cola 5¢ Ice Cold," white and yellow lettering on red background with vertical bottle in yellow bull's-eye, 1938, NM ....$400.00 C

Tin, "Drink Coca-Cola Fountain Service," red, green, and white lettering on yellow, red, and white background, 1950s, 28" x 12", NM...$575.00 C

Tin, "Drink Coca-Cola Ice Cold" in red arrow pointing right at bottle in white background, red & white, 1952, 27" x 19", NM ....$250.00 B

Tin, "Drink Coca-Cola Ice Cold" on red disc with bars, 1930s, 28" x 20", EX ....$300.00 C

Tin, "Drink Coca-Cola Ice-Cold" over "Delicious & Refreshing" on bottles with green background, 1940s, 28" x 20", EX...$250.00 C

Tin over cardboard with beveled edge, for use in China, rare, 11" x 8", EX, $675.00 C. *Courtesy of Bill Mitchell.*

Tin, painted, "Drink Coca-Cola," shoulders and head of girl drinking from a bottle, yellow and white lettering on red background, self framing, 1940, 34" x 12", EX, $475.00 D. *Courtesy of Muddy River Trading Co./Gary Metz.*

Tin, painted, "Take a case home today $1.00 plus deposit," 19½" x 27¾", VG, $235.00 C.

Tin, painted, "Drink Coca-Cola in Bottles 5¢," horizontally lettered, if this sign were EX to M, price would increase to the $1,000.00 – $1,200.00 range, 1900s, 34½" x 11¾", F, $400.00 C.

Tin, "Drink Coca-Cola in Bottles" button, all white lettering, 1955, 12", NM ....$300.00 C

Tin, "Drink Coca-Cola In Bottles" button with arrow shooting from right to left at about 2 and 8 o'clock, 1954, EX ....$550.00 C

Tin, "Drink Coca-Cola In Bottles" button with arrow shooting from right to left at about 2 and 8 o'clock, 1954, G..$375.00 C

Tin, "Drink Coca-Cola" in left and center with yellow dot bottle at lower right, 1940s, 28" x 20", EX ....$350.00 D

Tin, "Drink Coca-Cola" lettered in white over dynamic wave logo, 1980s, 24" x 18", EX ....$95.00 D

Tin, "Drink Coca-Cola" lettered in white over dynamic wave logo, 1980s, 24" x 18", G ....$75.00 D

Tin, "Drink Coca-Cola," marching bottles to left side of sign, 1937, 54" x 18", VG..................................$650.00 D

Tin, "Drink Coca-Cola" over yellow dot bottle, "5¢ Ice Cold" below, self framing, 1940s, 54" x 18", EX..$625.00 D

Tin, "Drink Coca-Cola," red background with yellow and white lettering featuring three receding bottles, 1930s, 54" x 18", EX..$750.00 C

Tin, "Drink Coca-Cola Sign of Good Taste," white and yellow on red, 1950s, 12" diameter, EX ....$300.00 D

Tin, "Drink Coca-Cola Sign of Good Taste," white and yellow lettering, 1950s, 24", EX ....$450.00 D

Tin, "Drink Coca-Cola Sign of Good Taste," white and yellow lettering, 1950s, 24", G ....$350.00 D

Tin, "Drink Coca-Cola," 24" iron frame, one side has a 16" button while the opposite side as a 10" plastic button with a small light which creates a back light, G........$775.00 B

Tin, "Drink Coca-Cola," white on red with bottle at right on white background, self framing, 1956, NM..$250.00 D

Tin, "Drink Coca-Cola," with smiling girl, self framing, 1940s, 28" x 20", NM ....$475.00 D

Tin, "Drink" over bottle, "Coca-Cola" under bottle, 1930s, 5" x 13", EX...$375.00 C

Tin, painted vertical, self framing, "Drink Coca-Cola, Take home a carton," with spotlighted early six pack, "Made in Canada 1942 by St. Thomas Metal Signs Ltd," white and yellow on red, 17" x 53½", 1942, EX, $750.00 B. *Courtesy of Collectors Auction Services.*

Tin, "Pause ... Drink Coca-Cola," considered to be rare due to the 1939 – 1940 cooler in the left-hand spotlight, all on red background, horizontal lettering, self framing, 1940, 42" x 18", EX, $2,400.00 B. *Courtesy of Muddy River Trading Co./Gary Metz.*

Tin, painted vertical sign, "Serve Coca-Cola at home," yellow and white lettering on red background with a six pack spotlighted in the center, 1951, 18" x 54", EX, $350.00 D. *Courtesy of Muddy River Trading Co./Gary Metz.*

Tin, "Pause" sign with bottle in spotlight, 1940, 18" x 54", VG, $775.00 B. *Courtesy of Muddy River Trading Co./Gary Metz.*

Tin, painted vertical sign, message "Take Home a Carton" at top over cardboard carton 6 for 25¢ in yellow spotlight over the message "Drink Coca-Cola" at bottom, 1930s, 18" x 54", G, $250.00 B. *Courtesy of Muddy River Trading Co./ Gary Metz.*

Tin, pilaster sign that advertises "Serve Coke at Home" with graphics of 25¢ six pack, original button with all connecting hardware, 1940s – 50s, 16" x 55", EX, $900.00 B. *Courtesy of Muddy River Trading Co./Gary Metz.*

Tin, "Drink," white on red with silver frame, 1950s, 34" x 18", EX ....$225.00 D

Tin, embossed, "Drink Coca-Cola," 1920, 18" x 5¾", VG...$475.00 C

Tin, embossed, "Drink Coca-Cola Delicious and Refreshing," 14" x 10", EX ....$350.00 D

Tin, embossed, "Drink Coca-Cola Delicious and Refreshing," 14" x 10", F.................................$235.00 C

Tin, embossed "Drink Coca-Cola In Bottles 5¢," white lettering on red, 1920s, 23" x 6", EX ....$475.00 B

Tin, embossed, "Drink Coca-Cola in Bottles 5¢," 1920, 23" x 6", VG..$375.00 B

Tin, embossed, "Drink Coca-Cola in Bottles 5¢," 1920, 23" x 6", NM ....$475.00 C

Tin, embossed "Drink Coca-Cola In Bottles 5¢" sign, red and white, 1930s, 23" x 6", EX......................$325.00 C

Tin, embossed, "Drink Coca-Cola" lettered in white on red with green border, 1920s, NM ....$825.00 B

Tin, embossed "Drink" sign by Dasco, in original wrapping paper, 1930s, 18" x 6", NM ....$395.00 D

Tin, embossed "Drink" sign with 1923 bottle on left side of sign, 1931, 27½" x 10", NM............................$1,600.00 B

Tin, embossed "Gas Today" sign with good colors, 1929, 28" x 20", G..$675.00 C

Tin, pilaster sign with decal of bottle in hand applied to plain front, minus the Coke button, 1940s, 16" x 40", VG, $160.00 B. *Courtesy of Muddy River Trading Co./Gary Metz.*

Tin, pilaster sign with the "Drink Coca-Cola" button at sign top and graphics of 1950s six pack, 1950s, near-mint, $700.00 B. *Courtesy of Muddy River Trading Co./Gary Metz.*

Tin, pilaster sign with plain "Drink Coca-Cola" button at top and plain bottle at center of the sign, 1948, EX, $625.00 B. *Courtesy of Muddy River Trading Co./Gary Metz.*

Tin, pilaster sign, rare version with the message "Refresh Yourself," under button, 16" x 52", 1950, EX, $1,400.00 B. *Courtesy of Muddy River Trading Co./Gary Metz.*

Tin, rack sign, "Take Home a carton ... 6 bottles 25¢," 18" x 9", 1930s, EX, $225.00 C. *Courtesy of Muddy River Trading Co./Gary Metz.*

Tin, pilaster sign with the message "Take home a carton of quality refreshment" with a "Drink" button at top, 1950s, 16" x 55", VG, $450.00 B. *Courtesy of Muddy River Trading Co./Gary Metz.*

Tin, self framed "Luncheonette" sign with advertising for both a bottle and a can with a fishtail "Coca-Cola," 59¼" x 23¼", EX, $375.00 C. *Courtesy of Collectors Auction Services.*

Tin, embossed, "Ice Cold Coca-Cola Sold Here," 1923 bottle inset at left, 1931, 28" x 20", M ....$950.00 D

Tin, embossed "Ice Cold Coca-Cola Sold Here," featuring 1916 bottle, 1926, 28" x 20", F ....$200.00 B

Tin, embossed, "Ice Cold Coca-Cola Sold Here," green and white trim, 1933, 19½" diameter, EX ....$475.00 C

Tin, embossed "Ice Cold Coca-Cola Sold Here," yellow and white on red, 1932, 29" x 19", F ....$375.00 C

Tin, embossed over cardboard with string holder, "Drink Coca-Cola," 1922, 8" x 4", EX ....$900.00 C

Tin, embossed sign featuring 1915 bottle, 1927, F ....$325.00 C

Tin, embossed sign featuring the 1923 bottle, 1920s, 28" x 20", F ....$295.00 D

Tin, "Enjoy Coca-Cola All the Year Round," with giant earth, 1982, 33" x 24", EX ....$225.00 C

Tin, "Enjoy Coca-Cola All the Year Round," with giant earth, 1982, 33" x 24", G ....$135.00 C

Tin, "Enjoy that Refreshing New Feeling," fishtail logo with rolled frame, 1960s, 54" x 18", NM ....$350.00 D

Tin, self framing fishtail logo sign with bottle at left and diamond can on right, 1960s, 54" x 18", NM, $850.00 B. *Courtesy of Muddy River Trading Co./Gary Metz.*

Tin, self framing fishtail logo sign with diamond can on left and bottle at right with advertising for "Delicatessen" at top, 1960s, 5' x 2', EX, $650.00 B. *Courtesy of Muddy River Trading Co./Gary Metz.*

Tin, self framing, new Betty, "Drink Coca-Cola" sign, yellow and white on red, 1940, 28" x 20", G, $250.00 C. *Courtesy of Muddy River Trading Co./ Gary Metz.*

Tin, self framing, horizontal oval, "Coca-Cola," girl in foreground offering a bottle, 1926, 11" x 8", VG, $950.00 D.

Tin, shadow bottle "Ice Cold" sign, hard to find, 1936, 18" x 54", G, $600.00 B. *Courtesy of Muddy River Trading Co./ Gary Metz.*

Tin, sidewalk sign featuring 24 bottle case "Take a case home today," 1957, EX, $250.00 D. *Courtesy of Muddy River Trading Co./Gary Metz.*

Tin, sidewalk, embossed, "Take home a carton," 1942, 20" x 28", EX, $400.00 C. *Courtesy of Gary Metz.*

Tin, "Enjoy That Refreshing New Feeling" on fishtail, self-framing, 1960s, 32" x 12", NM ....$275.00 D

Tin, featuring artwork of straight sided bottle on left side of sign, 1914, 27" x 19", G ....$1,700.00 B

Tin, featuring Elaine holding a glass, 1916, 20" x 30", G ....$4,000.00 B

Tin, fishtail, Coca-Cola fishtail in center with bottle at right hand, red, green, and white, vertical, 1960s, 56" x 32", NM ....$295.00 D

Tin, fishtail, "Enjoy that Refreshing New Feeling," bottle to right of fishtail, 1964, 28" x 20", NM.................$250.00 D

Tin, fishtail die cut, 1960s, 12" x 26", EX ....$325.00 D

Tin, fishtail die cut, 1960s, 12" x 26", VG ....$295.00 C

Tin, fishtail flange, "Enjoy that Refreshing New Feeling," 1962, 18" x 15", EX ....$295.00 D

Tin, fishtail flange, "Enjoy that Refreshing New Feeling," 1962, 18" x 15", G ....$225.00 C

Tin, fishtail horizontal, "Cold Drinks Drink Coca-Cola," with crushed ice, 1960, 24" x 15", NM ....$250.00 D

Tin, fishtail, horizontal, "Sign of the Good Taste," full-color bottle at right side of sign, all on white background with green trim on frame, 1959, 54" x 18", G ....$200.00 C

Tin, fishtail, horizontal, "Sign of the Good Taste," full-color bottle at right side of sign, white background with green trim on frame, 1959, 54" x 18", NM ....$300.00 D

Tin, sidewalk, embossed, "French Wine Coca," with 9" legs, close-up of center inset (right), 1885 – 1888, 27¾" x 19¾", VG, $7,500.00 B. *Courtesy of Muddy River Trading Co./Gary Metz.*

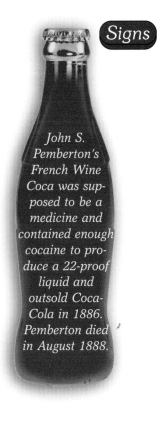

John S. Pemberton's French Wine Coca was supposed to be a medicine and contained enough cocaine to produce a 22-proof liquid and outsold Coca-Cola in 1886. Pemberton died in August 1888.

Tin, sidewalk insert sign with the message "things go better with Coke," 1960s, 20" x 28", VG, $500.00 B. *Courtesy of Muddy River Trading Co./Gary Metz.*

Tin, sidewalk "French Wine Coca" sign in original condition in original sidewalk frame. This cola was the forerunner of Coca-Cola. This sign is *extremely* rare, NOS, 1880s, sign 20" x 28" with frame 37" tall, NM, $10,000.00 B. *Courtesy of Muddy River Trading Co./Gary Metz.*

Tin, sidewalk insert sign with the message "Big King Size" and graphics of large bottle and fishtail logo at top, 1960s, 20" x 28", EX, $450.00 B. *Courtesy of Muddy River Trading Co./Gary Metz.*

Tin, fishtail, horizontal, with bottle on right sign with "Ice Cold" beside bottle, 1958, 54" x 18"..................$275.00 D

Tin, fishtail, self framed with bottle on right, "Drink Coca-Cola Enjoy that Refreshing New Feeling," horizontal, 1960s, 32" x 12", NM ....$250.00 D

Tin, fishtail sign "Drink Coca-Cola," horizontal, white lettering on red, 12" x 6", NM ....$195.00 C

Tin, fishtail sign with bottle on left and 12 oz. can on right, red, white, and green, 54" x 18", EX ....$300.00 D

Tin, fishtail, vertical, "Drink Coca-Cola" with bottle at bottom of sign, 1960, 18" x 54", NM ....$250.00 D

Tin, flange, "Drink Coca-Cola," 1941, 24" x 21", EX...$525.00 D

Tin, flange, "Drink Coca-Cola," 1941, 24" x 21", G...$400.00 C

Tin, flange, "Drink Coca-Cola, Ice Cold," flange forms arrow point, 1956, 18" x 22", M.......................$500.00 C

Tin, flat, "Refresh Yourself," 1927, 29" x 28", G ....$375.00 D

Tin, sidewalk sign featuring graphics of the fishtail logo at top with a six pack at bottom, "Take home a carton," 1959, 20" x 28", NM, $950.00 B. *Courtesy of Muddy River Trading Co./Gary Metz.*

Tin, sign advertising "Home Cooking Served with a Coke," Fay's Cafe, 1950s, 50" x 16", EX, $300.00 B. *Courtesy of Muddy River Trading Co./Gary Metz.*

Tin, sidewalk sign with the fishtail logo at top and graphics of a King Size six-pack at the bottom, 1958, 20" x 28", EX, $800.00 B. *Courtesy of Muddy River Trading Co./Gary Metz.*

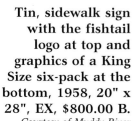

Tin, sign, "Coca-Cola with soda 5¢," a very rare sign and possibly one of a kind, manufactured by Tuchfarber Co., Cincinnati, 17" x 12", 1902, G, $7,200.00 B. *Courtesy of Muddy River Trading Co./ Gary Metz.*

Tin, sign "Enjoy Big King Size" over fishtail with bottle at right, 56" x 32", 1960s, EX, $375.00 B. *Courtesy of Muddy River Trading Co./Gary Metz.*

Tin, sign "Enjoy that Refreshing new Feeling" with fishtail logo and bottle, 56" x 32", 1960s, EX, $300.00 B. *Courtesy of Muddy River Trading Co./Gary Metz.*

Tin, French Canadian bottle sign, with 1916 bottle, 1920s, 28" x 20", F ....$225.00 C

Tin, French Canadian sign featuring 6 oz. bottle on right side, 1930s, 28" x 20", G ....$700.00 B

Tin, French six pack in spotlight, 1940s, 36" x 60", F ....$175.00 C

Tin, French, six pack in spotlight, 1942, 18" x 52", F ....$175.00 D

Tin, "Gas & Oil" on bottle side of fishtail logo, self framing, 1960s, 96" x 16", NM ....$475.00 D

Tin, girl with glass, gold beveled edge, 1920s, 8" x 11", EX...$900.00 D

Tin, girl with glass, gold beveled edge, 1920s, 8" x 11", G ....$750.00 B

Tin, "Grocery" over bottle with fishtail logo, 1960s, 28" x 20", F ....$125.00 C

Tin, "Grocery" over bottle with fishtail logo, 1960s, 28" x 20", VG ....$200.00 C

Tin, "Have a Coke," showing a spotlighted bottle in center with "Coca-Cola" at bottom all on red background, vertical, 1948, 18" x 54", EX ....$400.00 C

Tin, sign "Things go better with Coke" with a courtesy panel at top and graphics of bottle at right of sign, 1960s, 5' x 3', G, $275.00 B. *Courtesy of Muddy River Trading Co./Gary Metz.*

Tin, sign "Things go better with Coke" and graphics of hobbleskirt bottle, 1960s, 3' square, EX, $300.00 B. *Courtesy of Muddy River Trading Co./Gary Metz.*

Tin, sign "Things go better with Coke," with bottle at bottom, 18" x 54", 1960s, NM, $475.00 B. *Courtesy of Muddy River Trading Co./ Gary Metz.*

"Things go better with Coke" slogan debuted in 1963.

Tin, sign with bottle and the message "5¢ ice cold," 1936, EX, $2,700.00 B. *Courtesy of Muddy River Trading Co./Gary Metz.*

Tin, sign with decal of bottle, 16" x 50", 1940 – 1950s, EX, $425.00 B. *Courtesy of Muddy River Trading Co./Gary Metz.*

Tin, sign "Things go Better," featuring "Drink" paper cup, hard to find, red, green, and white, 1960s, 28" x 20", NM, $600.00 B. *Courtesy of Muddy River Trading Co./Gary Metz.*

Tin, sign "Things go better with Coke," with graphics of Coke glass, 1960s, 20" x 28", EX, $950.00 B. *Courtesy of Muddy River Trading Co./Gary Metz.*

Tin, "Have a Coke," tilted bottle on yellow dot, 1940s, 54" x 18", EX ....$400.00 C

Tin, heavy embossed,1923 bottle at each end, "Drink Coca-Cola" in center in white on red background, 1930s, EX ....$500.00 C

Tin, heavy embossed,1923 bottle at each end, "Drink Coca-Cola" in center in white on red background, 1930s, VG..$425.00 B

Tin, Hilda Clark, considered rare due to the fact this artwork is rarely found in the tin version, 1903, 16¼" x 19½", NM...$4,750.00 C

Tin, Hilda Clark, round, "Coca-Cola Drink Delicious and Refreshing," 1903, 6" diameter, VG ....$5,200.00 C

Tin, Hilda Clark, showing her drinking from a glass while seated at a table with roses and stationery, very rare, 1899, G ....$13,000.00 B

Tin, horizontal, "Drink Coca-Cola In Bottles," 1916 bottle at left of sign, 1920s, 35" x 12", G ....$225.00 D

Tin, sign with rolled edge, "Enjoy Big King Size ... Ice Cold Here," fishtail design, 1960s, 28" x 20", G, $250.00 D. *Courtesy of Patrick's Collectibles.*

Tin, sign with vertical fishtail over bottle, "Drink Coca-Cola ... Sign of Good Taste," 18" x 54", 1960s, EX, $350.00 B. *Courtesy of Muddy River Trading Co./ Gary Metz.*

Tin, sign with vertical fishtail over bottle, message in fishtail reads, "Drink Coca-Cola Enjoy That Refreshing New Feeling," self framing, 1960s, 18" x 54", VG, $300.00 B. *Courtesy of Muddy River Trading Co./ Gary Metz.*

Tin, sign with screen printed bottle in hand, "delicious and refreshing," most of these bottle in hand images are decals, 1954, 18" x 54", EX, $2,100.00 B. *Courtesy of Muddy River Trading Co./Gary Metz.*

Tin, six pack, embossed die cut, 1963, 3' x 2½', EX, $725.00 B. *Courtesy of Muddy River Trading Co./Gary Metz.*

Tin, six pack sign, "Take home a carton," 20" x 28", 1957, EX, $850.00 B. *Courtesy of Muddy River Trading Co./ Gary Metz.*

Tin, horizontal, "Drink Coca-Cola Ice Cold," with bottle at right, red and white, 1957, 28" x 20", EX ....$225.00 D

Tin, horizontal, "Drink Coca-Cola," red background, silver border on self frame, bottle in spotlight in lower right hand corner, 1946, 28" x 20", G ....$165.00 C

Tin, horizontal, "Drink Coca-Cola," red background, silver border on self frame, bottle in spotlight in lower right hand corner, 1946, 28" x 20", F ....$250.00 D

Tin, horizontal "Drink Coca-Cola" with bottle to right, red and white, 1954, 54" x 18", EX ....$185.00 C

Tin, horizontal embossed, "Drink Coca-Cola," 1923 bottle on left side, 35" x 12", EX ....$400.00 D

Tin, horizontal "Enjoy Coca-Cola" with bottle to right of message in white square, red and white, 1960s, 54" x 18", NM ....$270.00 C

Tin, horizontal, "Things go better with Coke," self framing, 1960s, 32" x 12", G ....$135.00 B

Tin, horizontal, "Things go better with Coke," self framing, 1960s, 32" x 12", NM.......................................$225.00 C

Tin, horizontal, "Things go better with Coke," self framing with full-color bottle on right, all on white background, 1960s, 54" x 18", EX ....$225.00 B

Tin, "Ice Cold Drinks," disc logo and cup, "Serve Yourself," 1960s, 27" x 22", NM.......................................$250.00 C

Tin, "Ice Cold Drinks Enjoy Coca-Cola," with cup of Coke and snowflakes, 1960, 27" x 22", NM ....$275.00 D

Tin, "Ice Cold" featuring '60s cup, white on blue, 1960s, 28" x 20", NM ....$595.00 D

Tin, six pack die-cut sign with spotlight on carton, hard to find, 1958, 11" x 12", NM, $1,500.00 B. *Courtesy of Muddy River Trading Co./Gary Metz.*

Tin, six pack, embossed die cut, featuring a King Size six pack, 1963, 3' x 2½', EX, $700.00 B. *Courtesy of Muddy River Trading Co./Gary Metz.*

Tin, six pack die-cut sign, featuring carrier with handle, advertising 6 for 25¢, 1950, 11" x 13", EX, $775.00 B. *Courtesy of Gary Metz.*

Tin, vertical pilaster sign with graphics of 1940s 6-pack carrier and bottles, "Serve Coke at Home," minus the button at top, 1947, 16" x 40", VG, $300.00 B. *Courtesy of Muddy River Trading Co./G ary Metz.*

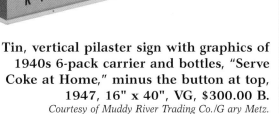

Tin, strip tacker type sign with "Drink Coca-Cola in bottles 5¢," 1922, 23½" x 6", NM, $1,350.00 B. *Courtesy of Muddy River Trading Co./Gary Metz.*

Tin, "Take Home a carton," self framing border, Canadian, 1950, 35" x 53", $625.00 B. *Courtesy of Muddy River Trading Co./Gary Metz.*

Tin, "turtle" sign, so called because of the shape, "Drink Coca-Cola The Delicious Beverage," 1920s, 20" x 15", G, $1,800.00 B. *Courtesy of Muddy River Trading Co./Gary Metz.*

Tin twelve pack die-cut sign in likeness of 12-pack carton, 1954, NM, $3,000.00 B. *Courtesy of Muddy River Trading Co./Gary Metz.*

Tin, "It's A Natural! Coca-Cola In Bottles," over bottle on red background, 1950s, 16" diameter, EX ....$375.00 D

Tin, "It's A Natural! Coca-Cola In Bottles," over bottle on red background, 1950s, 16" diameter, G............$300.00 C

Tin, Kay Displays sign, cardboard back plate, stand up featuring "Drink Coca-Cola," 1930s, 9" x 10", EX ..$650.00 C

Tin, Lillian Nordica, oval framed, "Coca-Cola Delicious and Refreshing," featuring Coca-Cola table and oval "Drink Coca-Cola 5¢," rare, 1904, 8½" x 10¼", F ......$3,500.00 C

Trolley car sign with graphics of a couple presenting a toast with Coke in glasses, 1927, 21" x 11", EX, $3,000.00 B. *Courtesy of Muddy River Trading Co./Gary Metz.*

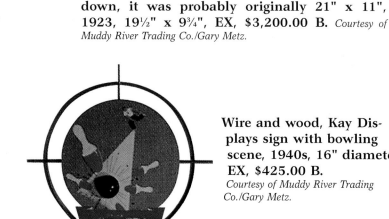

Trolley car sign with the ladies known as the four seasons, "Drink Coca-Cola delicious and refreshing all the year round," framed and matted which has cut the overall size of the sign down, it was probably originally 21" x 11", 1923, 19½" x 9¾", EX, $3,200.00 B. *Courtesy of Muddy River Trading Co./Gary Metz.*

Trolley car sign with graphics of pretty young girl with a bottle of Coke, "Absolutely Sanitary," very rare item, 1912, 21" x 11", F, $2,300.00 B. *Courtesy of Muddy River Trading Co./Gary Metz.*

Wire and wood, Kay Displays sign with bowling scene, 1940s, 16" diameter, EX, $425.00 B. *Courtesy of Muddy River Trading Co./Gary Metz.*

Tin, Lillian Nordica, self framed, embossed, promoting both fountain and bottle sales, 1904 – 05, G ....$4,000.00 C

Tin, "Let us put a Coke in your car," EX ....$150.00 C

Tin, octagonal, "Drink Coca-Cola" over bottle in circle, 1930s, 10" diameter, EX ....$500.00 D

Tin, oval, with French lettering "Buvez Coca-Cola Glace," Canadian, 1950s, 3' x 2', EX ....$250.00 D

Tin, over cardboard, featuring a straight sided bottle, rare and hard to find, white background, 1908, 6" x 13", F...$1,250.00 C

Tin, over cardboard, "Treat Yourself To A Coke," 1950 – 60s, EX ....$175.00 D

Tin, over cardboard, with "Drink Coca-Cola," featuring 1915 bottle, red lettering on white background, 1920s, 6" x 13", G ....$900.00 C

Tin, painted, "Coca-Cola," made in U.S.A/AAW 10-37, red background with white lettering and bottle in center outlined in green, 1934, 45" diameter, VG ....$375.00 D

Tin, painted, "Drink Coca-Cola in Bottles 5¢," horizontally lettered, 1900s, 34½" x 11¾",EX ....$950.00 C

Tin, painted litho, "Drink Coca-Cola In Bottles 5¢," bottle on each side, framed, 1907, 34½" x 12", EX......$675.00 D

Tin, painted litho, "Drink Coca-Cola In Bottles 5¢," bottle on each side, framed, 1907, 34½" x 12", F ....$425.00 C

Tin, painted, "Take a case home today, $1.00 deposit," 19½" x 27¾", EX ....$300.00 C

Tin, painted, "Take a case home today $1.00 deposit," 19½" x 27¾", VG ....$175.00 D

Tin, "Pause Drink Coca-Cola" on bottle in yellow center dot, 1940s, 54" x 18", EX...................................$425.00 D

Tin, "Pause, Drink Coca-Cola," tilted bottle on yellow dot, self framing, 1930s, 54" x 18", EX ....$275.00 D

Wire and tin, "Whatever you do," saddle on fence, 1960s, 14" x 18", EX, $215.00 C.

Wire and tin, "Wherever you go," skier coming down a snow slope, 1960s, 14" x 18", EX, $215.00 C.

Wire and tin, "Wherever you go," tropical island, 1960s, 14" x 18", EX, $215.00 C.

Wire and tin, "Whatever you do," fish jumping and fishing fly, 1960, 14" x 18", EX, $215.00 C.

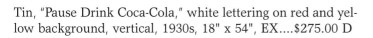

Tin, "Pause Drink Coca-Cola," white lettering on red and yellow background, vertical, 1930s, 18" x 54", EX....$275.00 D

Tin, "Pause Drink Coca-Cola," white lettering on red and yellow background, vertical, 1930s, 18" x 54", G......$200.00 D

Tin, pilaster sign, with six pack artwork and 16" button at top, 1948, 16" x 54", EX ....$675.00 C

Tin, raised frame "Drink" sign with 1923 bottle, 1942, 28" x 20", G ....$550.00 B

Tin, rectangular, man and woman with a bottle, "Drink Coca-Cola Delicious & Refreshing," all on red background, 1941, 28" x 20", NM ....$850.00 D

Tin, "Refresh Yourself, Drink Coca-Cola, Sold Here Ice Cold," 1927, 29" x 30", EX................................$300.00 D

Tin, "Refresh Yourself, Drink Coca-Cola, Sold Here Ice Cold," 1927, 29" x 30", G.............................$250.00 C

Tin, "Refresh Yourself Drink Coca-Cola Sold Here Ice Cold," trimmed in red and green, 1920s, 28" x 29", EX...$450.00 D

Tin, ribbon, die cut, "Sign of Good Taste," 1957, 3', EX...$225.00 D

Tin, ribbon, die cut, "Sign of Good Taste," 1957, 3', NM ....$275.00 C

Tin, round sign with bottle and logo, red, 1937, 46", NM ....$1,000.00 D

Tin, self framing "Drink" sign with couple holding bottle, woman in spotlight, 1942, 28" x 20", EX ....$550.00 D

Tin, self framing, horizontal oval, "Coca-Cola," girl in foreground of lettering offering a bottle, 1926, 11" x 8", F ....$250.00 D

Tin, self-framing rectangle, "Coca-Cola," oval inside rectangle framing girl presenting a bottle, 1926, 11" x 8½", EX ....$2,000.00 C

Tin, "Serve Coca-Cola at home," six pack highlighted at center of sign all on red background, vertical, 1950, 18" x 54", EX ....$475.00 D

Tin, "Serve Coca-Cola At Home," yellow dot six pack, 1950s, 54" x 18", G ....$225.00 C

Tin, "Serve Coca-Cola At Home," yellow dot six pack, 1950s, 54" x 18", NM ....$325.00 D

Tin, sidewalk, embossed, "Take home a carton," 1942, 20" x 28", G...$275.00 C

Tin, sidewalk sign "Big King Size" featuring fishtail over bottle all on green and white background, 1960s, 20" x 28", G ....$175.00 D

Tin, sidewalk sign, Big King Size, fishtail design with bottle, 1958 – 1960, 20" x 28", G ....$175.00 D

Window sticker, "Air Conditioned," 1950 – 1960s, EX, $8.00 C.

Wood arrow, "Drink Coca-Cola Ice Cold," silver painted bottle and arrow, 17" diameter, F, $500.00 D.
Courtesy of Gary Metz.

Wood and bent metal, carries the message "Drink Coca-Cola ... Please pay when served." This is an unusual double-sided flange sign, 1940 – 50s, 15" x 12", EX, $1,250.00 B.
Courtesy of Muddy River Trading Co./Gary Metz

Wood and glass counter top sign, carries the message "Coca-Cola Have a Coke," plastic crest at the top of the sign, not seen very often, 1948, 18" x 12", VG, $650.00 B.
Courtesy of Muddy River Trading Co./Gary Metz.

Wood composition Kay Displays medallion sign with the message "Please pay cashier" and a likeness of a glass on the top center, 1940s, 13" diameter, EX, $950.00 B.
Courtesy of Muddy River Trading Co./Gary Metz.

Wood composition medallion sign, "Lunch with us" with likeness of glass at top center, 1940s, 13" diameter, EX, $800.00 B.
Courtesy of Muddy River Trading Co./Gary Metz.

Tin, sidewalk sign "Delicious and refreshing," 1930s, 20" x 28", F ....$175.00 D

Tin, sidewalk sign "Drink Coca-Cola Ice Cold, Delicious and Refreshing," yellow, white, red, and green, 1939, 20" x 28", NM...$350.00 B

Tin, sidewalk sign featuring fishtail over bottle on green and white striped background, 1960s, NM ......$250.00 D

Tin, sign featuring straight sided bottle with wooden frame, 1914, 28" x 20", F ....$275.00 C

Tin, "Sign of Good Taste" button, white and yellow on red, 1950s, 12" diameter, F ....$250.00 C

Tin, "Sign of Good Taste," fishtail logo, with raised border, 1960s, 32" x 11", EX ....$250.00 D

Tin, "Sign of Good Taste, Ice Cold," fishtail logo and bottle, 1960s, 56" x 32", EX ....$300.00 D

Tin, "Sign of Good Taste" in fishtail with bottle at bottom on green and white striped background, 1960s, 16" x 41", EX..$325.00 C

Tin, "Sign of Good Taste," vertical fishtail, green rolled frame, 1960s, 18" x 54", NM ....$325.00 D

Tin, sign with man and woman in spotlight "Drink Coca-Cola," 1942, 56" x 32", NM ....$525.00 D

Tin, sign with woman with a bottle of Coca-Cola, "Drink Coca-Cola," 1942, 56" x 32", EX ....$475.00 D

Tin, six pack, die cut, "King Size, Coca-Cola," 1960s, VG..$325.00 C

Tin, six pack, die cut, "King Size, Coca-Cola," 1960s, G ....$225.00 D

Tin, six pack, die cut, red wire handle, 1950s, EX..$400.00 D

Tin, six pack, die cut, "6 for 25¢," 1950s, EX....$500.00 D

Wood, figural, die cut, "Coca-Cola" cooler, probably part of another sign, 1950s, EX, $275.00 C. *Courtesy of Gary Metz.*

Wood, glass, and chrome cash register topper, 11½" x 6", 1940s, EX, $900.00 B. *Courtesy of Muddy River Trading Co./Gary Metz.*

Wood, glass, and chrome cash register topper, a plain version sporting only the Coke name, 11½" x 5", 1940s, G, $475.00 B. *Courtesy of Muddy River Trading Co./Gary Metz.*

Tin, six pack, "Take home a Carton," with fishtail "Coca-Cola" at top of sign, 1958, 20" x 28", EX ....$550.00 B

Tin, "Take A Case Home Today, Quality Refreshment," red carpet with a yellow Coke case on it, 1950s, 28" x 20", NM ....$400.00 D

Tin, "Take a case home today," white and yellow lettering on red background, vertical, 1949, 20" x 28", NM ....$325.00 B

Tin, "Take Home A Carton," fishtail green border, 1960s, 28" x 20", EX ....$275.00 D

Tin, "Take Home A Carton" over six pack, Canadian, 1950s, 53" x 35", F ....$100.00 C

Tin, "Take Home A Carton" over six pack, Canadian, 1950s, 53" x 35", NM ....$575.00 D

Tin, "Take Home a Carton" sign, with six pack featured artwork, 1954, 20" x 28", NM ....$600.00 B

Tin, "Things Go Better With Coke" left of bottle, raised border, 1960s, 24" x 24", EX ....$275.00 D

Tin, "Things Go Better With Coke" on right, with disc logo at left, 1960s, 21" x 11", EX ....$300.00 D

Tin, "Things Go Better With Coke" on right, with disc logo at left, 1960s, 21" x 11", VG ....$250.00 C

Tin, "Things Go Better With Coke," red border, 1960s, 32" x 12", EX ....$225.00 D

Tin, "Things Go Better With Coke" with bottle, disc logo on both sides raised border, 1960s, 54" x 18", EX ....$300.00 D

Tin, "Things Go Better With Coke" with bottle, disc logo on both sides raised border, 1960s, 54" x 18", VG ....$250.00 C

Tin, twelve-pack, die cut, 1954, 20" x 13", NM ....$600.00 D

Tin, two-sided die cut triangle with hanging bracket, "Drink Coca-Cola" at top, white lettering on red background with "Ice Cold" at bottom over bottle, 1937, G ....$600.00 D

Tin, two-sided flange, "Ice Cold Coca-Cola Sold Here," white lettering on red and green background, 1920s, 12½" x 10", G ....$425.00 C

Tin, two-sided flange with attached 16" buttons at top of arrow, 1950s, G ....$725.00 D

Tin, two-sided rack, "Six bottles for 25¢, Take Home a Carton," 1937, 13" x 10", EX ....$325.00 B

Tin, vertical "Enjoy that Refreshing new taste" in fishtail with bottle at bottom on green & white stripe background, 1960s, 16" x 41", NM ....$350.00 D

Tin, vertical "Gas Today" sign, 1937, 18" x 54", F ....$350.00 D

Tin, vertical "Gas Today" sign, 1931, 18" x 54", EX ....$1,300.00 C

Tin, vertical "Pause" sign featuring bottle in spotlight in center, 1940, 18" x 54", VG ....$375.00 D

Tin, vertical, "Sign of Good Taste," fishtail logo at top over bottle, 1960s, 18" x 54", EX ....$275.00 C

Tin, vertical, "Take Home A Carton, Big King Size," six pack of big Cokes, self-framing, 1962, 20" x 28", EX ..$250.00 D

Wood, Kay Displays sign in likeness of shield with brass die cut filigree at top, graphics of bottle in center, 1940s, 19" x 20", G, $800.00 B. *Courtesy of Muddy River Trading Co./Gary Metz.*

Wood, Kay Displays with metal filigree, center graphics of marching Coke glasses, 1940, 9" x 11", EX, $525.00 B. *Courtesy of Muddy River Trading Co./Gary Metz.*

Wood, Kay Displays, "Lunch with us ... a tasty sandwich with Coca-Cola," difficult to find, 1940s, 9" x 13", EX, $2,900.00 B. *Courtesy of Muddy River Trading Co./Gary Metz.*

Wood, Kay Displays sign with "Pause" top line and "Drink Coca-Cola" and on last line is "Refresh," 1940s, 14" x 10½", EX, $2,900.00 B. *Courtesy of Muddy River Trading Co./Gary Metz.*

Tin, with button and bottle, Canadian, 1956, 28" x 20", EX ....$450.00 B

Wayne Gretzky, heavy cardboard life size stand up Coca-Cola poster, 1980s, EX.......................................$95.00 C

Window decal, "Drink Coca-Cola" with fretwork top, 1940, 25" x 12", EX ....$75.00 C

Window decal, "Drink Coca-Cola" with fretwork top, 1940, 25" x 12", M ....$110.00 B

Wood and masonite, hanging, "Drink Coca-Cola. Delicious ... Refreshing," with silhouette on left-hand side, 1941, 3' x 1', G ....$700.00 B

Wood and masonite, hanging, "Drink Coca-Cola. Delicious ... Refreshing," with silhouette on left-hand side, 1941, 3' x 1', NM...$950.00 C

Wood and masonite, Kay Displays industry "Work Refreshed" sign, 1940s, EX ....$375.00 C

Wood and masonite, Kay Displays "Refreshed Communication" sign, 1940s, EX ....$375.00 C

Wood and masonite, Kay Displays, "Refreshed Communication" sign, 1940s, VG ....$275.00 C

Wood arrow, "Drink Coca-Cola Ice Cold," silver painted bottle and arrow, 17" diameter, G ....$575.00 C

Wood, figural, die cut, "Coca-Cola" cooler, probably part of another sign, 1950s, G ....$135.00 C

Wood, "Here's Refreshment," bottle and horseshoe on plank, 1940s, F .... $150.00 C

Wood and masonite, Kay Displays transportation, work refreshed, 1940s, EX ....$350.00 D

Wood and masonite, Kay Displays work refreshed, agriculture, 1940, EX ....$275.00 D

Wood and masonite, Kay Displays work refreshed, science, 1940, EX ....$250.00 C

Wood and masonite, work refreshed, highlighting education, 1940, EX ....$250.00 C

Wood and plastic, "Drink Coca-Cola," advertising bar for Roden Soda Bar, unusual Canadian piece, 1940 – 1950s, 11" x 9", NM ....$300.00 C

Wood bottle, 3-D, silver bottle, red background, 1940s, 2' x 4', EX ....$275.00 C

Wood, "Drink Coca-Cola" above gold bottle and leaf designs, 1930s, 23" x 23", VG..........................$900.00 B

Wood, hand painted, truck sign double sided with the maker's name on one side, with original metal brackets, "Every Bottle Sterilized," white lettering on red background, 1920s, 10' x 1', F ....$450.00 D

Wood, Kay Displays, "Drink Coca-Cola," two glasses on top of red emblem, 1930s, 9" x 11", M....................$875.00 B

Wood, Kay Displays, metal at top showing glasses of Coca-Cola, 1930, EX ....$900.00 D

Wood, Kay Displays, "Please Pay Cashier," filigree on ends, 1930s, 22" x 12", EX ....$1,500.00 B

Wood and masonite, destroyer boat sign, 1940s, EX, $350.00 C.
Courtesy of Mitchell collection.

Wood and masonite, torpedo boat sign, 1940s, EX, $335.00 C.
Courtesy of Mitchell collection.

The five signs which make up this wartime set are Torpedo Boat, Destroyer, Battleship, Heavy Cruiser, and Aircraft Carrier.

Wood and masonite sign with metal arrow attached to the back and graphics of Coke bottle in spotlight at bottom, 1940s, 17" diameter, EX, $2,000.00 B.
Courtesy of Muddy River Trading Co./Gary Metz.

Wood, Kay Displays, "Please Pay Cashier" on two bars above "Drink" display, 1930s, 22" x 12½", G ....$1,950.00 B

Wood, Kay Displays, "Please Pay Cashier" with Coca-Cola at bottom, 22" x 12½", 1950, EX ....$450.00 D

Wood, Kay Displays, "Quick Service," 1930, 3" x 10", VG ....$2,100.00 B

Wood, Kay Displays, "Take some home today" double sided with button in center, 1940s, 3' x 1', F.............$600.00 C

Wood, Kay Displays, "While Shopping" with "Drink Coca-Cola" at center, 1930, 3" x 10", VG ....$1,500.00 B

Wood, Kay Displays, "While Shopping" with metal filigree at top and bottom, 1930s, 36" x 10", EX ....$1,500.00 B

Wood, Kay Displays, "While Shopping" with red "Drink Coca-Cola" below, 1930s, 10" x 3", EX ....$1,700.00 B

Wood, Kay Displays, with metal filigree at top with artwork of glasses in center, 1930s, 9" x 11½", NM ....$900.00 B

Wood, Kay Displays, "Ye What Enter Here" on board above emblem, 1940s, 39" x 11", EX..$500.00 D

Wooden medallion, Kay Displays, "Drink Coca-Cola," bottle with leaves at bottom, 1930s, EX, $1,300.00 D.

Wood, outdoor sign, weathered and worn advertising supplies, red and white on green, 1910s, 38" x 90", F ....$150.00 C

Wood, "Please Pay Cashier," cut out rope hanger, 1950s, 15" x 19", EX...$300.00 C

Wood, "Quick Service" on board with red "Drink Coca-Cola" emblem below, 1930s, 10" x 3", EX ......$2,000.00 D

Wood, "Quick Service" on board with red "Drink Coca-Cola" emblem below, 1930s, 10" x 3", F ....$600.00 B

Wood, "Resume Speed/Slow School Zone" two sided on diamonds, 1960s, 48", EX ....$900.00 B

Wood finish with chrome accents "Thirst asks nothing more," difficult to locate this piece, 38" x 10", G, $775.00 B. *Courtesy of Muddy River Trading Co./Gary Metz.*

Wood masonite "Take Home the new Home Case" sign with graphics of cardboard case in center spotlight, 1940s, 18" x 48", EX, $1,600.00 B. *Courtesy of Muddy River Trading Co./Gary Metz.*

"Thirst asks nothing more" introduced in 1938.

Wood and plastic, "Drink Coca-Cola" in fishtail sign, 15½" x 12", VG, $125.00 C.

Wood, round, pressed and raised, by Kay Displays, scarce, 13" diameter, G, $600.00 B. *Courtesy of Muddy River Trading Co./Gary Metz.*

Wood, "Here's Refreshment," bottle and horseshoe on plank, 1940s, EX, $350.00 C. *Courtesy of Bill Mitchell.*

Wood triangle double-sided sign with down arrow pointing to a bottle of Coke, 1940s, 24" x 28", G, $750.00 B. *Courtesy of Muddy River Trading Co./Gary Metz.*

Wood, Silhouette Girl, metal hanger, 1940, EX, $475.00 C. *Courtesy of Mitchell collection.*

Wood, "Slow School Zone," silhouette girl running, "Resume Speed" on back, 1957, 16" x 48", EX ..$595.00 C

Wood, "Yes," swimming girl miniature billboard, EX ....$200.00 C

Wood, Silhouette Girl, metal hanger, 1940, F ....$300.00 C

Wood, Silhouette Girl, metal hanger, 1940, P ....$150.00 D

Wood, School Zone, silhouette girl running, other side has bottle over button, 1957, 16" x 48", NM ....$2,000.00 C

Wood, "Yes," swimming girl miniature billboard, F ....$100.00 C

Bamboo calendar top from the Coca-Cola Bottler in Herrin, Illinois, with super graphics of the sun, low in the sky and a Japanese building in front of a mountain, extremely difficult to locate, 1920s, VG, $250.00 C. *Courtesy of Al and Earlene Mitchell.*

The Coca-Cola Company incorporated in 1892.

Calendar top, framed and matted with April tear sheet also in frame below image, 1903, G, $2,400.00 B. *Courtesy of Muddy River Trading Co./Gary Metz.*

Bamboo calendar top from the Coca-Cola Bottler in Herrin, Illinois, minus tear sheets, strong graphics of mountain scene and small village on water, difficult to locate good examples of this item, VG, $250.00 C. *Courtesy of Al and Earlene Mitchell.*

Calendar with fishtail top and replaceable bottom tear sheets, 1960s, EX, $475.00 B. *Courtesy of Muddy River Trading Co./Gary Metz.*

"Drink Coca-Cola," brass perpetual desk, M ..$300.00 C

Paper calendar with two months on each tear sheet, 11" x 17½", 1978, EX..$15.00 C

Paper, Jim Harrison calendar with that wonderful front page of the old lunch store, 1999, M..................$10.00 C

Paper tear sheet featuring a couple under a parasol with a couple of bottles, 12¼" x 16½", 1957, EX ....$15.00 C

Paper tear sheet featuring a young woman with a pair of boat oars, 22" x 12¼", 1957, EX ....$20.00 C

Perpetual desk showing day, month, and year, 1920, P...$35.00 D

Tin, embossed calendar holder with a new 1988 pad, with "Drink" fishtail at top, red and white, 1960s, 9" x 13", EX ....$140.00 C

Calendar top, missing the bottom pad area, 1909, 11" x 14", EX, $5,500.00 B. *Courtesy of Muddy River Trading Co./Gary Metz.*

Calendar top, featuring Hilda Clark, 7⅝" x 6", 1901, EX, $3,900.00 B. *Courtesy of Muddy River Trading Co./ Gary Metz.*

"Drink Coca-Cola," brass perpetual desk, VG, $195.00 C. *Courtesy of Mitchell collection.*

Calendar with one original tear sheet, 7" x 14", 1908, EX, $7,200.00 B. *Courtesy of Muddy River Trading Co./ Gary Metz.*

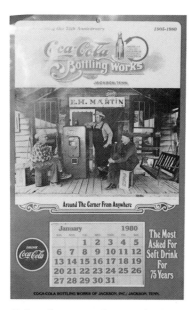

Calendars, 75th Anniversary bottlers' calendar from Jackson, Tennessee, 1980, EX, $35.00 C. *Courtesy of Mitchell collection.*

Original Betty calendar with the very scarce bottle version, has one original tear sheet, 1914, EX, $3,300.00 B. *Courtesy of Muddy River Trading Co./Gary Metz.*

Tin, fishtail calendar holder with daily tear sheets at bottom, red and white, 1960s, 9" x 13", G ....$175.00 C

Travel calendar compiled from the John Baeder postcard collection, 1997, EX ....$10.00 C

1891, from Asa Chandler & Co., featuring girl in period dress holding sport racquet with full pad moved to reveal full face of sheet, rare, EX ....$10,500.00 B

1904, Lillian Nordica standing by table with a glass, 7" x 15", F..$2,400.00 D

1905, Lillian Nordica standing beside table holding fan, table has a glass, framed, matted, and under glass, 7" x 15", G ....$3,700.00 C

1907, "Drink Coca-Cola Delicious Refreshing, Relieves Fatigue, Sold Everywhere 5¢," G....................$2,500.00 D

Tin, calendar holder with daily tear sheets at bottom featuring tin button at top, red and white, 1950s, 8" x 19", EX, $415.00 D.
Courtesy of Muddy River Trading Co./Gary Metz.

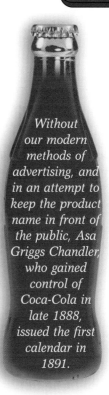

Perpetual desk showing day, month, and year, 1920, EX, $400.00 C.

1891, from Asa Chandler & Co. featuring girl in period dress holding a sport racquet with full pad moved to reveal full face of sheet, rare, G, $5,500.00 C.

Without our modern methods of advertising, and in an attempt to keep the product name in front of the public, Asa Griggs Chandler, who gained control of Coca-Cola in late 1888, issued the first calendar in 1891.

1897, "Coca-Cola at all Soda Fountains," all monthly pads displayed at once, 7" x 12", EX, $10,000.00 C.

1900, Hilda Clark at table with glass, all month pads displayed on front sheet, rare, 7" x 12", EX, $10,000.00 D.

1901, "Drink Coca-Cola at all Soda Fountains 5¢" with full monthly pad, framed, matted, and under glass, rare, EX, $5,500.00 C.

1902, "Drink Coca-Cola 5¢" with wrong month sheet, EX, $5,500.00 C.

1908, "Drink Coca-Cola Relieves Fatigue Sold Everywhere 5¢," top only, double this price if calendar is complete, 7" x 14", G ....$1,300.00 C

1911, The Coca-Cola Girl, "Drink Delicious Coca-Cola," framed, 10" x 17", Hamilton King, F ....$1,850.00 C

1912, "Drink Coca-Cola Delicious Refreshing," large version of this year's calendar, 12" x 30", King, EX ....$5,000.00 C

1912, "Drink Coca-Cola Delicious and Refreshing," King, P.................................$750.00 C

This piece of artwork is nicknamed the "Red Nordica" due to the dominance of the color red.

1904, Lillian Nordica standing by table with a glass, 7" x 15", EX, $4,000.00 D.

1905, Lillian Nordica standing beside table holding fan, table has a glass, framed, matted, and under glass, 7" x 15", EX, $5,000.00 C.

1906, Juanita, "Drink Coca-Cola Delicious Refreshing," framed, matted, under glass, 7" x 15", $5,000.00 D.

1907, "Drink Coca-Cola Delicious Refreshing, Relieves Fatigue Sold Everywhere 5¢" featuring woman in period dress holding up a glass of Coca-Cola, EX, $6,000.00 C.

1908, "Drink Coca-Cola Relieves Fatigue Sold Everywhere 5¢," top only, 7" x 14", EX, $3,000.00 C.

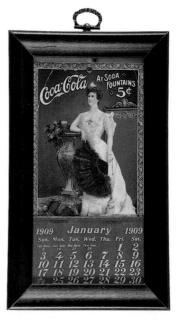

1909, Lillian Nordica beside tall table with a glass, full pad, framed under glass, 3¾" x 7", EX, $1,200.00 C. *Courtesy of Mitchell collection.*

1913, Top, girl in white hat with red ribbon, value would double if complete, rare piece matted and framed under glass, VG ....$2,500.00 C

1914, Betty, with full pad, F ....$400.00 C

1916, Elaine with glass, pad, 13" x 32", M ......$1,600.00 D

1916, World War I girl holding a glass; she also appears holding a bottle of another version, framed, 13" x 32", VG ....$1,200.00 C

1911, the Coca-Cola Girl, "Drink Delicious Coca-Cola," framed under glass, 10" x 17", Hamilton King, M, $4,600.00 B. *Courtesy of Mitchell collection.*

1912, "Drink Coca-Cola Delicious Refreshing," wrong pad, EX, $2,700.00 C.

1910, the Coca-Cola Girl with partial month pad matted, framed under glass, 8" x 17", King, EX, $5,200.00 B.

1914, Betty, top with monthly pad missing, this piece has the bottle featured which is rare, $2,200.00 C. *Courtesy of Mitchell collection.*

1913, top, girl in white hat with red ribbon, value would double if complete, rare piece matted and framed under glass, EX, $4,000.00 C. *Courtesy of Mitchell collection.*

1913, "Drink Coca-Cola Delicious Refreshing," girl drinking from flare glass with syrup line, 13" x 22", King, G, $2,500.00 C.

1914, Betty, full pad and original metal strip at top, VG, $1,450.00 C. *Courtesy of Muddy River Trading Co./Gary Metz.*

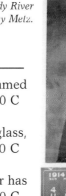

1917, Constance, with glass, full pad, matted and framed under glass, VG ....$1,750.00 C

1918, June Caprice with glass, framed under glass, VG ....$575.00 C

1918, two women at beach, one with a bottle, the other has a glass, 13" x 32", EX ....$4,500.00 C

1919, Knitting Girl, great artwork of girl with bottle and a knitting bag, full pad, 13" x 32", G ....$2,100.00 C

1915, Elaine, matted and framed with partial pad, VG, $1,450.00 C. *Courtesy of Muddy River Trading Co./Gary Metz.*

The model for this image was silent film star Faye Tincher. The image was also used on a 1916 tray.

1916, Elaine with bottle, partial pad, under glass in frame, 13" x 32", M, $2,000.00 C. *Courtesy of Mitchell collection.*

1916, the World War I Girl holding a glass, wrong pad, 13" x 32", M, $2,150.00 C.

1917, Constance, with glass, full pad, framed and matted under glass, EX, $2,550.00 C. *Courtesy of Mitchell collection.*

1919, Knitting Girl, great artwork of girl with bottle and a knitting bag, partial pad, framed under glass, 13" x 32", EX, $3,000.00 C. *Courtesy of Mitchell collection.*

1918, June Caprice with glass, framed under glass, G, $400.00 C. *Courtesy of Mitchell collection.*

1919, Marian Davis shown holding a glass, partial pad, framed, matted, under glass example of an early star endorsement, 6" x 10½", EX, $3,200.00 C.

1920, Garden Girl with bottle, 12" x 32", EX ....$1,950.00 C

1921, Autumn Girl, 12" x 32", EX ....$1,200.00 C

1922, Girl at baseball game with a glass, 12" x 32", EX ....$1,600.00 C

1923, Girl with shawl and a bottle with straw, full pad, 12" x 24", NM ....$1,300.00 C

1924, Smiling Girl holding a glass with a bottle close by, 12" x 24", beware of reproductions, EX ....$1,100.00 B

1925, Girl at party with white fox fur and a glass, 12" x 24", beware of reproductions, EX ....$850.00 C

1926, Girl in tennis outfit holding a glass, with a bottle sitting by the tennis racquet, 10" x 18", G ....$850.00 C

1920, Garden Girl with a bottle, actually at a golf course, framed under glass, 12" x 32", M, $2,600.00 C. *Courtesy of Mitchell collection.*

1921, Autumn Girl promoting fountain sales, partial pad, framed under glass, 12" x 32", M, $1,700.00 C. *Courtesy of Mitchell collection.*

1922, girl at baseball game with glass, framed under glass, 12" x 32", NM, $2,100.00 C. *Courtesy of Mitchell collection.*

1923, girl with shawl promoting bottle sales, full pad, framed under glass, 12" x 24", VG, $950.00 C. *Courtesy of Mitchell collection.*

1924, smiling girl in period dress holding a glass with a bottle close by, framed under glass. 12" x 24", M, $1,400.00 C. **Beware of reproductions.** *Courtesy of Mitchell collection.*

1925, girl at party wearing white fox fur and promoting fountain sales, framed under glass, 12" x 24", M, $1,100.00 C. **Beware of reproductions.** *Courtesy of Mitchell collection.*

1926, girl in tennis outfit holding a glass, with a bottle sitting by the tennis racquet, framed under glass, 10" x 18", VG, $1,100.00 C. *Courtesy of Mitchell collection.*

1927, girl in sheer dress holding a glass, partial pad, framed under glass, Taylor's Billiard Parlor, 12" x 24", M, $1,800.00 C. *Courtesy of Mitchell collection.*

1927, "The Drink that Makes The Whole World Kin," VG ....$900.00 C

1927, "The Drink that Makes The Whole World Kin," with bottle in oval frame at lower left, EX ....$975.00 C

1927, "The Drink that Makes The Whole World Kin," with bottle in oval frame at lower left, promoting bottle sales, framed under glass, M, $1,150.00 C. *Courtesy of Mitchell collection.*

1928, lady in evening wear holding glass, partial pad, framed under glass, 12" x 24", M, $1,000.00 C. *Courtesy of Mitchell collection.*

1929, flapper girl in green dress with string of beads displaying both glass and bottle, full pad, framed under glass, 12" x 24", M, $1,075.00 C. *Courtesy of Mitchell collection.*

1930, woman in swimming attire sitting on rock with canoe in foreground with bottles, display partial pad, framed under glass, 12" x 24", M, $1,200.00 C. *Courtesy of Mitchell collection.*

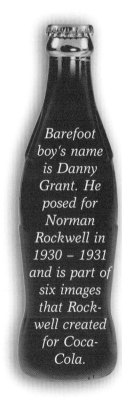

Barefoot boy's name is Danny Grant. He posed for Norman Rockwell in 1930 – 1931 and is part of six images that Rockwell created for Coca-Cola.

1931, boy at fishing hole with dog, sandwich, and a bottle, full pad, framed under glass, 12" x 24", Rockwell, M, $950.00 C. *Courtesy of Mitchell collection.*

1929, Flapper girl in green dress, string of beads, glass and bottle, full pad, 12" x 24", EX ....$800.00 C

1930, Woman in swimming attire sitting on rock with canoe in foreground with bottles, partial pad, 12" x 24", EX ....$775.00 D

1933, The Village Blacksmith with full pad, 12" x 24", Frederic Stanley, EX...$700.00 C

1934, Girl on porch playing music for elderly gentleman with cane, full pad, 12" x 24", Rockwell, EX ..$500.00 C

1935, Boy with a bottle sitting on a stump fishing, full pad, 12" x 24", Rockwell, beware of reproductions, VG ....$500.00 C

1936, 50th Anniversary, older man at small boat and a young girl enjoying a bottle, full pad, 12" x 24", N.C. Wyeth, VG ....$550.00 C

1937, Boy walking, fishing pole over his shoulder, holding bottles, 12" x 24", EX ....$550.00 C

1941, Girl wearing ice skates sitting on log, displaying a bottle, full pad displays two months at same time, VG ....$250.00 C

1928, Lady in evening wear holding glass, full pad, 12" x 24", VG...$975.00 C

1942, "America Love It or Leave It" from Brownsville, Tennessee, featuring a drum and fife attachment, with monthly pads, G ....$75.00 C

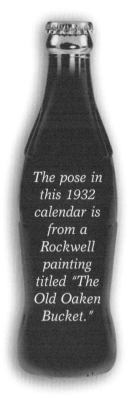

The pose in this 1932 calendar is from a Rockwell painting titled "The Old Oaken Bucket."

1932, young boy sitting at well with a bucket full of bottles and a dog sitting up at his feet, full pad, framed and under glass, 12" x 24", Rockwell, M, $825.00 C. *Courtesy of Mitchell collection.*

1933, Village Blacksmith will full pad, framed and under glass, 12" x 24", Frederic Stanley, M, $775.00 C. *Courtesy of Mitchell collection.*

1934, girl on porch playing music for elderly gentleman with cane, full pad, framed under glass, 12" x 24", Rockwell, M, $750.00 C. *Courtesy of Mitchell collection.*

This image was the last of six pieces produced for Coke by Rockwell and was printed on nearly two million calendars.

1935, "Out Fishin'," boy sitting on a stump fishing with a bottle, full pad, framed under glass, 12" x 24", Rockwell, M, $750.00 C. Beware of reproductions. *Courtesy of Mitchell collection.*

1943, Military nurse with a bottle, full pad displays two months at same time, VG ....$300.00 C

1943, Pocket, "Tastes like Home," small, with all months shown on one front sheet, sailor drinking from a bottle, G ....$40.00 C

1945, Boy Scout in front of the Scout Oath, Rockwell, M ....$550.00 D

1945, Girl in head scarf with snow falling in the background, full pad, VG ....$250.00 C

1946, Boy Scout den chief showing younger Cub Scout how to tie a knot, Rockwell, VG ....$450.00 D

1948, Girl in coat and gloves, holding a bottle, full pad, VG ....$250.00 C

1936, 50th Anniversary, older man at small boat and a young girl enjoying a bottle, full pad, framed under glass, 12" x 24", N.C. Wyeth, M, $825.00 C. *Courtesy of Mitchell collection.*

1937, boy walking with fishing pole over his shoulder, holding a couple bottles, framed under glass, 12" x 24", M, $750.00 C. *Courtesy of Mitchell collection.*

1938, girl sitting in front of blinds with a bottle, full pad, framed under glass, Crandall, M, $695.00 C. *Courtesy of Mitchell collection.*

1939, girl starting to pour Coca-Cola from bottle into glass, unmarked, full pad, framed under glass, M, $550.00 C. *Courtesy of Mitchell collection.*

1940, woman in red dress with a glass and a bottle, full pad, framed and under glass, VG, $525.00 C. *Courtesy of Mitchell collection.*

1941, girl wearing ice skates sitting on a log and displaying a bottle, full pad that displays two months at once, EX, $375.00 C. *Courtesy of Mitchell collection.*

1942, boy and girl with bottles building snowman, full pad displays two months at once, VG, $325.00 C. *Courtesy of Mitchell collection.*

1952, "Coke adds Zest," full calendar pad, VG ..$135.00 C

1953, "Work Better Refreshed," full pad, VG ....$125.00 C

1953, Boy Scout, Cub Scout, Explorer Scout in front of Liberty Bell, Coca-Cola Bottling Works, Greenwood, Mississippi, Rockwell, VG ....$275.00 C

1942, "America Love It or Leave It" from Brownsville, Tennessee, featuring a drum and fife attachment with monthly pads, EX, $135.00 C. *Courtesy of Mitchell collection.*

1943, pocket, "Tastes like Home," small, with all months shown on one front sheet, sailor drinking from a bottle, EX, $55.00 C. *Courtesy of Mitchell collection.*

1943, pocket, "Here's to our G.I. Joes," two girls toasting with bottles, EX, $55.00 C. *Courtesy of Mitchell collection.*

1943, military nurse with a bottle, full pad displays two months at once, EX, $475.00 C. *Courtesy of Mitchell collection.*

1944, woman holding a bottle, full pad, EX, $300.00 C. *Courtesy of Mitchell collection.*

1945, girl in head scarf with snow falling in the background, full pad, EX, $325.00 C. *Courtesy of Mitchell collection.*

1947, girl holding snow skis with mountains in background, full pad, EX, $350.00 C. *Courtesy of Mitchell collection.*

1948, girl in coat and gloves holding a bottle, full pad, EX, $325.00 C. *Courtesy of Mitchell collection.*

1954, "Me, too!" 1953 Santa cover sheet, full pad, G ....$85.00 C

1954, Reference edition with full pad featuring Santa with bottle, VG ....$85.00 C

1955, Reference edition with Santa holding a bottle, M ....$35.00 C

1956, "There's nothing like a Coke," full pad, EX ....$125.00 C

1957, "The pause that refreshes," girl holding ski poles and bottle, VG ....$75.00 C

1958, Snow scene of a boy and girl with a bottle, "Sign of Good Taste," full pad, EX ....$135.00 C

1949, girl in red cap with a bottle, full pad, M, $275.00 C. *Courtesy of Mitchell collection.*

1950, woman with a serving tray full of bottles, full pad, M, $295.00 C. *Courtesy of Mitchell collection.*

1951, girl at party holding a bottle, with colorful streamers in background, full pad, M, $195.00 C. *Courtesy of Mitchell collection.*

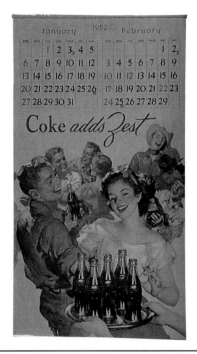

1952, "Coke adds Zest," party scene with a girl serving bottles from tray, full calendar pad, M, $175.00 C. *Courtesy of Mitchell collection.*

1953, "Work Better Refreshed," work scenes with woman in center in work scarf holding a bottle, full pad, M, $175.00 C. *Courtesy of Mitchell collection.*

1960, "Be Really Refreshed," VG.........................$50.00 C

1960, Reference with puppies in Christmas stockings, VG ....$15.00 D

1961, Santa reference calendar, VG....................$15.00 C

1963, Reference edition with Santa Claus, holding a bottle, in middle of electric train display in front of Christmas tree with helicopter flying around his head, VG ....$25.00 C

1964, Japanese girl pictured on front, full pad, EX ....$375.00 B

1964, Reference featuring Santa standing by a fireplace with his list and a bottle, VG ....$20.00 C

1964, "Things go better with Coke," featuring a woman reclining on a couch while a man is offering her a bottle, EX ....$75.00 C

128

This Boy Scout calendar was commissioned by the Boy Scouts of America, not Coca-Cola, and was published by Brown & Bigelow, the largest calendar publisher in the country.

1953, Boy Scout, Cub Scout, and Explorer Scout in front of the Liberty Bell, Coca-Cola Bottling Works, Greenwood, Mississippi, matted and framed under glass, Rockwell, EX, $425.00 D. *Courtesy of Mitchell collection.*

1954, sports scene in background with woman in foreground holding a bottle, full calendar pad, M, $195.00 C. *Courtesy of Mitchell collection.*

1955, woman in hat holding a bottle, full pad, M, $225.00 C. *Courtesy of Mitchell collection.*

1956, "There's nothing like a Coke," full pad, featuring girl pulling on ice skates, M, $145.00 C. *Courtesy of Mitchell collection.*

1957, "The pause that refreshes," girl holding ski poles and a bottle, EX, $100.00 C. *Courtesy of Mitchell collection.*

1958, snow scene of a boy and girl with a bottle, "Sign of Good Taste," full pad, M, $185.00 C. *Courtesy of Mitchell collection.*

1965, Reference edition with Santa and children, VG ....$20.00 C

1967, "For the taste you never get tired of," featuring five women with trophy, full pad, VG ....$35.00 C

1967, Reference edition with Santa Claus sitting at desk with a bottle, G ....$15.00 C

1968, "Coke has the taste you never get tired of," girl looking at 45rpm record and holding a bottle, with full pad, EX ....$65.00 C

1968, Reference edition of Santa on ladder, M ..$30.00 D

1969, Reference edition showing Holiday Greetings, bottle on front, EX ....$12.00 C

1958, reference edition with "Sign of Good Taste" with flowers against a brick background, M, $25.00 C. *Courtesy of Mitchell collection.*

1959, birds sitting on branch with a Coke button under branch, reference version, Athos Menaboni, M, $35.00 D. *Courtesy of Mitchell collection.*

1959, girl being offered a bottle in front of a sports scene, full pad, G, $140.00 C. *Courtesy of Mitchell collection.*

1960, "Be Really Refreshed," featuring man and woman holding skis, each with a bottle, full pad, M, $95.00 C. *Courtesy of Mitchell collection.*

1960, reference with puppies in Christmas stockings, EX, $25.00 C. *Courtesy of Mitchell collection.*

1961, "Coke Refreshes You Best," woman being offered a bottle, full pad, M, $85.00 C. *Courtesy of Mitchell collection.*

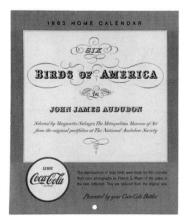

1962, reference of Birds of America, M, $35.00 C. *Courtesy of Mitchell collection.*

1962, "Enjoy that Refreshing New Feeling," boy holding bottle and offering other hand to dance with a young woman, M, $80.00 C. *Courtesy of Mitchell collection.*

1970, "It's the real thing," Coca-Cola presented its new image here, one that many collectors don't care to collect, so the demand for 1970 or newer calendars is not great ... yet! G .... $15.00 C

1970, Reference edition featuring Santa with a bottle, EX .... $15.00 C

1970s, Tin holder with wave logo at top and tear-off day sheets on bottom, EX .... $70.00 D

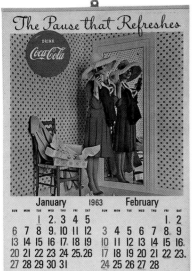

1963, "The Pause that Refreshes," with a woman looking at new clothes in a door mirror, M, $90.00 C.
Courtesy of Mitchell collection.

1964, "Things go better with Coke," featuring a woman reclining on a couch while a man is offering her a bottle, M, $85.00 C.
Courtesy of Mitchell collection.

1965, "Things go better with Coke," a couple relaxing by a log cabin, each with a bottle, $85.00 C. *Courtesy of Mitchell collection.*

1966, man pictured holding serving tray with food and bottles over woman's head, full pad, "Things Go Better with Coke," M, $90.00 C. *Courtesy of Mitchell collection.*

1967, "For the taste you never get tired of," featuring five women with trophy, full pad, M, $65.00 C. *Courtesy of Mitchell collection.*

1968, "Coke has the taste you never get tired of," girl looking at 45rpm record and holding a bottle, with full pad, M, $75.00 C.
Courtesy of Mitchell collection.

1971, Shadow box with full pad, M ....$40.00 D

1972, Cloth featuring Lillian Nordica, VG.........$10.00 D

1972, featuring crafts & hobbies to enjoy with the real thing, Coke, M ....$20.00 D

1974, 1927 reproduction, reverse image, full pad, M ....$25.00 D

1978, Air-borne snow skier, full pad, M ....$20.00 D

1980, Sports scenes, full pad, M ....$20.00 D

1969, reference edition showing Holiday Greetings with bottles on front, M, $15.00 C. *Courtesy of Mitchell collection.*

1969, "Things go better with Coke," featuring boy whispering into girl's ear while both are seated at a table enjoying a bottle, full pad, M, $75.00 C. *Courtesy of Mitchell collection.*

1970, "It's the real thing," Coca-Cola presented its new image here, one that many collectors don't care to collect, so demand for 1970 or newer calendars is not great — yet! M, $35.00 C. *Courtesy of Mitchell collection.*

1972, cloth featuring Lillian Nordica, EX, $12.00 C.

1973, cloth with Lillian Nordica standing by Coca-Cola table, EX, $10.00 D.

1975, scenes of America showing backpackers, with full pad, M, $25.00 C. *Courtesy of Mitchell collection.*

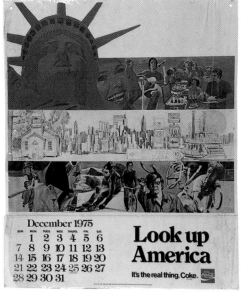

1976, "Look up America," "It's the real thing — Coke," with full pad, M, $45.00 C. *Courtesy of Mitchell collection.*

1979 Olympic torch, full pad, M, $20.00 C. *Courtesy of Mitchell collection.*

1981, "Have a Coke and a smile," full pad with scenes of America at top, EX, $20.00 C. *Courtesy of Mitchell collection.*

1982, Four women around piano, full pad, M ..$20.00 D

1983, Iced down bottles in front of a bonfire, full pad, M ....$20.00 D

Candles TV tray, 1961, 18¾" x 13½", EX, $15.00 D.

Change, "Drink a Bottle of Carbonated Coca-Cola," 1903, 5½" diameter, EX, $5,000.00 C.

Top left: Change, "Drink Coca-Cola Delicious Refreshing," Juanita, 1900s, 4" diameter, EX, $1,000.00 D.

Top right: Change, World War I Girl, 1916, 4⅜" x 6⅛", EX, $400.00 C.

Bottom left: Change, "Drink Coca-Cola, Relieves Fatigue," 1907, EX, $775.00 C.

Bottom right: Change, featuring Betty, 1914, EX, $450.00 C.

Courtesy of Mitchell collection.

Top left: Change, Hamilton King model enjoying a glass, 1913, 4¼" x 6", EX, $625.00 C.

Top right: Change, oval commemorating the St. Louis World's Fair, 1909, 4¼" x 6", EX, $650.00 C.

Bottom left: Change, oval, last change tray issued in United States, 1920, EX, $450.00 C.

Bottom right: Change, featuring the Coca-Cola Girl, 1910, King, EX, $600.00 C.

Courtesy of Mitchell collection.

Canadian, 1957, 14¼" x 10½", EX ....$150.00 C

Change, "Drink a Bottle of Carbonated Coca-Cola," 1903, 5½" diameter, G ....$2,500.00 C

Hilda Clark posed for Coca-Cola from 1899 until 1904 – 1905.

Change, Hilda Clark at table with stationery holding a glass in a glass holder, 1903, 6" diameter, EX, $2,300.00 B.

Change, Hilda Clark, metal, 1903, 4" diameter, EX, $2,400.00 D.

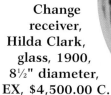

Change, Hilda Clark with flowers, 1901, 6" diameter, EX, $2,500.00 C.

Change receiver, Hilda Clark, glass, 1900, 8½" diameter, EX, $4,500.00 C.

Change, Hilda Clark seated at table with glass, 1900, 6" diameter, EX, $3,700.00 D.

Change, featuring Hilda Clark, round, 1903, 6" diameter, VG ....$1,800.00 B

Change, featuring the Coca-Cola Girl by Hamilton King, 1909 – 1910, 4⅜" x 6⅛", VG.............................$350.00 B

Change, featuring the Coca-Cola Girl by Hamilton King, 1909 – 10, 4⅜" x 6⅛", G....................................$250.00 C

Change, featuring the Coca-Cola Girl, 1910, King, VG...$425.00 C

Change, Hilda Clark, 1901, 6" diameter, VG ..$1,250.00 B

Change receiver, ceramic, "The Ideal Brain Tonic" with red lettering, 1890s, 10½" diameter, VG...............$4,500.00 C

Change receiver, ceramic, with dark lettering and red line outline "The Ideal Brain Tonic, For Headache and Exhaustion," 1899, F ....$2,800.00 C

Change receiver, glass, "Drink Coca-Cola 5¢," 1907, 7" diameter, VG ....$775.00 C

Change receiver, Griselda Change, 1905, 13" x 13", NM ....$975.00 D

Change receiver, glass, "Drink Coca-Cola 5¢," 1907, 7" diameter, EX, $1,250.00 C.

Change receiver, Griselda Change, 1905, 13" x 13", EX, $875.00 D.

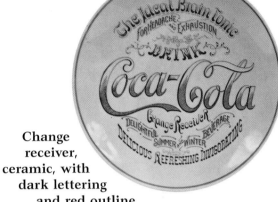

Change receiver, ceramic, with dark lettering and red outline "The Ideal Brain Tonic, For Headache and Exhaustion," 1899, EX, $5,700.00 C.

Commemorative bottlers serving tray from the Lehigh Valley with artwork of plant, 1981, EX, $15.00 C. *Courtesy of Mitchell collection.*

Serving, Autumn Girl, this model is featured on the 1922 calendar, rectangular, 1920s, 10½" x 13¼", EX, $1,000.00 C. *Courtesy of Mitchell collection.*

Serving, Betty, manufactured by Stelad Signs, Passaic, New Jersey, oval, 1914, 12½" x 15¼", EX, $900.00 C. Beware of reproductions. *Courtesy of Mitchell collection.*

Serving, boy and dog, boy is holding sandwich and a bottle, 1931, 10½" x 13¼", Rockwell, EX, $900.00 C. *Courtesy of Mitchell collection.*

Change receiver, Hilda Clark, glass, 1900, 8½" diameter, VG ....$3,500.00 D

Christmas serving tray; there are many variations of this tray, 1973, VG ....$15.00 D

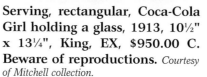

Serving, Coca-Cola Girl, oval, 1913, 12¼" x 14¼", King, EX, $975.00 C. *Courtesy of Mitchell collection.*

Serving, rectangular, Coca-Cola Girl holding a glass, 1913, 10½" x 13¼", King, EX, $950.00 C. **Beware of reproductions.** *Courtesy of Mitchell collection.*

Serving, Canadian commemorative with the English version, with Lillian Nordica, 1968, 10½" x 13¼", EX, $85.00 C. *Courtesy of Mitchell collection.*

Serving, "Drink Coca-Cola, Delicious and Refreshing," girl on dock, Sailor Girl, 1940, 13¼" x 10½", NM, $625.00 B. *Courtesy of Buffalo Bay Auction Co.*

Serving, "Coca-Cola" with good litho by Western Coca-Cola Bottling Company of Chicago, Illinois, without the sanction of the Coca-Cola Company, 1908, EX, $5,500.00 D. *Courtesy of Muddy River Trading Co./ Gary Metz.*

Serving, "Drink Coca-Cola, Refreshing Delicious," featuring Hilda Clark, 1900, 9¼" diameter, EX, $7,500.00 B.

"Drink Coca-Cola, Delicious Refreshing," red background with yellow and white lettering, fairly rare, 1940 – 1950s, 12¾" diameter, EX ....$450.00 C

General Merchandise, new, painted by Jeanne Mack, inspired by a real location in Georgia where rural neighbors would gather for an ice cold "Coke," 17½" x 12¾", 1997, NM ....$15.00 C

Serving, Autumn Girl, rectangular, 1920s, 10½" x 13¼", VG ....$775.00 C

Serving, Betty, manufactured by Stelad Signs, Passaic, New Jersey, oval, 1914, 12½" x 15¼", beware of reproductions, G ....$200.00 C

Serving, boy and dog, boy is holding sandwich and a bottle, 1931, 10½" x 13¼", Rockwell, VG ....$775.00 C

Serving, Captain James Cook bicentennial, produced to celebrate the landing at Nootka Sound, B.C, "Coca-Cola" on back, 1978, EX ....$35.00 D

Serving, "Drink Coca-Cola Relieves Fatigue," oval, 1907, 10½" x 13¼", EX, $2,500.00 C. *Courtesy of Mitchell collection.*

Serving, featuring a couple receiving curb service, 1927, 13¼" x 10½", G, $775.00 C. *Courtesy of Mitchell collection.*

Serving, featuring Betty, rectangular, 1914, 10½" x 13¼", EX, $825.00 C. Beware of reproductions. *Courtesy of Mitchell collection.*

Serving, featuring a pull cart with a picnic basket, 1958, 13¼" x 10½", EX, $25.00 C. *Courtesy of Mitchell collection.*

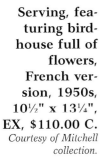

Serving, featuring bird-house full of flowers, French version, 1950s, 10½" x 13¼", EX, $110.00 C. *Courtesy of Mitchell collection.*

Serving, featuring Elaine (modeled by film star Faye Tincher), manufactured by Stelad Signs Passaic Metal Ware Company, Passaic, New Jersey, rectangular, 1916, 8½" x 19", EX, $675.00 C. Beware of reproductions. *Courtesy of Mitchell collection.*

Serving, Captain James Cook bicentennial, produced to celebrate landing at Nootka Sound, B.C, "Coca-Cola" on back, 1978, NM ....$45.00 D

Serving, "Coca-Cola" with good litho by Western Coca-Cola Bottling Company of Chicago, Illinois, without the sanction of the Coca-Cola Company, 1908, G ....$3,200.00 C

Serving, Coca-Cola Girl holding a glass, 1913, 10½" x 13¼", King, beware of reproductions, G ....$550.00 C

Serving, Curb Service for fountain sales, 1928, EX ....$900.00 B

Serving, "Drink Coca-Cola, Delicious and Refreshing," Sailor Girl, 1940, 13¼" x 10½", VG.................$300.00 C

Serving, featuring model Paulene Moore on arm of chair in party dress, Hostess, 1936, 10½" x 13¼", EX, $475.00 C. *Courtesy of Mitchell collection.*

Serving, featuring girl on beach in chair with a bottle, 1932, 10½" x 13¼", EX, $650.00 C. *Courtesy of Mitchell collection.*

Serving, featuring girl with ice skates on log and a bottle, 1941, 10½" x 13¼", EX, $375.00 C. *Courtesy of Mitchell collection.*

Serving, featuring movie star Madge Evans, manufactured by American Art Works, Inc., Coshocton, Ohio, 1935, 10½" x 13¼", EX, $475.00 D. *Courtesy of Mitchell collection.*

Serving, featuring Lillian Nordica on Canadian commemorative, 1968, 10½" x 3¼", EX, $85.00 C. *Courtesy of Mitchell collection.*

Serving, featuring red-haired woman in yellow scarf with a bottle, 1950s, 10½" x 13¼", EX, $225.00 C. Beware of reproductions. *Courtesy of Mitchell collection.*

Serving, "Drink Coca-Cola Relieves Fatigue," oval, 1907, 10½" x 13¼", G ....$1,000.00 C

Serving, "Drive-In," "Drink Coca-Cola" in fishtail logo "Goes good with food" under logo "Drive in for Coke" on rim, a hard to find piece, 1959, VG ....$150.00 C

Serving, Edmonton, rectangular, 1978, 10½" x 13¼", EX ....$35.00 C

Serving, Elaine, 1916, 8½" x 19", VG ....$450.00 D

Serving, featuring a couple receiving curb service, 1927, 13¼" x 10½", NM ....$925.00 C

Serving, featuring a pull cart with a picnic basket, 1958, 13¼" x 10½", G ....$15.00 C

Serving, featuring Betty, rectangular, 1914, 10½" x 13¼", beware of reproductions, VG ....$650.00 C

Serving, featuring Maureen O'Sullivan and Johnny Weissmuller both holding bottles, 1934, 13¼" x 10½", EX, $975.00 C. Beware of reproductions. *Courtesy of Mitchell collection.*

Serving, featuring girl running on beach with bottles in each hand, 1937, EX, $375.00 C. Beware of reproductions. *Courtesy of Mitchell collection.*

Model Verna Clair, whose real name is Josephine Moore, was the "Running Girl" model.

Serving, featuring the Coca-Cola Girl, this was the first rectangular tray used by the Coca-Cola Company by American Art Works, Inc., 1909, 10½" x 13¼", King, EX, $1,200.00 C. Beware of reproductions. *Courtesy of Mitchell collection.*

Serving, featuring the girl at party, 1921, 10½" x 13¼", G, $500.00 C. *Courtesy of Mitchell collection.*

Serving, featuring the movie star, Frances Dee, 1933, 10½" x 13¼", EX, $575.00 C. *Courtesy of Mitchell collection.*

Serving, featuring birdhouse full of flowers, French version, 1950s, 10½" x 13¼", VG.............................$35.00 D

Serving, featuring bottle of Coca-Cola with food, Mexican, 1970, 13¼", M ....$25.00 D

Serving, featuring Elaine, manufactured by Stelad Signs Passaic Metal Ware Company, Passaic, New Jersey, rectangular, 1916, 8½" x 19", beware of reproductions, VG ....$475.00 C

Serving, featuring girl at party, 1921, 10½" x 13¼", VG ....$350.00 C

Serving, featuring girl on arm of chair in party dress, Hostess, 1936, 10½" x 13¼", VG ....$325.00 C

Serving, featuring girl on beach in chair with a bottle, 1932, 10½" x 13¼", VG....................................$475.00 C

Serving, featuring girl running on beach with bottle in each hand, 1937, beware of reproductions, G ..$150.00 D

Serving, featuring ice skater with bottle on log, 1941, 10½" x 13¼", VG ....$275.00 C

139

Serving, featuring the Smiling Girl holding a glass, this tray can have either a brown or maroon border, add $200.00 for maroon tray, 1924, 10½" x 13¼", EX, $750.00 C. *Courtesy of Mitchell collection.*

Serving, featuring the Summer Girl, manufactured by the H.D. Beach Company Coshocton, Ohio, 1922, 10½" x 13¼", EX, $850.00 C. *Courtesy of Mitchell collection.*

Serving, featuring woman in rain coat with umbrella and a bottle, French version, 1950s, 10½" x 13¼", G, $150.00 C. *Courtesy of Mitchell collection.*

Serving, Flapper Girl, 1923, 10½" x 13¼", EX, $435.00 C. *Courtesy of Mitchell collection.*

Serving, French, featuring food and bottles on table, 1957, EX, $100.00 C. *Courtesy of Mitchell collection.*

Serving, girl in afternoon with a bottle, produced by American Art Works Inc., Coshocton, Ohio, 1938, 10½" x 13¼", EX, $350.00 C. *Courtesy of Mitchell collection.*

Serving, featuring Lillian Nordica on Canadian commemorative, 1968, 10½" x 13¼", VG ....$65.00 C

Serving, featuring Maureen O'Sullivan and Johnny Weissmuller, 1934, 13¼" x 10½", beware of reproductions, G...$400.00 C

Serving, featuring movie star Madge Evans, manufactured by American Art Works, Inc., Coshocton, Ohio, 1935, 10½" x 13¼", VG....................................$375.00 C

Serving, featuring red-haired woman in yellow scarf with a bottle, 1950s, 10½" x 13¼", beware of reproductions, VG ....$125.00 C

Serving, featuring the Coca-Cola Girl; this was the first rectangular tray used by the Coca-Cola Company by American Art Works, Inc., 1909, 10½" x 13¼", King, beware of reproductions, VG..........................$850.00 C

Serving, featuring the movie star, Frances Dee, 1933, 10½" x 13¼", G ....$350.00 C

Serving, featuring the Smiling Girl holding a glass, 1924, 10½" x 13¼", VG ....$525.00 C

Serving, featuring the Summer Girl, 1922, 10½" x 13¼", VG ....$675.00 C

Serving, girl in yellow swim suit holding bottle, promoting bottle sales, produced by American Art Works Inc., Coshocton, Ohio, 1929, 10½" x 13¼", EX, $750.00 C.

Serving, Garden Girl, 1920, 10½" x 13¼", EX, $900.00 C. *Courtesy of Mitchell collection.*

Serving, Garden Girl, 1920, 13¼" x 16½", EX, $875.00 C. *Courtesy of Mitchell collection.*

Serving, girl on a spring board, 1939, 10½" x 13¼", EX, $350.00 C. *Courtesy of Mitchell collection.*

Serving, Hilda Clark, "Drink Coca-Cola Invigorating, Refreshing, Delicious," 1899, 9¼" diameter, EX, $10,500.00 D.

Serving, Hilda Clark, round, 1903, 9½" diameter, NM, $3,200.00 B. *Courtesy of Muddy River Trading Co./Gary Metz.*

Serving, Flapper Girl, 1923, 10½" x 13¼", G....$125.00 C

Serving, Garden Girl, 1920, 13½" x 16½", VG..$400.00 C

Serving, girl in afternoon with a bottle, produced by American Art Works Inc., Coshocton, Ohio, 1938, 10½" x 13¼", VG ....$200.00 C

Serving, girl in swim suit holding bottle, promoting bottle sales, 1929, 10½" x 13¼", VG ....$600.00 C

Serving, girl on a spring board, 1939, 10½" x 13¼", VG ....$250.00 C

Serving, girl with glass and bottle, Mexican, round, 1965, 13¼" diameter, M..$115.00 D

Serving, "Hambly's Beverage Limited," featuring World War I girl, 60th anniversary, 1977, EX ....$25.00 D

Serving, "Here's a Coke for you," more than three versions of this tray, 1961, 13¼" x 10½", VG ....$20.00 D

Serving, Juanita, bottle version, 1906, 10½" x 13¼", EX ....$2,500.00 D

Serving, Juanita, oval, "Drink Coca-Cola, In Bottles 5¢, at Fountains 5¢," 1906, 10½" x 13¼", VG..........$1,750.00 C

Serving, Lillian Nordica, "Drink Carbonated Coca-Cola in Bottles 5¢ Delicious Refreshing," oval, 1905, 10½" x 13", G...$2,000.00 C

Serving, Juanita, oval, "Drink Coca-Cola, In Bottles 5¢, at Fountains 5¢," 1906, 10½" x 13¼", EX, $2,500.00 D.

Serving, "Here's a Coke for you," more than three versions of this tray, 1961, 13¼" x 10½", EX, $30.00 C. *Courtesy of Mitchell collection.*

Serving, Lillian Nordica, "Drink Coca-Cola at Soda Fountains, Delicious Refreshing," oval, 1905, 10½" x 13", EX, $4,000.00 D.

Serving, miscellaneous items, French version, 1950s, 10½" x 13¼", G, $110.00 C.

Serving, promoting bottle sales, bobbed hair girl drinking from bottle with a straw, 1928, 10½" x 13¼", EX, $750.00 C. *Courtesy of Mitchell collection.*

Serving, Menu Girl, French version, 1955 – 1960, 10½" x 13¼", EX ....$175.00 D

Serving, Menu Girl holding a bottle in her hand, 1950s, 10½" x 13¼", VG ....$75.00 D

Serving, Menu Girl, English version, 1950s, 10½" x 13¼", EX ....$125.00 C

Serving, oval, Hilda Clark, 1903, 15" x 18½", EX ....$5,100.00 B

Serving, pansy garden, 1961, 13¼" x 10½", EX ....$30.00 B

Serving, promoting bottle sales, bobbed hair girl drinking from bottle with a straw, 1928, 10½" x 13¼", VG ..$650.00 C

Serving, promoting bottle sales, girl in red swim cap and white swim suit with towel, 1930, EX, $475.00 C. *Courtesy of Mitchell collection.*

142

Serving, promoting fountain sales, girl on phone, "meet me at the soda fountain," 1930, 10½" x 13¼", EX, $500.00 C.
Courtesy of Mitchell collection.

Serving, promoting fountain sales with soda person, 1928, 10½" x 13¼", EX, $675.00 B.
Courtesy of Mitchell collection.

Serving, round, "Drink a Bottle of Carbonated Coca-Cola, The Most Refreshing Drink in the World," 1903, 9¾" dia., EX, $6,500.00 D. Beware of reproductions.

Serving, sports couple, 1926, 10½" x 13¼", EX, $850.00 C. Beware of reproductions.
Courtesy of Mitchell collection.

Serving, St. Louis Fair, oval, 1909, 13½" x 16½", EX, $2,800.00 C.
Courtesy of Mitchell collection.

Serving, promoting bottle sales, girl in red swim cap and bathing suit with a towel, 1930, G ....$275.00 C

Serving, promoting bottle sales, 1929, 10½" x 13¼", F..$450.00 C

Serving, promoting fountain sales, girl on phone, "meet me at the soda fountain," 1930, 10½" x 13¼", VG ....$375.00 C

Serving, promoting fountain sales with soda jerk, 1928, 10½" x 13¼", F ....$225.00 C

Serving, rectangular, covered bridge with "Coca-Cola" on side, Summer Bridge, 1995, Jim Harrison, EX ....$15.00 D

Serving, rectangular, "Goodwill Bottling Std.," logo in lower right, 1979, EX..$15.00 D

Serving, red-haired girl with wind in hair on solid background, 1950, beware of reproductions, EX.....$200.00 C

Serving, two women at car with bottles, because of metal needed in the war effort this was the last tray produced until after World War II, 1942, EX, $400.00 C; G, $104.00 B. *Courtesy of Mitchell collection.*

TV, assortment, 1956, 18¾" x 13½", EX, $15.00 D.

Serving, Victorian Girl, "Drink Coca-Cola, Refreshing, Delicious," woman drinking from a glass, 1897, 9¼" diameter, EX, $14,000.00 B.

TV, Thanksgiving, 1961, 18¾" x 13½", EX, $20.00 C.

TV, Duster Girl, 1972, 10¾" x 14¾", EX, $15.00 C.

Tray, commemorative Alabama/Auburn tray, 1975, EX, $30.00 C. *Courtesy of Mitchell collection.*

Serving, round, "Drink a Bottle of Carbonated Coca-Cola, The Most Refreshing Drink in the World," 1903, 9¾" diameter, NM ....$7,000.00 C

Serving, round, featuring University of Indiana basketball, 1976, EX ....$25.00 D

Serving, sports couple, 1926, 10½" x 13¼", beware of reproductions, VG ....$725.00 B

Serving, St. Louis Fair, oval, 1909, 13½" x 16½", VG ....$1,800.00 C

Serving, two women at car with bottles, because of metal needed in the war effort this was the last tray produced until after World War II, 1942, NM ....$425.00 C

Serving, with Garden Girl, 1920, 10½" x 13¼", VG ....$650.00 C

St. Louis Fair, 1909, 10½" x 13¼", EX ....$1,500.00 C

TV, assortment, 1956, 18¾" x 13½", VG ....$10.00 C

TV, Duster Girl, 1972, 10¾" x 14¾", VG ....$10.00 C

TV, Thanksgiving, 1961, 18¾" x 13¾", VG........$15.00 D

Victorian Girl, "Drink Coca-Cola, Refreshing, Delicious," woman drinking from a glass, 1897, 9¼" diameter, F ....$3,500.00 C

Alphabet Book of Coca-Cola,
1928, EX, $110.00 C.
Courtesy of Mitchell collection.

Alphabet Book of Coca-Cola, 1928, VG ....$70.00 C

Book, *100 Best Posters*, hard cover, 1941, EX ....$65.00 D

Book cover, "America is Strong ... because America is Good!" Dwight Eisenhower on front, 1950s, VG...............$15.00 C

Book cover for school book, 1940 – 50s, white and red, NM ....$15.00 C

Book, *Illustrated Guide to the Collectibles of Coca-Cola*, Cecil Munsey, 1972, EX ....$85.00 C

Book, *Illustrated Guide to the Collectibles of Coca-Cola*, Cecil Munsey, 1972, NM...$100.00 C

Book, *Pause For Living*, bound copy, 1960s, red, EX ....$15.00 C

Book, six bottle carton with dealer info, 1937, EX ....$20.00 C

Book, sugar ration, 1943, EX ....$30.00 D

Book, *The 5 Star Book*, 1928, EX ....$45.00 D

Book, *The Six Bottle Carton for the Home*, illustrated, 1937, EX ....$240.00 C

Book, *The Wonderful World of Coca-Cola*, NM ......$85.00 D

Book, *When You Entertain*, by Ida Bailey Allen, 1932, EX..$20.00 D

Booklet, "Coolers for Coca-Cola" with pictures, 1941, EX..$95.00 C

Book cover, "America is Strong ... because America is Good!" with Dwight Eisenhower on front, 1950s, EX, $20.00 C. *Courtesy of Mitchell collection.*

Book cover for school book, 1940 – 50s, white and red, EX, $10.00 C. *Courtesy of Mitchell collection.*

Book cover, national insignia of planes, 1940s, EX, $35.00 C. *Courtesy of Mitchell collection.*

Book cover, Planets and the Stars, 1960s, EX, $25.00 C. *Courtesy of Mitchell collection.*

Booklet, *Easy Hospitality*, 1951, EX ....$15.00 D

Booklet, *Easy Hospitality*, 1951, VG ....$10.00 C

Booklet, *Facts*, 1923, EX ....$65.00 D

Booklet, *Flower Arranging*, 1940, EX....................$15.00 C

Booklet, *Homes and Flowers*, 1940, EX ....$12.00 D

Booklet, *Know Your War Planes*, 1940s, EX ....$65.00 D

Booklet, *Know Your War Planes*, 1940s, P ....$35.00 D

Booklet, *Pure and Healthful*, 1915, G ....$35.00 B

Booklet, *The Charm of Purity*, 1920s, EX..............$35.00 C

Booklet, *The Coca-Cola Bottler*, 1940, EX ....$40.00 C

Booklet, *The Coca-Cola Bottler*, 1940, P ....$20.00 C

Booklet, *The Romance of Coca-Cola*, 1916, EX ......$95.00 C

Booklet, *The Romance of Coca-Cola*, 1916, F..........$45.00 D

Booklet, *Transportation by Coca-Cola*, 15 pages with different types of transportation, a school educational tool, 15 pages, 1940s, EX ....$25.00 D

Booklet with woman in front of sun dial on front and bottle in hand on back cover, with original envelope, 1923, EX..$45.00 D

Bottlers' magazine, *The Red Barrel*, 1940, EX ....$20.00 D

Bottlers' magazine, *The Red Barrel*, 1940, P ....$10.00 D

Bottling plant guide for educational tours of the plant, 1950s, EX ....$15.00 C

Bulletin book for route men, 1950 – 1960s, VG ....$30.00 D

Card hologram, Cal Ripken, McDonald's, and Coke, 1991, NM ....$15.00 D

Carton wrap, "Holiday Hospitality," 1940s, M ......$20.00 D

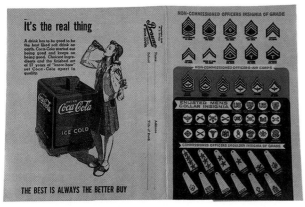

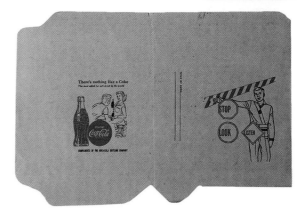

Book cover showing military rank insignias, 1940s, EX, $25.00 C. *Courtesy of Mitchell collection.*

Book cover, "There's nothing like a Coke," school boy, 1940s, EX, $25.00 C. *Courtesy of Bill Mitchell.*

Booklet, *The Charm of Purity*, 1920s, $45.00 C. *Courtesy of Mitchell collection.*

Check, Globe Bank and Trust Co., 1907, EX, $20.00 C.

Check, Coca-Cola Bottling Works with bottling plant on left side of check at Sixth and Jackson, Paducah, Kentucky, 1915, EX, $65.00 C.

Check, Coca-Cola Bottling Works banner at top and eagle on top of world globe on left side of check, 1905, EX, $25.00 C. *Courtesy of Mitchell collection.*

Check, Globe Bank & Trust Co., Paducah, Kentucky, signed by Paducah bottler Luther Carson, 1908, while most checks are valued in the $5.00 – 15.00 range, this one is higher due to bottler's signature, EX, $110.00 C. *Courtesy of Mitchell collection.*

Cap saver bag, for saving caps to redeem for cash from bottler at Bethlehem, Pennsylvania, red and white, 2½" x 5", EX ....$20.00 C

Catalog sheet, Roy G. Booker Coca-Cola jewelry from "Gifts In Fine Jewelry," 1940, NM ....$75.00 C

Catalog, The All-Star Mechanical Pencil Line, featuring Coca-Cola and other drink lines, 1941, M ....$45.00 D

Christmas card with "Seasons Greetings" under silver ornament, 1976, red, M......................................$10.00 D

Circus cut out for kids, still uncut in one sheet, 1927, EX ....$350.00 C

Circus cut out for kids, uncut in one sheet, 1932, NM ....$275.00 C

Coca-Cola money roll, quarters, M ....$6.00 C

Coca-Cola money roll, halves, VG ....$6.00 C

Comic book, "Refreshment Through The Ages," 1951, EX...$30.00 D

Coca-Cola News, 3rd edition, dated April 15, 1896, very hard to find, 1896, 6" x 8", NM, $135.00 C. *Courtesy of Muddy River Trading Co./Gary Metz.*

Contest paper ticket pad, 1960s, 3" x 5", NM, $5.00 C. *Courtesy of Sam and Vivian Merryman.*

Coupon for 5¢, VG, $15.00 C.

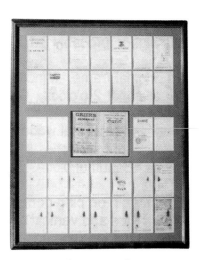

Grier's Almanac featuring a large amount of advertising from Coca-Cola, and Asa Chandler, druggist, matted and framed, rare and hard to find, 1891, F, $1,500.00 C. *Courtesy of Muddy River Trading Co./Gary Metz.*

Invitation to attend the opening of the Paducah, Kentucky, Coca-Cola plant, with picture of the bottling plant at top of sheet, 1939, G, $35.00 C. *Courtesy of Mitchell collection.*

Menu sheet, blank, "Today's Special" with graphics of icy Coke in a cup at bottom, NOS, 1960s, 9½" x 12", NM, $5.00 C. *Courtesy of Sam and Vivian Merryman.*

Comic book, "Refreshment Through The Ages," 1951, P ....$8.00 D

Comic trade card featuring woman in bathtub and serving bottles from a serving tray, 1905, beware of reproductions, VG .... $800.00 D

Convention packet, 14th annual Coca-Cola Convention at Philadelphia, 1988, F ....$20.00 C

Convention packet, 14th annual Coca-Cola Convention at Philadelphia, 1988, MIB ....$35.00 C

Coupon, 1900, EX ....$400.00 C

Coupon, featured 12 pack, 1950s, EX ....$15.00 C

Coupon, featured 12 packs, 1950s, F ....$8.00 D

Coupon for 5¢, EX ....$25.00 D

Coupon, for free six pack with return of empty six pack featuring Santa Claus, issued from bottling company in Youngstown, Ohio, white lettering on light green background with Santa in 4-color, 6" x 3", EX ....$10.00 C

Coupon, for six free bottles of Coke with purchase of 12 pack, red and green on white, 6" x 3½", G ....$10.00 C

Coupon, free bottle of Coke, 1920s, EX ....$20.00 C

Coupon, free Coke at soda fountain, 1908, EX..$225.00 B

Coupon, "Free 6 Bottles of Coca-Cola," pictures six pack with wire handle, 1950s, EX ....$10.00 C

Menu sheet from the 1930s – 1950s in a menu holder from the 1960s, 1930s – 1960s, VG, $45.00 C. *Courtesy of Mitchell collection.*

Newspaper, *Paducah Sun-Democrat*, June 18, 1939, advertising the opening of a new bottling plant, F, $75.00 C. *Courtesy of Mitchell collection.*

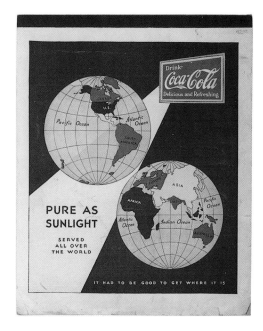

Notebook pad with super graphics on front cover, "Drink Coca-Cola" box in upper corner, "Pure as Sunlight Served All Over the World" and graphics of both sides of the globe, 1930s, VG, $25.00 C. *Courtesy of Sam and Vivian Merryman.*

Our America, Iron and Steel, poster number three in a series of four posters, great graphics but demand for educational material has remained low, 1946, EX, $25.00 C. *Courtesy of Mitchell collection.*

Coupon, good for six pack of Coke when five are accumulated, red, and green lettering on light green background, 3½" x 2", EX ....$10.00 C

Coupon, Hilda Clark, 1901, EX ....$500.00 D

Coupon, Lillian Nordica, 1905, 6½" x 9¾", EX ....$250.00 C

Coupon, "Refresh yourself," free at Roberts & Echols, Glendale, California, 1920s, 5" x 2", EX...........$45.00 D

Coupon, "Take home a carton," 1930s, EX ....$39.00 D

Coupon, "This card entitles an adult to one glass of Coca-Cola free," 1890s, EX ....$250.00 B

Coupon, "This Card Entitles You To One Glass of Coca-Cola," 1903, EX ....$400.00 B

Coupon, "Wholesome Refreshment" with red-headed boy drinking from a bottle with a straw, 1920s, EX ..$100.00 D

Coupons, "Refresh Yourself" with bottle in hand, 1920s, EX ....$75.00 C

Coupons, soda person "Refresh Yourself," 1927, 2¼" x 4", EX ....$85.00 B

Display sheet for cartons, "Match the brides for fun and prizes," for 35-cap display, 1967, EX.................$30.00 C

"Our America" educational poster, chart four in the electricity series, distributed to schools for teaching aids, great graphics, but low in demand, 1940s, EX, $25.00 D. *Courtesy of Creatures of Habit.*

Paper adjustable, "Drink Coca-Cola" sun visor, red on white, NM, $10.00 D. *Courtesy of Rare Bird Antique Mall/ Jon & Joan Wright.*

Driver's license holder featuring bottle in hand from Terra Haute, Indiana, dark blue lettering on light blue background, 2" x 3½", EX ....$25.00 C

Driver's route book, EX ....$15.00 D

Educational pamphlet, "American Glass" used in classrooms and distributed by The Coca-Cola Bottling Company, 15 pages, 1945, EX..$18.00 C

Educational pamphlet, distributed by The Coca-Cola Bottling Company, one of a series of four, this one on American oil, also originally had posters for classroom, 15 pages, 1944, EX ....$35.00 D

Famous Doctors Series, set of six heavy folders, complete, of individual figure approximately $35.00 each, 1932, EX ....$250.00 C

Halloween promotional package for dealers, 1954, EX..$35.00 D

Health record, *My Daily Reminder*, compliments of Sanford Coca-Cola Bottling Co., Sanford, N.C., 1930s, EX ..$25.00 D

Health record, *My Daily Reminder*, compliments of Sanford Coca-Cola Bottling Co., Sanford, N.C., 1930s, G ..$15.00 C

Holder for gas ration book, "Drink Coca-Cola in Bottles," G..$25.00 D

Information kit, New York World's Fair, "The Coca-Cola Company Pavilion," 1964, NM...........................$65.00 D

Kit, merchandising for cooler, 1930, M ....$85.00 D

Letter, Asa G. Chandler, matted and framed, 1889, EX ....$250.00 C

Magazine, *Pause for Living*, single copy, 1960, EX ....$10.00 C

Magazine, *The Coca-Cola™ Bottler*, 1940s, EX ....$20.00 C

Magazine, vest pocket, complete set of 52, 1928, NM ....$500.00 D

Menu, for soda fountain, matted and framed, 1902, 4⅛" x 6⅛", EX ....$600.00 B

Menu, Hilda Clark, rare, 1901, 11¾" x 4", EX..$1,200.00 B

Menu, Hilda Clark, soda menu, matted and framed, hard to find, 1903, 4⅛" x 6⅛", EX ....$650.00 B

Menu, Lillian Nordica, matted and framed, 1904, 4⅛" x 6½", EX ....$650.00 B

Menu sheet, "Today's Menu" featuring artwork of button and glass in lower page corners, green on white, 1950s, 6" x 11", EX...$8.00 D

Menu sheet, "Today's Menu" featuring "goes good with food," artwork of glass in red banner at bottom, green on white, 1950s, 6" x 11", EX ....$10.00 D

Note pad, celluloid, 1902, 2½" x 5", EX ....$600.00 B

Note pad, green alligator cover, "Compliments the Coca-Cola Co." stamped on front in gold, 1906, EX ..$225.00 D

The Coca-Cola caravan truck is 64' long and has 25,000 lights.

Paper border display wrap with graphics of Christmas light-up Coke truck, 1996, EX, **$50.00 C.**
Courtesy of Sam and Vivian Merryman.

Paper border with Diet Coke messages, used mainly to cover display bases, full roll, unused, EX, **$30.00 C.**
Courtesy of Sam and Vivian Merryman.

Paper border, corrugated paper display covering with Super Bowl graphics, full unused roll, 1991, EX, **$35.00 C.** *Courtesy of Sam and Vivian Merryman.*

Paper border of corrugated paper used to hide store display bases, full unused roll, graphics of the sun logo used in the Red Hot Summer promotions and colorful lettering promoting the Olympics, EX, **$30.00 C.** *Courtesy of Sam and Vivian Merryman.*

Note pad, Hilda Clark, matted and framed, 1903, 2½" x 5", EX ....$600.00 C

Note pad holder, calfskin, 1946, EX....................$30.00 D

Note pad, leather covered, 1905, 2¾" x 4½", EX ....$225.00 D

Note pad, pocket size, white lettering on red, 1943, 4" x 6", EX...$45.00 D

Note pad with boy and dog, 1931, 10" x 7", Rockwell, EX...$45.00 D

Notebook, "Coca-Cola Advertised Schedule," 1980, EX ....$20.00 C

Olympiad Records wheel, 1932, EX..................$125.00 D

Opera program presented by Columbus Coca-Cola Bottling Co., 1906, EX..$125.00 C

Paper border, corrugated paper for store display use, full unused roll, EX, **$30.00 C.** *Courtesy of Sam and Vivian Merryman.*

Paper border, corrugated paper for displays with graphics of Santa in chair, full unused roll, EX, **$30.00 C.** *Courtesy of Sam and Vivian Merryman.*

Paper border, corrugated paper display cover, full unused roll, graphics of baseball batter and the message "Major League Baseball," 1960s, EX, **$35.00 C.** *Courtesy of Sam and Vivian Merryman.*

Paper border, corrugated paper display material, full unused roll, graphics for 38th Grammy Awards and Diet Coke Uncapped, 12" x 97", EX, **$35.00 C.** *Courtesy of Sam and Vivian Merryman.*

Paper book cover featuring the girl drinking from a bottle in front of what appears to be a Westinghouse cooler, opposite is a patriot man, 1940s, EX ....$20.00 C

Placemats, "Around The World," set of four, 1950s, EX ....$25.00 C

Pocket secretary, hardbound, 1920s, EX.............$35.00 D

Punch card for a "Bottle Coke" Special, with punches of 1, 2, 3, 4, and 5 cents manufactured by W. H. Hardy Co., Eau Claire, Wisconsin, 1900, VG ....$10.00 C

Report card holder with 1923 bottle, 1930s, EX ..$85.00 D

Report card holder with 1923 bottle, 1930s, P ......$15.00 D

Return ticket showing price of returned bottle deposit, NM ....$25.00 C

Route coupon from Paducah, Kentucky, VG........$20.00 C

Sack for popcorn from Jungleland with "Drink Coca-Cola" logo in center featuring artwork of tiger face, orange, red, black, 4" x 15", EX ....$15.00 D

School kit, *Man & His Environment*, 1970s, EX ..$25.00 D

Score pad, American Women's Volunteer Service, 1940s, EX ....$20.00 C

Score pad, American Women's Volunteer Service, 1940s, F ....$8.00 C

Paper border, corrugated paper display border with graphics for Super Bowl XXXV, full unused roll, EX, $35.00 C. *Courtesy of Sam and Vivian Merryman.*

Paper border, corrugated display paper promoting the "One & Only Taste," EX, $30.00 C. *Courtesy of Sam and Vivian Merryman.*

Paper border wrap for displays promoting Coca-Cola Classic, 6" tall, NM, $35.00 C. *Courtesy of Sam and Vivian Merryman.*

Paper carton stuffer with perforated paper doll cut out, EX, $10.00 C.

Paper employee safety responsibility card, message "Central States Safety ... Pour It On," 1996, G, $5.00 C. *Courtesy of Sam and Vivian Merryman.*

Paper, St. Louis Cardinals souvenir score card, art of vendor on back with St. Louis products that make the game more enjoyable, EX, $30.00 C. *Courtesy of Mitchell collection.*

Score pad for playing cards, six pack in spotlight "easy to serve, good with food," green on white, 4" x 11", EX..$12.00 D

Sheet music, cover and song sheet, "I'd Like to Buy the World A Coke™," 1971, 8½" x 11½", EX...............$25.00 D

Sheet music, "It's the Real Thing," 1969, EX........$15.00 C

Sheet music, "It's the Real Thing," 1969, M........$30.00 D

Sheet music, "Rum & Coca-Cola," Jeri Sullivan, EX ....$25.00 C

Slide chart for figuring profits on sales of Coca-Cola, M ....$30.00 D

Souvenirs, Confederate Bank note, 1931, EX ....$85.00 D

The Real Coke, The Real Story, hardback, 195 pages, first edition with dustcover, 1986, NM ....$18.00 C

Paper, St. Louis Cardinals Official Score Card and Program, with artwork of stadium vendor with Coke bottle, G, $20.00 C. *Courtesy of Mitchell collection.*

Return ticket showing price of returned bottle deposit, G, $15.00 C. *Courtesy of Mitchell collection.*

Rand McNally Auto Road Map of Illinois with a Coca-Cola advertisement on the back cover, 1920s, $40.00 C. *Courtesy of Mitchell collection.*

Route coupon from Paducah, Kentucky, EX, $25.00 C. *Courtesy of Mitchell collection.*

Score pads, "Spotter," "Drink Coca-Cola Delicious and Refreshing," and military nurse in uniform, 1940, EX, $15.00 each C. *Courtesy of Mitchell collection.*

Score card for St. Louis National League, Robison Field, 1916, EX, $30.00 C. *Courtesy of Mitchell collection.*

Sheet music for "The Coca-Cola Girl" by Howard E. Way, published by The Coca-Cola Company, Atlanta, framed, 1927, VG, $350.00 C. *Courtesy of Mitchell collection.*

Toonerville cut out, still uncut and in one piece, 1930, M .... $75.00 C

Writing tablet, flags, 1960s, EX .... $10.00 D

Sheet music of "My Old Kentucky Home," featuring Juanita on cover with a glass, 1906, EX, $850.00 B.

Price tag, unused NOS, with Coca-Cola Classic graphic at top, 4" x 8", NM, $5.00 C. *Courtesy of Sam and Vivian Merryman.*

Sheet music, "Rock Me to Sleep Mother," with Juanita on cover drinking from a glass, 1906, EX, $875.00 C.

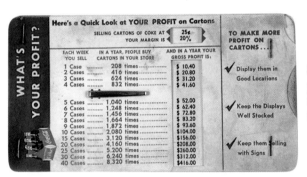

Slide chart for figuring profits on sales of Coca-Cola, G, $20.00 C. *Courtesy of Mitchell collection.*

Slide information booklet, Kit Carson, 1950s, VG, $45.00 C. *Courtesy of Mitchell collection.*

Wildflower study cards for schools, complete set consists of 20 cards and envelopes, 1920 – 30, VG, $60.00 set D.

Writing tablet, landmarks of the U.S.A, 1960s, EX ....$10.00 D

Writing tablet, Pure As Sunlight, 1930s, EX ....$30.00 D

Writing tablet, Pure As Sunlight, 1930s, F ....$15.00 D

Writing tablet, wildlife of the United States, 1970s, EX...$12.00 D

Writing tablet, wildlife of the United States, 1970s, G...$10.00 D

Writing tablet, with Silhouette Girl, 1940s, EX..$20.00 D

Writing tablet, with Silhouette Girl, 1940s, VG..$18.00 C

Cardboard fold out from the Atlanta Coca-Cola Bottling Company, EX, $60.00 C.

Bamboo with front and back graphics, "Keep Cool, Drink Coca-Cola," Oriental lady drinking a glass of Coca-Cola on opposite side, 1900, VG, $225.00 C. *Courtesy of Mitchell collection.*

Cardboard with rolled paper handle, "Drink Coca-Cola the Pause that Refreshes," 1930, $175.00 C. *Courtesy of Mitchell collection.*

Cardboard fold out from the Coca-Cola Bottling Co., Bethlehem, Pennsylvania, 1950s, EX, $55.00 C.

Cardboard on wooden handle, "Enjoy Coca-Cola," 1960s, EX, $20.00 C.

Cardboard with rolled paper handle, with poem on cover, 1930s, EX, $195.00 C.

Bamboo with front and back graphics, "Keep Cool, Drink Coca-Cola," Oriental lady drinking a glass of Coca-Cola on opposite side, 1900, F ....$95.00 C

Cardboard and wood with picture of a mother and child, "Drive with care, protect our loved ones," EX ....$125.00 D

Cardboard fold out from the Coca-Cola Bottling Co., Bethlehem, Pennsylvania, 1950s, VG ....$45.00 C

Cardboard with wooden handle, "Drink Coca-Cola" with bottle in spotlight, 1930s, VG ....$45.00 C

Cardboard with wooden handle, "Buy by the carton, 6 for 25¢," Memphis, Tennessee, 1930s, EX, $185.00 C.

Cardboard with wooden handle, "Drink Coca-Cola" with bottle in spotlight, 1930s, EX, $140.00 C. *Courtesy of Mitchell collection.*

"Drink Coca-Cola" featuring a spotlighted bottle with wooden handle, 1930s, EX, $85.00 C. *Courtesy of Mitchell collection.*

Paper on wooden handle, manufactured by Franklin-Cora Co., Richmond, Virginia, "Chew Coca-Cola Gum," red lettering on white background, 1912 – 1916, VG, $2,000.00 B.

Cardboard with wooden handle from the Coca-Cola Bottling Works of Greenwood, Mississippi, "Enjoy Coca-Cola," 1960s, EX, $35.00 C.

"Quality carries on, Drink Coca-Cola" with bottle in hand, 1950, EX, $65.00 C. *Courtesy of Mitchell collection.*

Rolled paper handle, "Drink Coca-Cola The Pause That Refreshes," Coca-Cola Bottling Co., Martin, Tennessee, EX, $115.00 C. *Courtesy of Mitchell collection.*

Property of Church, donated by Ruston Coca-Cola Bottling Co., Ruston, Louisiana, 1920s, EX, $135.00 C. *Courtesy of Mitchell collection.*

Wicker, compliments of Waycross Coca-Cola Bottling Co., 1950s, EX, $95.00 C. *Courtesy of Mitchell collection.*

"Refresh Yourself" was introduced in 1923.

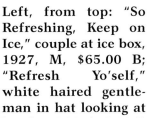

Left, from top: "So Refreshing, Keep on Ice," couple at ice box, 1927, M, $65.00 B; "Refresh Yo'self," white haired gentleman in hat looking at bottle, 1928, $75.00 D; "Be prepared, be refreshed," Boy Scout at cooler with a bottle in each hand, 1940s, M, $350.00 B.

Right, from top: "And one for you," girl on blanket holding bottle, 1934, $95.00 D; Dog and boy with fishing pole, drinking from a bottle, 1930s, $100.00 D; "Good with food, Try It," plate of food with two bottles, 1930s, M, $55.00 D.

50th Anniversary, 1936, NM ....$85.00 D

50th anniversary of Coca-Cola, "Made In USA, 1936," 7¾" x 3½", 1936, EX ....$25.00 B

"A pure drink of natural flavors," 1929, EX ....$150.00 B

"A pure drink of natural flavors," 1929, G ....$50.00 C

"Be Prepared," 1950, G ....$75.00 C

"Be prepared, be refreshed," featuring a Boy Scout offering a Coke from lift top cooler, 7¾" x 3½", 1950, EX ....$200.00 B

Blotter with likeness of young boy on bicycle drinking a bottle of Coke, "The Pause That Refreshes," G ....$75.00 C

Bottle in hand over the earth, 1958, EX..............$25.00 D

Bottle in hand over the earth, 1958, VG..............$15.00 C

Bottle, large, "Over 60 million a Day," 1960, EX..$20.00 D

Bottle, large, "Over 60 million a Day," 1960, VG..$15.00 D

Bottle, paper label, "The Most Refreshing Drink in the World," 1904, EX ....$350.00 B

Boy Scout blotter, NOS, with a picture of Boy Scout in front of a wet box cooler drinking a Coca-Cola, 7¾" x 3½", 1942, G ....$250.00 C

Boy Scout commemorative blotter, 7¾" x 3¼", 1942, F ....$35.00 B

Boy Scouts, "Wholesome Refreshment," 1942, EX ....$95.00 C

Blotter with the advertising "Restores Energy ... Drink Coca-Cola ... Strengthens the Nerves," 1926, EX, $125.00 C.

Canadian blotter with ruler and protractor markings on edges, hard to find piece, 1930s, NM, $275.00 B. *Courtesy of Muddy River Trading Co./Gary Metz.*

"Friendliest drink on earth" blotter with bottle in hand and world globe, 1956, 8" x 4", NM, $35.00 C. *Courtesy of Sam and Vivian Merryman.*

"I think it's swell" with graphics of girl lying on her stomach looking at a magazine with an ad of the Sprite Boy, G, $35.00 C. *Courtesy of Sam and Vivian Merryman.*

Boy Scouts, "Wholesome Refreshment," 1942, VG ....$75.00 C

Canadian, 1940, NM ....$30.00 D

"Carry A Smile Back To Work Feeling Fit," 1935, M ....$95.00 B

Coca-Cola being enjoyed by a policeman, 1938, G ....$30.00 C

Coca-Cola, policeman enjoying, 1938, EX ....$45.00 C

"Coke knows no season," bottle in hand with snow scene in background, 7¾" x 3½", 1947, NM ....$6.00 B

"Cold," dated 1937 in lower left corner, has a Coke bottle in front of a Cold banner, deep, blue background, 7¾" x 3½", 1937, G ....$18.00 B

"Cold Refreshment," 1937, EX ....$35.00 C

"Completely Refreshing," with disc upper left, 1942, EX ....$35.00 C

"Completely Refreshing," girl on blanket with bottle of Coke, 7¼" x 3¾", 1942, NM ....$15.00 C

Couples at a party, Canadian, 1955, EX ....$25.00 D

"Delicious and Refreshing," fountain service, 1915, EX ....$185.00 B

"Delicious, Refreshing, Invigorating," 1909, red and white, EX...$120.00 C

"Drink Coca-Cola," Atlanta, 1904, EX.............$400.00 B

"Drink Coca-Cola," Chicago, 1904, EX ....$120.00 D

159

"Over 60 million a day" with graphics of bottle and "Drink" button, 1960, 3½" X 7¾", NM, $25.00 C. *Courtesy of Sam and Vivian Merryman.*

Paper blotter with girl on beach, 5¾" x 2½", EX, $35.00 B. *Courtesy of Collectors Auction Services.*

Paper blotter with man on bicycle, 7¾" x 3½", EX, $150.00 B. *Courtesy of Collectors Auction Services.*

Paper blotter with Sprite Boy and a bottle of Coke, 7¾" x 3½", EX, $25.00 C. *Courtesy of Sam and Vivian Merryman.*

"Drink Coca-Cola," with Sprite Boy beside a bottle of Coke, 7¾" x 3½", 1951, VG ....$13.00 B

"Drink ... Delicious & Refreshing All Soda Fountain 5 cents," 1915, EX ....$175.00 B

Fountain sales, 1913, EX ....$85.00 B

Four folks enjoying bottles of Coca-Cola in a close setting, Canadian, 1955, EX ....$10.00 C

"Friendliest drink on earth," a bottle in hand, 1956, 4" x 8", EX ....$25.00 C

Girl in boat, 1942, EX ....$35.00 D

Girl lying on her stomach, 1942, NM ....$55.00 D

"Good," Sprite Boy with bottle of Coke in snow bank, with bottle in upper left corner, "Drink Coca-Cola in bottles," 7¾" x 3½", 1953, G ....$10.00 C

"How about a Coke," three ladies each with bottles of Coke, 7¾" x 3½", 1944, NM ....$18.00 B

"I think it's swell," 1944, 3½" x 7½", F ....$30.00 D

"I think it's swell," featuring a young girl reading an ad for Coca-Cola, 7¾" x 3½", 1942, EX ....$45.00 D

"I think it's swell," girl, 1942, VG ....$35.00 D

"Over 60 million a day," with large bottle in foreground, 3½" x 7¾", 1960, VG ....$12.00 C

Policeman with bottle, 1938, EX ....$75.00 D

"Pure and Healthful," with a paper label on each side to promote bottle sales, 1913, EX ....$95.00 D

"Pure and Healthful," with bottles on both sides, 1916, G ....$65.00 D

"The pause that refreshes," 1930, EX, $45.00 B. *Courtesy of Muddy River Trading Co./Gary Metz.*

"Pure as Sunlight," "Drink Coca-Cola, Delicious and Refreshing," "Litho in USA 1931 Courier Journal Lith Louisville," 1931, EX ....$125.00 B

"Refresh Yourself," 1926, EX ....$85.00 D

"Refreshing & Delicious" disc, 1940, EX ....$35.00 D

"Restores Energy," 1906, red and white, EX....$130.00 B

"The Coca-Cola Company of Canada Limited Lithographed in Canada 1942," 7¼" x 3¾", 1942, F ....$18.00 C

"The Drink Everyone Knows," 1939, EX ....$45.00 D

"The Greatest Pause On Earth," 1940, EX ....$75.00 D

"The most refreshing drink in the world," 1905, EX ....$225.00 C

"The Pause That Refreshes," 1929, EX ....$110.00 C

"The Pause That Refreshes," 1930, NM ....$85.00 C

"The Pause That Refreshes," 1931, EX ....$225.00 B

Three girls with bottles, disc at right, 1944, NM..$35.00 C

"Wherever thirst goes," "Drink Coca-Cola," woman in rowboat holding a bottle of Coca-Cola, 5" x 3" (smaller than usual), 1942, M ....$21.00 B

Coca-Cola Bottling Co., No. 1 at Paducah, Kentucky, with picture of bottling plant at Sixth and Jackson St., 1920s, $85.00 C. *Courtesy of Mitchell collection.*

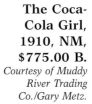

The Coca-Cola Girl, 1910, NM, $775.00 B. *Courtesy of Muddy River Trading Co./Gary Metz.*

Auto delivery truck with an even loaded bed and five men on board, 1913, EX ....$135.00 B

Bobby Allison & Coke, 1970s, NM......................$15.00 D

Bottling plant showing interior, 1905, EX ....$135.00 B

Coca-Cola™ girl, 1910, Hamilton King, EX ......$700.00 B

Duster girl, 1911, 3½" x 5½", EX ....$700.00 B

Exterior of a bottling plant showing the truck fleet in front of building, 1906, EX ....$155.00 C

Folding, "Have You a Hobby?" showing a youngster on a rocking horse, 1910, EX....................................$175.00 D

Folding, "Will You Have It — When They Call?" 1913, EX...$150.00 D

Free six bottles with wire handled carton commemorating 65th Anniversary, 1950s, EX ....$25.00 D

Horse-drawn delivery wagon, 1900, EX ....$135.00 B

Horse-drawn delivery wagon with a Coca-Cola umbrella, 1913, EX ....$145.00 D

Interior of store, 1904, EX ....$100.00 B

International truck, 1940s, VG...........................$40.00 D

International truck, 1940s, F ....$8.00 C

Motorized delivery wagon with three men standing beside it, 1915, EX ....$125.00 B

Piccadilly Circus with large Coca-Cola ad, 1950s, EX...$8.00 C

Photo truck loaded with case of Coca-Cola in snow, framed, 1910, 8" x 10", black and white, EX ..$125.00 D

Postcard featuring picture of DuQuoin, Illinois, bottling plant, NM ....$45.00 D

Postcard from Charleston, Illinois, good for free bottle of Coke, red lettering on white, 5" x 3", G ....$20.00 D

International truck, VG, $45.00 C.
Courtesy of Mitchell collection.

The Coca-Cola Pavilion at the New York World's Fair, 5½" x 3½", 1964, EX, $20.00 C.

Piccadilly Circus, London, with lift flap in center and large Coca-Cola sign on side of building, $20.00 C.

Race car of Bobby Allison, 1973, EX ....$15.00 D

Postcard of Poplar Bluff, Missouri, featuring Main Street and a large Coca-Cola sign on top of a building, 1945, EX ....$15.00 C

Postcard with bottle in hand in center, "Drink ... The Pause That Refreshes," EX..$15.00 C

Store showing bar with ceramic dispensers and pool table, 1904, EX ....$100.00 D

The Fulton Coca-Cola Bottling Co., 1909, EX..$150.00 B

Trifold, showing profit for selling Coca-Cola, featuring a teacher at blackboard, 1910s, EX ....$450.00 B

Trifold, showing profits sitting on top of globe, 1913, EX..$225.00 D

Weldmech truck, 1930, EX ....$25.00 D

Advertisement from the *Chicago Daily News*, full page, 1908, EX, $15.00 B. *Courtesy of Muddy River Trading Co./Gary Metz.*

Magazine ad featuring Lillian Nordica and a coupon at bottom, 1904, NM, $135.00 B. *Courtesy of Muddy River Trading Co./Gary Metz.*

Magazine, "Even the bubbles taste better," 1956, VG, $12.00 D.

Magazine, Christmas ad for "We'll trim the tree. Free," with graphics of a cold bottle of Coke in front of a Christmas scene, 1967, 8½" X 11", VG, $15.00 C. *Courtesy of Sam and Vivian Merryman.*

American, man and woman toasting each other with flare glasses inside a large flare glass, NM ....$20.00 D

"Baseball and Coke grew up together," young boy in uniform with a bottle, framed, 1951, 12" x 15", NM ....$15.00 D

Delineator, featuring a city scene, 1921, EX........$25.00 D

Delineator, featuring a city scene, 1921, VG ......$10.00 D

Delineator, with Coke logo on side of building in city setting, 1921, EX ....$10.00 C

"Drink," glass on ledge, 1917, EX ....$20.00 D

"Face the Day Refreshed," woman at table, "Drink ..." button upper left, framed, 1939, 12" x 15", EX ....$30.00 D

"Get together with refreshment," couple at soda fountain, "Drink ..." button upper right, matted and framed, 1941, 12" x 15", NM ....$20.00 D

Girl with flare glass, 1910s, EX ....$25.00 D

Girl with muffler, 1923, NM ....$25.00 D

"Has Character," featuring soda person, 1913, VG ..$15.00 D

Human Life, color, lady in arrow, 1910, F............$20.00 D

Human Life, color, lady in arrow, 1910, NM........$85.00 D

Human Life, color, "Come In" with arrow encircling soda fountain, 1909, NM ....$65.00 D

Ladies' Home Journal, "Enjoy Thirst," girl with straw and bottle, 1923, EX...$25.00 D

Ladies' Home Journal, "Enjoy Thirst," girl, straw and bottle, 1923, NM ....$40.00 D

Ladies' Home Journal, girl with background showing golfers, 1922, EX ....$30.00 D

Ladies' Home Journal, girl, background showing golfers, 1922, NM ....$40.00 D

Ladies' Home Journal, snow scene and skiers with flare glass in hands, 1922, EX ....$20.00 D

Ladies' Home Journal, snow scene and skiers with flare glass in hand, 1922, NM ....$30.00 D

Ladies' Home Journal, "Thirst Knows No Season" with calendar girl, December 1922, EX ....$25.00 D

National Geographic, cover, back, "You Taste Its Quality," February 1951, F, $12.00 D.

National Geographic with Edgar Bergen and Charlie McCarthy, 1950, G, $15.00 C.

The Coca-Cola Company began advertising in National Geographic in 1933. Through 1965, the company placed 188 ads in the publication. With the exception of June and October 1933, all ads were on the back cover.

Ladies' Home Journal, "Thirst Knows No Season" with calendar girl, December 1922, NM ....$35.00 D

Ladies' Home Journal, with ski scene, "Thirst Knows No Season," 1922, EX ....$10.00 C

"Let's Get a Coca-Cola," featuring couple under a fountain service sign, framed, 1939, 12" x 15", EX ....$20.00 D

Magazine ad showing an elaborate soda fountain surrounded by women and children, double page, 9" x 13½", 1905, EX ....$225.00 C

Magazine, buggy, 1906, EX ....$40.00 D

Magazine, featuring Lillian Nordica and a Coke, matted and framed, 1904, EX ....$110.00 B

Magazine, golfing couple, 1906, EX ....$110.00 B

Magazine, "Scorching Hot Day," arrow above test, 1909, EX...$55.00 D

Magazine, "Scorching Hot Day," arrow above test, 1909, VG ....$35.00 D

Massengale, lady and maid, 1906, EX ....$110.00 B

Massengale, lady and maid, 1906, G ....$50.00 D

National Geographic Coca-Cola ads, full set, EX..$315.00 C

Newspaper, black and white print of early fountain scene with logo circle arrow, 18" x 21", EX ....$20.00 C

Paper advertisment showing a factory whistle and a Coke vending machine, "Inviting workers everywhere to the pause that refreshes with ice cold Coca-Cola," 10" x 13", 1950s, EX ....$10.00 C

"Pause and refresh," three girls in car, "Drink ..." button upper right, 1938, 12" x 15", NM......................$25.00 D

"Pause ... and shop refreshed," couple of ladies at table with glasses, 1940, 12" x 15", NM ....$20.00 D

People waiting behind counter, matted and framed, 1905, 14" x 10", EX ....$120.00 B

"Refreshment through the years," with "Drink ..." button lower right, 1951, 12" x 15", EX ....$15.00 D

Saturday Evening Post, skier, "The Answer to Thirst," EX..$10.00 C

Saturday Evening Post, water skier, EX ....$15.00 D

Seated girl, 1915, 14" x 19", EX ....$155.00 D

"Through 65 Years," one side 1886 fountain service, other side 1951 fountain service, framed, 1951, 12" x 15", NM ....$65.00 C

Woman's World, 1920, EX ....$45.00 D

165

The ad at right is from Haddom Sundblom's painting titled "Daddy's Home." The baby being held is Kay Dell Knarr.

National Geographic back page, "Christmas together ... Have a Coca-Cola," 1945, 6¾" x 10", G, $8.00 C.

Paper, back cover ad from *The Railway Journal*, advertising Coke for 5¢, artwork of engineer and fireman in ICRR locomotive, 8½" x 11", 1929, G, $35.00 C.

The Housekeeper cover, front and back, August 1909, framed, 1909, VG, $150.00 C. *Courtesy of Mitchell collection.*

The Housewife cover, front and back, June 1910, framed, The A.D. Poster Co., Publisher, New York, 1910, G, $185.00 C. *Courtesy of Mitchell collection.*

Book, 1942 advertising price list, 1942, EX, $235.00 C. *Courtesy of Muddy River Trading Co./Gary Metz.*

Book, 1943 price list for advertising, 1943, EX, $235.00 B. *Courtesy of Muddy River Trading Co./Gary Metz.*

Book, 1944 advertising price list, 1944, EX, $275.00 B. *Courtesy of Muddy River Trading Co./Gary Metz.*

Bottlers' advertising price list, 1935, EX, $235.00 C. *Courtesy of Mitchell collection.*

Bottlers' advertising price list, 1933, EX, $250.00 C. *Courtesy of Mitchell collection.*

Bottlers' advertising price list, 50th Anniversary, 1936, EX, $350.00 C. *Courtesy of Mitchell collection.*

Book, 1942 advertising price list, 1942, VG..........$195.00 D

Book, 1943 advertising price list, 1943, NM ....$265.00 C

Book, 1944 advertising price list, 1944, NM ....$300.00 C

Book, *At Work Handbook Manual*, EX ....$325.00 C

Book, detailing refrigeration, and sales displays, 1950s, EX ....$225.00 C

Book, *Universal Beverage*, explaining fountain and bottle service, with Elaine, 1915, EX ....$175.00 C

Booklet, *Profitable Soda Fountain Operation*, 1953, EX ....$75.00 C

Booklet, *Profitable Soda Fountain Operation*, 1953, P ....$25.00 C

Bottlers' advertising price list, January 1932, F ..$90.00 D

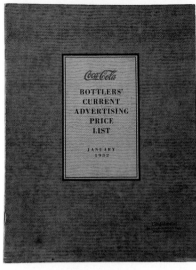

Bottlers' advertising price list, January 1932, EX, $250.00 C. *Courtesy of Mitchell collection.*

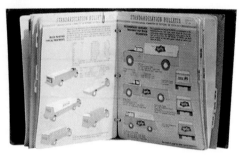

Bulletins book with Coca-Cola bulletins from the '50s and '60s featuring some great information, 1950s, G, $100.00 C. *Courtesy of Muddy River Trading Co./Gary Metz.*

Chronological History of the Coca-Cola Company, brief history of one of the world's most successful companies, with graphics of Coca-Cola products at bottom, VG, $25.00 C. *Courtesy of Sam and Vivian Merryman.*

Coca-Cola Refreshment Activation Kit with fold out information, NM, $250.00 C. *Courtesy of Sam and Vivian Merryman.*

Fact sheet from bottlers book for cooler radio, 1950s, VG, $75.00 C. *Courtesy of Mitchell collection.*

Fountain installation manuals in a three ring binder, 1970s, NM, $200.00 C. *Courtesy of Sam and Vivian Merryman.*

Gold Service display book, EX, $75.00 C. *Courtesy of Sam and Vivian Merryman.*

Bottlers' advertising price list, 1933, VG ....$225.00 D   Bottlers' advertising price list, 1935, VG ....$225.00 D

Handbook used for sales preparation in retail stores, white lettering on red, 1950s, EX, $30.00 C. *Courtesy of Muddy River Trading Co./Gary Metz.*

Marketing programs book for the offical soft drink of summer promotion, NM, $200.00 C. *Courtesy of Sam and Vivian Merryman.*

Manual with programs and merchandising items, such as 100th anniversary pins, in three ring binder with graphics on front, "Enjoy Coca-Cola 100," 1986, EX, $250.00 C. *Courtesy of Sam and Vivian Merryman.*

Paul Flum advertising supply book for a range of Coke items, such as the floor standing store point of purchase drink cooler in the shape of an older vending machine, EX, $55.00 C. *Courtesy of Sam and Vivian Merryman.*

"Pause for Living," winter 1954 with graphics of full table party items and a man ready to cook, VG, $20.00 C. *Courtesy of Sam and Vivian Merryman.*

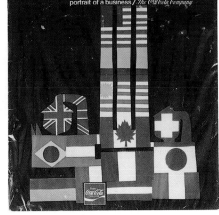

Portrait of a Business/The Coca-Cola Company, NM, $125.00 C. *Courtesy of Sam and Vivian Merryman.*

Bottlers' advertising price list, 50th Anniversary, 1936, P ....$125.00 D

Cardboard, page from a salesman's manual, heavy, rare and somewhat unusual, 12½" x 18½", EX ....$450.00 D

Handbook, *Comprehensive Advertising Price Lists of Items from the 60s,* 1960s, EX ....$150.00 C

Service manual and parts catalog for VMC, manufactured Vendolator Mfg. Co. in leatherette book, 1950s, 8" x 9", EX..$300.00 D

Price list with great colors and period graphics in book form, 1941, EX, $325.00 B. *Courtesy of Muddy River Trading Co./Gary Metz.*

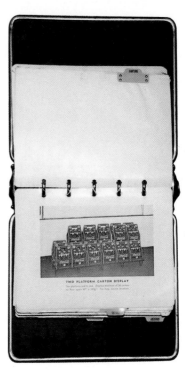

Salesman merchandise book, hardback 5-ring binder, 1942, EX, $400.00 D. *Courtesy of Chief Paduke Antiques Mall.*

Southern Area Coca-Cola Merchandising Standards manual, EX, $135.00 C. *Courtesy of Sam and Vivian Merryman.*

Sports Manual with graphics of various sports scenes on the front with a "Drink" button, VG, $75.00 C. *Courtesy of Sam and Vivian Merryman.*

In 1894, Joseph Biedenharm was given the right to bottle Coca-Cola and installed bottling equipment behind his soda fountain.

Biedenharm Candy Co., Vicksburg, Mississippi, embossed lettering, block print on crown top bottle, 1900s, aqua, EX, $375.00 C.

Biedenharm Candy Co., Vicksburg, Mississippi, embossed block print, Hutchinson Bottle, 1894 – 1902 aqua, EX, $675.00 C.

Biedenharm Candy Co., Vicksburg, Mississippi, with script "Coca-Cola" on base edge, all embossed, 1905, aqua, EX, $175.00 C.

75th Anniversary, Paducah Coca-Cola Bottling Company, Inc., 1978, 10 oz., clear, EX ....$25.00 D

75th Anniversary, Paducah Coca-Cola Bottling Company, Inc., 1978, 10 oz., clear, VG ....$15.00 D

75th Anniversary, Thomas Bottling Company, 1974, amber, EX ....$75.00 C

75th Anniversary, Thomas Bottling Company, 1974, amber, G...$55.00 D

America's Cup, 1987, NM ....$45.00 D

American Airlines LE commemorative bottle, 8 oz., NM ....$155.00 D

Analyst-Portfolio Managers Meeting, limited edition of 408 bottles produced, 1996, M ....$250.00 D

Annie Oakley Days LE commemorative, 1985, NM ....$80.00 D

Atlanta Christian College, 1987, 10 oz., NM ......$12.00 D

Atlanta Falcons, NM ....$10.00 D

Atlanta Olympics, 1996, NM ....$8.00 D

Atlanta Olympics LE commemorative issued to celebrate the upcoming Olympic to be held in Atlanta in 1996, 8 oz., 1991, EX ....$12.00 C

Baskin Robbins LR commemorative bottle, NM ....$150.00 D

Biedenharm Candy Company with applied paper label and "Coca-Cola" in script on bottle shoulder, 1905, aqua, EX...$400.00 D

Bill Elliot #94, limited edition, commemorative bottle, full, 6½ oz., NM ....$8.00 C

Birmingham, Alabama, straight sided bottle with Coca-Cola inscribed on the base, 6½ oz., 1920s, G ......$35.00 C

Block print "Coca-Cola" in center of bottle body, fluted above and below name, EX ....$25.00 D

Block print on base, embossed, 6½ oz., aqua, EX ..$35.00 D

Bobby Labonte #18 limited edition, commemorative bottle, 6½ oz., NM ....$8.00 C

Block print embossed on base with fluted sides, 7 oz., clear, EX, $40.00 D.

Block print embossed on shoulder, bottle is unusual due to size and color, 32 oz., green, EX, $75.00 D.

Block print embossed on side in circle from Sedalia, Missouri, 6½", aqua, EX, $45.00 C.

Block print on shoulder, C.C.B. Co. from Raton, New Mexico, embossed, 6 oz., aqua, EX, $35.00 C.

Bottles, Martha's Vineyard, limited edition commemorative bottle, full, 8 oz., 1997, NM ....$9.00 C

Brickyard 400 Nascar Inaugural at Indianapolis, NM ....$55.00 D

Buddy Holly Music Festival, LE bottle issued to commemorate the Lubbock, TX, festival, full, 8 oz., 1997, NM ....$5.00 B

California State Fair LE commemorative bottle, 1995, NM ....$10.00 D

Cal Ripken, "The Record Breaking Year," NM ....$15.00 D

Can, alternating red and white diamonds, red "Coca-Cola" next to white "Coke" on center diamond, 1960s, VG...$50.00 C

Can, experimental fashioned to feel like bottle, red and white Coca-Cola logo, not put into production, 1990s, 12 oz., NM ....$4.50 C

Can, fashioned to feel like a bottle, white with the dynamic wave logo, experimental only, not put into production, 1970s, 12 oz., NM...$350.00 C

Can from St. Martin advertising "Carnival 1997" with dynamic wave trademark, 11¼ oz., 1997, EX........$5.00 C

Can that has it all, crimped steel Tab, lemon lime banner, EX ....$20.00 C

Carolina Panthers #1, NM ....$8.00 D

Casey's General Store 25th Anniversary 1968 – 1993, NM ....$145.00 D

Charleston, South Carolina, straight sided bottle with Coca-Cola inscribed on the base, 6½ oz., 1920s, EX......$35.00 C

Chattanooga 100 years, LE gold cap bottle, issued to commemorate the world's first bottler and 100 years of service, full, 8 oz., 1999, NM ....$5.00 C

Chattanooga, Tennessee, limited edition commemorative gold cap bottle, celebrating the first 100 years of bottling that began in Chattanooga, distributed in limited numbers around the Chattanooga area only, 8 oz., NM ......$6.00 C

Clear syrup with metal lid, "Drink Coca-Cola" with outline etched in bottle, 1920s, clear, VG.........................$475.00 D

Clemson, 1981, NM...$10.00 D

Coca-Cola safe truck driving rodeo limited edition commemorative, M ....$160.00 D

Coca-Cola Enterprises LE bottle issued to employees to commemorate their 10th anniversary, full, 8 oz., 1996, NM ....$20.00 B

Coca-Cola racing family, limited edition commemorative bottle with center reading "1999 The Coca-Cola Racing Family," 8 oz., 1999, NM ....$4.00 C

Bottles, six pack of bottles with original carrier showing one year to go until the Olympics, 1995, EX, $35.00 D. *Courtesy of Pleasant Hill Antique Mall & Tea Room/Bob Johnson.*

Can, waxed paper, a prototype can that was never put into production, dynamic wave contour, red, 12 oz., EX, $135.00 B. *Courtesy of Collectors Auction Services.*

Canadian with white lettering on clear glass with screw on top, 40 oz., clear, EX, $35.00 C.

Can with the diamond pattern, unopened, red, 12 oz., EX, $75.00 B. *Courtesy of Collectors Auction Services.*

Commemorative Hutchinson style, Coca-Cola 1894 – 1979, 1979, 7¼", M ....$130.00 D

Commemorative reproduction of 1927 bottle used on luxury liners, green glass with green and red label, foil covered neck and top, 1994, M...$75.00 D

25th Anniversary, 1974, EX, ...$100.00 C

Convention, 50th Anniversary National Soft Drink Association, 1969, EX..$100.00 C

Convention, 1976, EX..$45.00 C

Convention, 1981, EX..$40.00 C

Convention, Anaheim, California, 1977, EX........$75.00 C

Convention, Anaheim, California, 1985, EX........$40.00 C

Convention, Atlanta, Georgia, 1978, EX.............$45.00 C

Convention, Atlanta, Georgia, 1982, EX.............$40.00 C

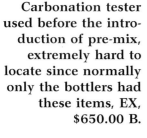

Carbonation tester used before the introduction of pre-mix, extremely hard to locate since normally only the bottlers had these items, EX, $650.00 B.

Ceramic syrup jug with paper label, tall, two-color stoneware, hardest to find, 1900s, 10" tall, VG, $2,600.00 B. Beware of reproductions. *Courtesy of Muddy River Trading Co./Gary Metz.*

Contour can issued to feel similar to the Coke bottle that is so well known, limited issue on a trial basis, didn't work, 12 oz., 1990s, $6.00 C.

From left: Double diamond with script "Coca-Cola" inside diamond from Toledo, Ohio, 1900 – 1910, 6 oz., amber, EX, $155.00 C; Script "Coca-Cola" on bottom edge of front side, on reverse "This bottle our private property & protected by registration under Senate Bill No. 130 approved June 7th, 1911," Dayton, Ohio, 1900 – 1910, 6 oz., amber, EX, $225.00 C; Script "Coca-Cola" inside arrow circle, Louisville, Kentucky, 1910s, 6 oz., amber, EX, $145.00 C; Script "Coca-Cola" on shoulder of bottle with vertical arrow, Cincinnati, Ohio, registered on bottom in block print, 1910s, 6 oz., amber, EX, $135.00 C.

Convention, Atlanta, Georgia, 1988, EX.............$30.00 C	Convention, Atlantic City, N.J., 1966, EX............$50.00 C
Convention, Atlanta, Georgia, 1994, EX, ...$25.00 C	Convention, Chicago, Illinois, 1953, EX ....$100.00 C
Convention, Atlantic City, N.J., 1952, EX..........$125.00 C	Convention, Chicago, Illinois, 1964, EX ....$55.00 C
Convention, Atlantic City, N.J., 1958, EX............$95.00 C	Convention, Chicago, Illinois, 1972, EX ....$45.00 C
Convention, Atlantic City, N.J., 1962, EX............$65.00 C	Convention, Chicago, Illinois, 1980, EX ....$40.00 C

Embossed script "Coca-Cola" at edge of base with unusual shoulder, clear, EX, $85.00 C.

Glass straight-sided first version throw-away bottle with embossed diamond, 1960s, 10 oz., NM, $25.00 C. *Courtesy of Sam and Vivian Merryman.*

Gold, 50th Anniversary 1899 – 1949, Everett Pidgeon in bottle cradle, 1949, EX, $200.00 C. *Courtesy of Mitchell collection.*

Benjamin Franklin Thomas and Joseph Whitehead formed The Coca-Cola Bottling Company under an agreement signed July 21, 1899, by Asa Chandler.

Convention, Chicago, Illinois, 1984, EX ....$40.00 C

Convention, Chicago, Illinois, 1987, EX ....$30.00 C

Convention, Chicago, Illinois, 1990, EX ....$25.00 C

Convention, Chicago, Illinois, 1992, EX ....$25.00 C

Convention, Cleveland, Ohio, 1956, EX ....$95.00 C

Convention, Dallas, Texas, 1963, EX ....$60.00 D

Convention, Dallas, Texas, 1975, EX ....$55.00 D

Convention, Dallas, Texas, 1979, EX ....$45.00 C

Convention, Dallas, Texas, 1986, EX ....$35.00 C

Convention, Detroit, Michigan, 1960, EX...........$80.00 C

Convention, Detroit, Michigan, 1968, EX ....$50.00 D

Convention, Houston, Texas, 1967, EX................$50.00 C

Convention, Houston, Texas, 1971, EX................$45.00 C

Convention, Houston, Texas, 1983, EX...............$40.00 C

Convention, Las Vegas, Nevada, 1989, EX ....$30.00 C

Convention, Miami, Florida, 1955, EX...............$95.00 C

Convention, Miami, Florida, 1965, EX................$50.00 D

Convention, Miami, Florida, 1973, EX................$45.00 C

Convention, Philadelphia, Pennsylvania, 1954, EX..$95.00 C

Convention, Philadelphia, Pennsylvania, 1970, EX..$95.00 C

Convention, San Francisco, California, 1950, EX..$700.00 C

Convention, San Francisco, California, 1961, EX..$700.00 C

Convention, St. Louis, Missouri, 1959, EX ....$85.00 C

Convention, Washington, D.C., 1951, EX..........$125.00 C

Convention, Washington, D.C., 1957 ....$90.00 C

Cub Foods, NM ....$30.00 D

Dale Earnhardt Sr. and Jr., with artwork of both drivers cars on front and back, "Coca-Cola 500 Montegi, Japan, November 21, 1998," 8 oz., 1998, NM ....$3.00 C

Dallas Cowboys silver season commemorative, 1984, 10 oz., M ....$75.00 D

Dallas Cowboys Silver Season LE, commemorating 25 years in the NFL, along with record, 10 oz., 1984, NM ....$25.00 C

There are well over 5,000 embossed hobbleskirt bottles known.

Glass display 1923 Christmas bottle with display cap, 1930s, 20" tall, F, $250.00 B.
Courtesy of Muddy River Trading Co./Gary Metz.

In all, 56 bottles were produced to celebrate the 100th anniversary of Coca-Cola.

Gold, 100th Anniversary, 1986, EX, $55.00 C. *Courtesy of Mitchell collection.*

Dallas Cowboys Super Bowl XXX commemorative, 8 oz., M ....$70.00 D

Dallas Cowboys Super Bowl XXVII, LE commemorative bottle, 8 oz., 1993, NM ....$20.00 C

Denver Broncos LE Commemorative issued to celebrate the win of Super Bowl XXXII, 8 oz., 1998, NM ....$4.00 C

Denver Broncos LE commemorative bottle, issued to commemorate the back-to-back Super Bowl Championships, 8 oz., 1999, NM ....$5.00 C

Detroit Red Wings, NM......................................$5.00 D

Display bottle with cap and patent date, 1923, 20" tall, EX ....$450.00 C

DollyWood LE commemorative bottle issued to celebrate the park's 12th anniversary, 8 oz., 1997, NM ......$25.00 C

Domino's commemorative, M ....$75.00 D

Easter Seals commemorative, M ....$30.00 D

Elvis Presley's Graceland limited edition commemorative bottle, full, 8 oz., 1998, NM..................................$6.00 C

Elvis "Still Rockin," limited edition, commemorative, neck has "Graceland 15th Anniversary," body has a guitar and reads "Elvis Still Rockin," 8 oz., 1997, NM. ....$10.00 C

Embossed 24 set, yellow wooden case with red lettering, 1920s, 24 bottle case, yellow, EX ....$175.00 D

Emergency Coca-Cola bottle, bottle in oak box with plexiglas front and a small mallet to break glass in case of emergency, 8 oz., NM ....$30.00 B

Emma Sanson, Alabama State 5-A Champions, Gadsden, Alabama, 10 oz., 1984, M ....$15.00 C

England Royal Wedding, featuring Union Jack flag with screw-on cap, 7-29-81, 8 oz., M ....$75.00 D

Florida Forest Festival, 1995, NM ....$45.00 D

Florida Marlins, 1994, NM ....$8.00 D

Gator Bowl, NM ....$5.00 D

George C. Snyder D•A•Y commemorative, issued only to plant stockholders to honor founder of bottling plant in Charlotte, N.C., 1-30-96, 8 oz., M.....................$395.00 C

Georgia State Champions, East Marietta 1983 All Stars World Champions, 10 oz., 1983, NM ....$7.00 B

Georgia Tech National Football Champions LE, issued to commemorate the Yellow Jackets #1 victory, season schedule and scores, 10 oz., 1990, EX ....$6.00 C

The 10 oz. tall commemorative bottle was phased out in 1992 in favor of an 8 oz. hobbleskirt bottle.

Miniature perfume bottle with glass stopper, 1930s, clear, EX, $75.00 C. Beware of reproductions.

Metal syrup can designed for cruise ship use, 1940s, one gallon, G, $250.00 B. *Courtesy of Muddy River Trading Co./Gary Metz.*

Limited edition 4-H bottle, "Kentucky Leadership Center, Developing Leaders for Kentucky's Youth," 10 oz., 1986, EX, $45.00 C.

Georgia Tech 75th Anniversary, 1984, NM..........$12.00 C

Girlstown 50th Anniversary and Cal Farley's Boy's Ranch 60th Anniversary limited edition commemorative bottle, full, 8 oz., 1999, NM ....$15.00 C

Glass jug with diamond paper label, 1910, one gallon, clear, EX ....$250.00 C

Glass jug with hoops at neck and embossed lettering, "Coca-Cola" in script, fairly rare, 1900s, one gallon, clear, EX ....$1,200.00 C

Glass jug with paper label, 1960s, one gallon, clear, EX..$15.00 D

Glass jug with round paper label, 1910s, one gallon, clear, EX ....$300.00 B

Glass quart Coca-Cola bottle with paper diamond label and twist top, no return, quart, EX...........................$40.00 C

Glass syrup jug with applied label, 1950, one gallon, clear, VG ....$25.00 D

Gold bottle of Bellingrath Gardens & Homes, Mobile, Alabama, limited edition, NM ....$40.00 D

Gold commemorative, 3-bottle set, from Atlanta, Georgia, in display case, 1996, M ....$135.00 D

Gold dipped, "Bottled from the one millionth gallon December 22, 1959, by the Coca-Cola Bottling Co., Memphis, Tennessee," 1959, NM...............................$45.00 D

Mold made of solid iron, for 10 oz. no return bottle, very heavy, EX, $475.00 C.

Guam Liberation Day ....$10.00 D

Happy Holidays, 1994, NM ....$5.00 D

Hardee's LE commemorative celebrating opening of the 3,000th restaurant, 1988, NM ....$60.00 D

Hardee's three great years LE commemorative, 1982 – 1985, 1985, NM...$30.00 D

Hardee's 35th anniversary LE commemorative, NM ....$85.00 D

Hawaii Mickey Mouse Toontown limited edition, 1994, NM ....$20.00 D

Head Yai, Thailand, new bottling plant, rare, 1993, 10 oz., NM ....$100.00 D

House for Coca-Cola August 3, 1977, 10 oz., 1977, NM ....$15.00 C

Hutchinson style, "Birmingham Coca-Cola Bottling Co.," "DOC 13" on back, 1894, 7", NM ....$1,000.00 B

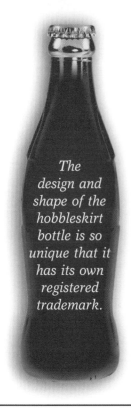

The design and shape of the hobbleskirt bottle is so unique that it has its own registered trademark.

Left: Oklahoma Anniversary, regular capped, gold dipped with white lettering, dated 1903 – 1967 on reverse, only 1,000 made make this a fairly scarce item, 1967, 6½ oz., gold, EX, $150.00 C.

Right: Regular capped gold dipped, embossed lettering, these were made for individual bottlers for special occasions, 6 oz., gold, EX, $65.00 C.

National Convention, 75th Anniversary Hutchinson style bottle, fairly scarce, 1961, light aqua, EX, $250.00 D.

Independent Grocers Alliance, 70th anniversary commemorative, only 960 produced, 1996, M ....$115.00 C

Iowa Hawkeyes Rose Bowl, limited edition commemorative bottle, never opened, has both Coke and Hawkeyes logos, 10 oz., 1982, NM ....$10.00 C

Jacksonville Jaguars limited edition commemorative No. 1, M ....$5.00 D

Jacksonville Jaguars limited edition commemorative No. 2, M ....$5.00 D

Jacksonville Jaguars limited edition commemorative No. 3, M ....$5.00 D

Jeff Gordon 1995 Winston Cup Champion LE commemorative with stats on neck and face, 8 oz., 1995, NM ....$20.00 C

Jeff Gordon #24, limited edition commemorative bottle, neck reads 1995 Winston Cup Champion (second of two Jeff Gordon Coke bottles), body of bottle reads Jeff Gordon 7 Wins – 8 Poles – 2610 Laps Led, 8 oz., 1995, NM ....$20.00 C

Jeff Gordon Winston Cup Champion, 1995, NM ..$12.00 C

Kennesaw College National Softball Champs, 50 cases produced, M ....$35.00 C

KC Chiefs 35th AFL-NFL 35th Anniversary LE bottle, 8 oz., 1993, NM ....$8.00 C

Kyle Petty #44 LE commemorative bottle, has likeness of Petty over checkered flag on bottle center, 8 oz., NM ....$10.00 C

Lamp with embossed "Coca-Cola" base, 1970s, 20", EX........................$6,000.00 B

Lamp with embossed "Coca-Cola" base, 1970s, 20", G ....$3,500.00 C

Leaded glass display bottle, 1920s, 36" tall, EX..$9,500.00 C

Long John Silver's LE commemorative, 8 oz., NM ....$95.00 C

Los Angeles Olympics set in boxes with tags, 1984, EX........................$100.00 D

Mardi Gras, 1996, NM ....$10.00 D

McDonald's 40th partners, M..........................$120.00 C

McDonald's Hawaii I, M ....$60.00 D

McDonald's Hawaii II, M ....$60.00 C

Mexican Christmas commemorative, 1993, M ....$26.00 D

Mexican Christmas commemorative, 1994, EX ..$21.00 D

Mexican Christmas bottle, 1996, M ....$22.00 D

Mexico, Christmas with Santa and girl, NM ....$8.00 D

"Root" commemorative bottle is a reissue of the original bottle design of 1915, the original bottle bottoms were plain, the reissue is marked; only 5,000 of the reissues were made, 1965, EX, $425.00 C. *Courtesy of Mitchell collection.*

Premix, 1920s, green, EX, $65.00 C. *Courtesy of Mitchell collection.*

"Property of Coca-Cola Bottling Co., La Grange, Texas," in block print on body with embossed ribbon on shoulder, 6 oz., aqua, EX, $60.00 C. *Courtesy of Mitchell collection.*

Rubber display bottle, 43" tall, 1940s, G, $850.00 B. *Courtesy of Muddy River Trading Co./Gary Metz.*

Mickey Mouse Hawaii Toontown limited edition commemorative, given away with $200 grocery purchase in Hawaii between May and July 1994, M ....$15.00 C

Miniature six pack of gold-plated metal bottles, 1970, EX...$20.00 D

Monsanto experimental with screw-on lid in various colors, 1960, EX ....$40.00 C

Nahunta Fire Dept. LE commemorative, M ....$80.00 C

Nantucket Island, bottle issued to commemorate the island, full, never opened, 8 oz., 1997, NM ....$5.00 C

NASCAR limited edition commemorative bottle with a checkered flag and "Official Soft Drink of NASCAR," 8 oz., 1998, NM ....$8.00 C

Nashville, Tennessee, LE commemorative bottle with Coca-Cola in Hebrew and the Star of David on one side and English on the other side, full, 6½ oz., EX ....$12.00 C

National Champions Georgia Bulldogs, LE commemorative bottle, with season schedule and final scores, full, 10 oz., 1980, EX ....$10.00 C

New Coke, Houston Coca-Cola Bottling Company, with the introduction of New Coke, one side shows the 100 years of success, the other celebrates the introduction of the new product, 10 oz., 1985, NM ....$15.00 C

New Super Bowl 2000 LE commemorative bottle in a special commemorative tube, issued for the Atlanta, 2000, Super Bowl, 8 oz., 1999, M ....$35.00 C

Newbern, N.C., straight sided, green tinted bottle, some good air bubbles, 6½ oz., 1920s, G ....$35.00 C

North Dakota Centennial limited edition commemorative bottle, empty, 10 oz., EX ....$10.00 C

North Dakota, embossed Coke with bottle in diamond, 10 oz., NM ....$25.00 D

Orange T, LE issued to celebrate the '98 winning season of Tennessee, full, 8 oz., 1997, NM ....$10.00 C

Original paper label with script "Coca-Cola Beverage," reproduction labels are available, 1900 – 1910, aqua, EX ....$350.00 C

Original paper label with script "Coca-Cola Beverage," reproduction labels are available, 1900 – 1910, aqua, F ....$100.00 C

Orlando World Cup, NM ....$10.00 D

Paul "Bear" Bryant LE commemorative bottle, issued when the coach won his 315th game, likeness of Bryant and milestones on bottle, full, 10 oz., 1981, NM ....$20.00 C

Pete Rose, NM ....$100.00 C

Piggly Wiggly 50th Anniversary LE bottle, hard to find, distribution based on Piggly Wiggly employees and best 100 customers, 8 oz., 1999, NM ....$7.00 C

Pharmor, NM ....$275.00 D

Phoenix Coyotes hockey LE commemorative bottle with picture of moon, new, M ....$5.00 D

In 1996, 126 8 oz. commemorative bottles were produced.

From left: Script "Coca-Cola" at bottom from any location, 1910s, 6 oz., amber, EX, $85.00 C.

Script "Coca-Cola" on base edge, "Bottling WKS 2nd Registered" in block print at bottom of base, 1910s, 6½ oz., amber, EX, $115.00 C.

Script "Coca-Cola" midway from any location, 1910s, 6 oz., amber, EX, $85.00 C.

Script "Coca-Cola" on shoulder from any location, 1910s, 6 oz., amber, EX, $95.00 C.

Script "Coca-Cola" embossed on body with embossed art around name, 1910 – 1920s, aqua, $105.00 C. *Courtesy of Mitchell collection.*

Script "Coca-Cola" in shoulder from Verner Springs Water Co., Greenville, South Carolina, 9", aqua, VG, $45.00 C.

Syrup can with paper label, red and white, 1940s, one gallon, EX, $300.00 D.

"Property of Coca-Cola Bottling Co., La Grange, Texas," in block print on body with embossed ribbon on shoulder, 6 oz., aqua, G......................$20.00 D

Republican National Convention LE commemorative, 1996, M..............................$30.00 C

Robinson Humphrey American Express, Inc., 90th Anniversary, LE commemorative bottle, 10 oz., 1984, NM..............................$10.00 B

Ronald McDonald House charity commemorative, 1996, M..............................$105.00 C

Ron Carew LE commemorative, NM..................$25.00 C

Root Commemorative in box with gold clasp, 1965, aqua, EX..............................$450.00 D

Root Commemorative in box with silver clasp, 1971, aqua, EX..............................$350.00 D

Rose Bowl and Pac 10 Champions, 10 oz., 1987, NM..............................$30.00 C

Sam Houston Bicentennial Birthday limited edition commemorative bottle, with likeness of Sam Houston beside a star, banner that reads "1793 – Bicentennial Birthday Celebration – 1993," 8 oz., 1993, NM......................$5.00 C

San Diego, California, LE commemorative bottle issued to celebrate the 75th anniversary of the bottler, unopened, full and in the original box, 10 oz., 1985, NM....$20.00 C

San Diego Padres, 1993, EX..............................$5.00 C

San Diego Padres, 1993, NM..............................$8.00 D

San Francisco 49ers, NM......................$8.00 D

Santa Claus Christmas bottle carrier sleeve, Santa Claus & Christmas Greetings, 1930s, M......................$1,900.00 B

Straight sided block print bottle with large S on body and starting up neck "Coca-Cola Bottling Co. Decatur, 9 oz., VG, $35.00 C. *Courtesy of Sam and Vivian Merryman.*

Super Bowl 2000 bottle with original single cardboard carton, 2000, 8 oz., NM, $75.00 C. *Courtesy of Sam and Vivian Merryman.*

Script "Coca-Cola" in shoulder from Verner Springs Water Co., Greenville, S.C., 9", aqua, EX .... $55.00 C

Script "Coca-Cola" inside arrow circle, Louisville, Kentucky, 1910s, 6 oz., amber, G .... $75.00 D

Script "Coca-Cola" on shoulder and Biedenharm in script on base, all lettering is embossed, 1900s, aqua, F .... $150.00 C

Seltzer, clear, from Coca-Cola Bottling Co., Cairo, Illinois, with applied color labeling featuring Ritz boy with tray, EX $175.00

Seltzer, from Bradford Pennsylvania Bottling Company, blue, VG .... $125.00 D

Seltzer, green fluted for Rock Springs Coca-Cola Bottling Company, Rock Springs Wyoming, green, VG .. $240.00 D

Seltzer, top marked "Coca-Cola B. Co. R.t. Ill.," 1930s, amber, NM .... $200.00 D

Seltzer, with etched lettering, dark blue, EX .... $175.00 D

Six miniature perfume bottles in miniature '50s style case, 1950s, EX .... $160.00 C

Show East, Atlantic City, LE commemorative bottle, only 100 cases were supposedly made, issued for the movie convention which is annual, full, 8 oz., 1995, NM .... $75.00 B

Small tray bottle for toy cooler, 1951, 3½" tall, VG .... $10.00 C

Small tray bottle for toy cooler, 1951, 3½" tall, EX .... $15.00 D

Southwest Airlines commemorative featuring artwork of wings on bottle, 8 oz., M .... $125.00 C

St. Louis Rams, NM .... $10.00 D

Standard top, with "Coca-Cola" in block print from Mt. Vernon, IL, embossed at base, 6 oz., aqua, EX .... $15.00 D

Straight-sided amber marked "Made at Williamstown, New Jersey," "Made by Williamstown Glass Company," made by mold, very rare, 1905 – 1910, 3¼" tall, EX .... $3,200.00 B

Styrofoam display, 1961, 42" tall, VG .... $225.00 C

Super Bowl XXVIII, NM .... $10.00 D

Super Bowl XXIX, Joe Robbie Stadium, Jan. 25, 1995, LE commemorative bottle, 8 oz., 1995, NM .... $3.00 C

Syrup bottle with wreath logo, with original jigger cap, nice heavy transfer onto bottle, 1910, NM .... $700.00 B

Syrup can with paper label, 1930s, one gallon, red, EX .... $200.00 D

Syrup can with paper label featuring Coca-Cola glass, 1940, EX .... $325.00 D

Syrup can with paper label red on white, 1950s, one gallon, VG .... $175.00 D

Syrup, applied label and original cap, EX ...... $1,000.00 C

Syrup, with "Drink Coca-Cola" inside etched ribbon with bow at bottom, metal lid, 1910, clear, EX .... $800.00 C

Syrup keg with paper label on end, 1930s, 5-gallon, F, $100.00 B. *Courtesy of Muddy River Trading Co./Gary Metz.*

White lettering on clear glass with tight fitting plastic top, used as a display piece, 1960s, 20" tall, clear, EX, $75.00 D.

Tri-State Area Council Boy Scouts of America, 1953, green, EX, $230.00 C. *Courtesy of Mitchell collection.*

Syrup, with original metal cap, 1920s, EX, $675.00 C. *Courtesy of Mitchell collection.*

Syrup, with fired-on foil label, red lettering on white label, 1920s, NM ....$775.00 C

Syrup, with foil label red script lettering on white background with gold outline, with original metal lid, 1920, blue, EX.............................$850.00 C

Syrup, with paper label "Coca-Cola" in block lettering, metal lid, 1900, clear, EX ....$700.00 C

Tab, paper label with screw top, clear, with red label, white lettering, 32 oz., G ....$12.00 B

"Tell City, IND," green, 28 oz., 1937, 12", NM ....$40.00 C

Test for 16 oz., "QC" on bottom for quality control, original sticker, scarce due to unusual size, 1940 – 1960s, 16 oz., NM ....$90.00 C

The Atlanta Coca-Cola Bottling Company, Christmas limited edition commemorative bottle, only 3,000 made, 8 oz., 1999, NM...$50.00 B

The Coca-Cola Bottling Company, six-sided body, 1920 – 1930, aqua, EX ....$95.00 C

"Tour the World with Caps from Coke," bottle cap collection three, fold-out folder, 1950s, VG ....$90.00 C

Ty Cobb commemorative, birthplace Banks County, 8 oz., NM ....$75.00 D

Ty Cobb LE commemorative five-piece: The Georgia Peach; Royston Lodge Remembers; First in the Hall of Fame; The Boy, the Man, the Legend; Birthplace, Banks County, NM ....$1,375.00 C

Ty Cobb, limited edition, commemorative bottle, only 1,000 of these bottles were made, numbered, NRFB, still in original presentation box, 6½ oz., NM ....$40.00 C

Tyber Island Centennial limited edition commemorative, 10 oz., M..$8.00 C

University of Georgia, 4-H LE, commemorating Rock Eagle, world's largest 4-H center with 30 years of service, 1954 – 1984, full, 10 oz., 1984, EX.....................$10.00 C

Valdosta 100th anniversary, limited edition commemorative bottle, neck reads, "2nd Bottling Plant In The World," center "Valdosta Coca-Cola Co. 100th Anniversary 1897 – 1997," 8 oz., 1997, NM ....$8.00 C

Varsity 70th Anniversary, LE commemorative bottle, 1928 – 1998, 8 oz., 1998, NM....................................$55.00 B

Wal-Mart 25th Anniversary, limited edition commemorative bottle, 10 oz., 1987, NM ....$25.00 C

Wal-Mart Christmas, 1994, NM ....$5.00 C

White Castle 75th anniversary LE commemorative bottle, NM ....$85.00 C

World of Coca-Cola 5th anniversary limited edition commemorative, 8 oz., M ....$6.00 D

World Cup USA Soccer, LE bottle sold in a tube bank, full, 8 oz., 1994, NM ....$10.00 B

Wooden keg with paper label, 1920 – 1930, 10-gallon, VG ....$225.00 B

Wooden keg with paper label on end, 1920 – 1930s, 5-gallon, VG ....$200.00 B

World Series, Dizzy Dean Graduate League Aug. 4-8, Rossville, Georgia, LE commemorative issued by the Chattanooga, Tennessee, Coca-Cola Bottling Co., 10 oz., 1982, NM ....$15.00 C

York Rite Masonry, NM....................................$25.00 D

Young Presidents commemorative, M ....$55.00 D

50th Anniversary, gold-dipped with plastic stand, 1950s, EX, $250.00 B. *Courtesy of Muddy River Trading Co./Gary Metz.*

Arrow flare, small, acid etched with syrup line at bottom, "Drink Coca-Cola 5¢," 1912 – 1913, $875.00 B. *Courtesy of Muddy River Trading Co./ Gary Metz.*

Anniversary glass given to John W. Boucher, 1936, NM, $375.00 B. *Courtesy of Muddy River Trading Co./Gary Metz.*

Bell, "Drink Coca-Cola," 1940 – 1960s, $20.00 C. *Courtesy of Mitchell collection.*

Bell, with "Enjoy," set of four different sizes, EX, $25.00 D.

Flare, modified, "Coca-Cola," 1926, EX, $200.00 C; Bell with trademark in tail of C, 1930 – 40s, $65.00 C; Flare with syrup line, "Drink Coca-Cola," 1910s, EX, $450.00 C. *Courtesy of Mitchell collection.*

Pewter, bell-shaped, scarce, 1930s, EX, $375.00 C. *Courtesy of Muddy River Trading Co./ Gary Metz.*

Bell, "Enjoy Coca-Cola," 1970s.............................$8.00 C

Flare, "Bottle Coca-Cola," 1916, EX ....$550.00 B

Flare with syrup line, 1900s, EX ....$450.00 C

Information paper showing all the strong points of the glass, VG ....$15.00 C

Pewter, "Coca-Cola," with original leather pouch, 1930s, EX ....$750.00 B

Glass holder, "Coca-Cola," new, EX, $25.00 C. *Courtesy of Mitchell collection.*

Glass holder, silver, 1900, VG, $2,400.00 B. Beware of reproductions. *Courtesy of Muddy River Trading Co./Gary Metz.*

Sandwich plate, "Drink Coca-Cola Refresh yourself," 1930s, 8¼", NM, $1,200.00 B. *Courtesy of Muddy River Trading Co./ Gary Metz.*

"Drink Coca-Cola Good with food," Wellsville China Co., 1940 – 1950s, 7½", VG, $750.00 B. *Courtesy of Muddy River Trading Co./Gary Metz.*

Dish, square, "Coca-Cola" world, 1960s, 11½" x 11½", EX, $135.00 C.

Sandwich plate, "Drink Coca-Cola Refresh Yourself," Knowles China Co., 1931, NM, $775.00 B. *Courtesy of Muddy River Trading Co./Gary Metz.*

Sugar bowl complete with lid, "Drink Coca-Cola," 1930, M, $375.00 C; Creamer, "Drink Coca-Cola," 1930s, VG, $325.00 C. *Courtesy of Mitchell collection.*

Dish, round, world, 1967, 7", EX ....$125.00 C

Display bottle with original tin lid, 1923 bottle, 20" ....$260.00 D

Novelty advertising bowl with likeness of billboard advertising in center by W. S. George, 5⅛" diameter, EX ....$25.00 C

Pitcher, red lettered "Coca-Cola" on glass, M ....$55.00 C

Plate, Swedish, 1969, 8¼" x 6¼", EX ....$100.00 C

Dark headed woman facing forward with her head slightly to the left and looking upward, 10", EX, $375.00 D.

Western Coca-Cola™ Bottling Co., featuring long haired woman body forward with head and eyes to the right wearing a white drape covering off the shoulders, 1908 – 1912, EX, $450.00 C.

Western Coca-Cola™ Bottling Co., featuring brunette with red hair scarf holding a pink rose, 1908 – 1912, EX, $450.00 C.

Western Coca-Cola™ Bottling Co., featuring woman with auburn colored hair with a red adornment on the right side of her head, 1908, 10", EX, $375.00 C.

Western Coca-Cola™ Bottling Co., featuring dark haired woman turned at an angle to the plate, 1908, 10", EX, $375.00 D.

Western Coca-Cola™ Bottling Co., featuring woman with long red hair and off the shoulder apparel, 1908 – 1912, 10", EX, $425.00 C.

Western Coca-Cola™ Bottling Co., featuring dark haired woman with low drape across shoulders, 1908, 10", EX, $400.00 C.

Western Coca-Cola™ Bottling Co., if any art plate is in its original shadow box frame value can be doubled, 1908 – 1912, EX, $1,100.00 C. *Courtesy of Mitchell collection.*

Western Coca-Cola™ Bottling Co., featuring dark haired woman with yellow head piece, 1908 – 1912, 10", EX, $375.00 C.

Western Coca-Cola™ Bottling Co., profile of dark haired woman with red head piece and yellow blouse, 1908 – 1912, 10", EX, $400.00 C.

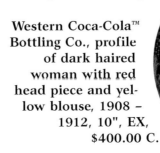

Celluloid and metal pocket mirror with the Hamilton King Coca-Cola girl on the front, 1911, 1¾" x 2¾", F, $195.00 C. *Courtesy of Muddy River Trading Co./Gary Metz.*

Celluloid and metal pocket mirror featuring Elaine, 1916, 1¾" x 2¾", G, $225.00 C. *Courtesy of Muddy River Trading Co./Gary Metz.*

Pocket mirror featuring the Coca-Cola girl, 1910, 1¾" x 2¾", EX, $375.00 B. *Courtesy of Muddy River Trading Co./Gary Metz.*

"Drink Coca-Cola in Bottles," Coca-Cola Bottling Co, Madisonville, Kentucky, 1920 – 1930s, 8" x 17½", $550.00 C. *Courtesy of Mitchell collection.*

Celluloid and metal, "Drink Coca-Cola," 1908, 1¾" x 2¾". Beware of reproductions. EX...........................$1,200.00 C

Celluloid and metal, "Drink Coca-Cola," Elaine, 1916, 1¾" x 2¾", NM ....$625.00 C

Celluloid and metal, "Drink Coca-Cola 5¢," 1914, 1¾" x 2¾", EX ....$650.00 C

Celluloid and metal, "Drink Coca-Cola," Golden Girl, 1920, 1¾" x 2¾", beware of reproductions, EX ....$700.00 C

Celluloid and metal, "Drink Delicious Coca-Cola" with the Coca-Cola girl, 1911, 1¾" x 2¾", Hamilton King, beware of reproductions, NM..$550.00 C

Celluloid and metal, girl on beach beside parasol, much sought after piece, 1922, 1¾" x 2¾", EX ....$1,750.00 D

Celluloid and metal, Juanita, 1906, 1¾" x 2¾", beware of reproductions, EX ....$625.00 C

Celluloid and metal, "Relieves Fatigue," 1907, 1¾" x 1¾", EX..$600.00 D

Celluloid and metal, St. Louis Fair, 1909, 1¾" x 2¾". Beware of reproductions. EX ....$650.00 D

Celluloid and metal, the Coca-Cola Girl, 1910, 1¾" x 2¾", Hamilton King, NM ....$575.00 C

Commemorative wall mirror featuring Hilda Clark produced for the 75th anniversary of the Chicago Coca-Cola Bottling Co., 1976, 28½" x 41", NM ....$425.00 C

In frame under glass "Drink Coca-Cola in Bottles Delicious Refreshing," 1930s, 8" x 12", EX ....$175.00 D

Pemberton and Chandler with ceramic dispenser in center, 1977, M...$50.00 D

Pocket, "Coca-Cola Memos, 50th Anniversary, 1886 – 1936," 1936, EX..$200.00 D

Pocket, "Coca-Cola Memos, Delicious and Refreshing," 1936, EX ....$225.00 C

Glass, Silhouette Girl, with thermometer, 1939, 10" x 14¼", VG, $850.00 B. *Courtesy of Muddy River Trading Co./Gary Metz.*

Pocket mirror, "Wherever you go you will find Coca-Cola at all fountains 5¢," 1900s, G, $900.00 C. *Courtesy of Mitchell collection.*

Pocket mirror, folding cardboard cat's head, "Drink Coca-Cola in bottles" on inside cover, 1920, EX, $825.00 C. *Courtesy of Mitchell collection.*

Cardboard pre-mix counter unit thermometer with mercury scale on left then comparison chart of thermometer reading to regulator setting, 1960s, VG, $65.00 C. *Courtesy of Mitchell collection.*

"Drink Coca-Cola, Delicious and Refreshing," Silhouette Girl, 1930s, 6½" x 16", EX, $475.00 C. *Courtesy of Mitchell collection.*

Embossed die cut with 1923 Christmas bottle, 1931, VG, $210.00 B. *Courtesy of Muddy River Trading Co./Gary Metz.*

Masonite, "Thirst knows no season," 1940s, 6¾" x 17", EX, $475.00 C. *Courtesy of Mitchell collection.*

Metal, die cut bottle thermometer, 1956, 5" x 17", NM, $160.00 B. *Courtesy of Muddy River Trading Co./Gary Metz.*

Metal and plastic 12" Pam style with bottle outline in center on red background, outside circle is in green with black numbers, 1950s, EX $450.00 C. *Courtesy of Muddy River Trading Co./Gary Metz.*

Metal, "Drink Coca-Cola in Bottles, Quality Refreshment," features button at top, 1950s, EX, $195.00 C. *Courtesy of Mitchell collection.*

Desk free-standing in leather case with a round dial, hard to find, 1930s, 3¼" x 3¼", EX ....$1,500.00 C

Dial, with gold bottle outline on red center button, black numbers on face, 1908, 12" diameter, NM ....$375.00 C

Leather front, self-standing desk, 1930s, 3¼" x 3¼", EX ....$1,600.00 C

Liquid crystal readout design showing temp in both Celsius and Fahrenheit, scarce, 1970s, 10¼" square, NM ....$175.00 C

Metal and plastic, Pam, "Drink Coca-Cola Be Really Refreshed," with fishtail, 1960s, 12" diameter ..$500.00 C

Metal "cigar" thermometer, red and white, 1950s, 30" tall, F ....$130.00 C

Metal, embossed Spanish bottle thermometer, 1950s, 6" x 18", EX, $150.00 B. *Courtesy of Muddy River Trading Co./Gary Metz.*

Metal French Canadian bottlers' thermometer, logo at top left with scale on left next to bottle, "Leo Aboussafy," 6" x 16", NM, $350.00 B. *Courtesy of Muddy River Trading Co./Gary Metz.*

Metal, gold version double bottle, "Drink Coca-Cola," metal composition, 1942, 7" x 16", EX, $495.00 C. *Courtesy of Mitchell collection.*

Metal, stand-up, calculated in Celsius and Fahrenheit, 1940s, VG, $45.00 C. *Courtesy of Mitchell collection.*

Oval, Christmas bottle, 1938, 6¾" x 16", EX, $300.00 C. *Courtesy of Mitchell collection.*

Plastic, "Enjoy Coca-Cola" vertical scale type thermometer, 7" x 18", G, $30.00 C. *Courtesy of Sam and Vivian Merryman.*

Plastic, "Enjoy Tab," vertical scale thermometer with message box at bottom, EX $45.00 C.

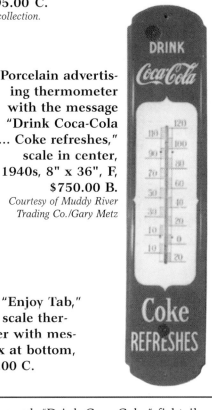

Porcelain advertising thermometer with the message "Drink Coca-Cola ... Coke refreshes," scale in center, 1940s, 8" x 36", F, $750.00 B. *Courtesy of Muddy River Trading Co./Gary Metz*

Metal framed mirror with thermometer on left side and Silhouette Girl across bottom, 1930s, EX ....$450.00 C

Metal, round, "Enjoy Coca-Cola," white on red, EX ....$95.00 C

Metal, round, "Things Go Better With Coke," red on white, 1960s, EX ....$160.00 C

Metal, "Things go better with Coke," 1960, 12", M ....$110.00 D

Plastic and metal, round, "Drink Coca-Cola," fishtail with green on white, 1960s, NM ....$375.00 C

Plastic and metal, round, "Drink Coca-Cola in Bottles," white on red, VG ....$110.00 C

Porcelain, all red, French version of the Silhouette Girl, 1939, 5½"x18", M..$525.00 C

Porcelain, French, Silhouette Girl, with green and yellow background, VG ....$240.00 B

Porcelain, Canadian, Silhouette Girl, with red and yellow background, 1942, VG, $450.00 C. *Courtesy of Muddy River Trading Co./Gary Metz.*

Porcelain, Canadian, Silhouette Girl, with yellow and green background, M, $1,700.00 B.

Porcelain, French, Silhouette Girl, with red and yellow background, G, $240.00 D.

Round Pam front dial thermometer with the messages "things go better with Coke" at top and "Drink Coca-Cola" at bottom, 1960s, 12" diameter, NM, $250.00 B. *Courtesy of Muddy River Trading Co./ Gary Metz.*

Round metal and glass dial type thermometer, message reads "Drink Coca-Cola in Bottles," 1950s, 12" diameter, EX, $250.00 B. *Courtesy of Muddy River Trading Co./Gary Metz.*

Round metal and glass dial type thermometer, "Drink Coca-Cola ... Sign of Good Taste," Robertson, 1950s, 12" diameter, EX, $135.00 C. *Courtesy of Mitchell collection.*

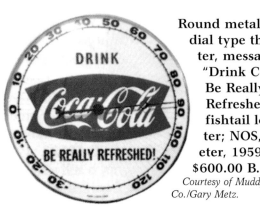

Round metal and glass dial type thermometer, message reads "Drink Coca-Cola Be Really Refreshed," with fishtail logo in center; NOS, 12" diameter, 1959, NM, $600.00 B.
Courtesy of Muddy River Trading Co./Gary Metz.

Porcelain, Silhouette Girl, red and green version, 1939, 5½"x18", EX..$625.00 C

Porcelain, "Thirst Knows No Season," green background with red dot at top and Silhouette Girl at bottom, 1939, 18", EX ....$600.00 D

Round, "Drink Coca-Cola," "Be Really Refreshed!," with fishtail logo, 1960s, 12" diameter, NM ....$475.00 C

Round, "Drink Coca-Cola In Bottles," white on red with glass face, 1950s, 12", VG.................................$225.00 C

Round, "Drink Coca-Cola, Sign of Good Taste," 1957, 12" diameter, NM ....$155.00 D

Tin, "Drink Coca-Cola in Bottles," Phone 612, Dyersburg, Tennessee, with minder notations for oil, grease, and battery, 1940s, VG, $50.00 C. *Courtesy of Mitchell collection.*

Round metal and glass dial type thermometer, message reads "Enjoy Coca-Cola," 1960s, 12" round, EX, $155.00 D. *Courtesy of Muddy River Trading Co./Gary Metz.*

Wooden, "Coca-Cola 5¢" good graphics, red on white, 1905, 5" x 21", G, $400.00 B. *Courtesy of Muddy River Trading Co./Gary Metz.*

Wooden, "Drink Coca-Cola in Bottles 5¢ Everywhere," V.O. Colson Co., Paris, Illinois, 1910s, VG, $675.00 C. *Courtesy of Mitchell collection.*

Thermometer, rare prototype, 15" square, EX, $650.00 B. *Courtesy of Muddy River Trading Co./Gary Metz.*

Tin, "Coke Refreshes," white on red, 1950, 8" x 36", NM ....$2,600.00 C

Tin, double bottle, 1941, VG ....$325.00 D

Tin, embossed bottle, 1936, G ....$160.00 D

Wooden, "Coca-Cola 5¢," 1905, F ....$275.00 C

Aluminum six pack carrier with separated bottle compartments, "Coca-Cola" is embossed on side, 1940 – 1950s, EX, $95.00 C. *Courtesy of Mitchell collection.*

Aluminum six pack carrier with wood and wire handle, red lettered "Drink Coca-Cola," 1950s, EX, $125.00 C. *Courtesy of Mitchell collection.*

Aluminum six pack king size carrier with wire handle, red lettered "Drink Coca-Cola" and "King Size," 1950, EX, $115.00 C. *Courtesy of Mitchell collection.*

Aluminum six pack with wire handle, separated bottle compartments, "Delicious Refreshing Coca-Cola" in white on red center panel, 1950s, EX, $65.00 C. *Courtesy of Mitchell collection.*

Bent wood with rounded corners and flat wood handle, 1940s, VG, $135.00 C. *Courtesy of Mitchell collection.*

Cardboard, showing "Season's Greetings" and holly leaves, 1930s, VG, $55.00 C. *Courtesy of Mitchell collection.*

Cardboard, red and white, will hold four Family Size bottles, NOS, 1958, NM ....$25.00 D

Cardboard, six pack "Money back bottles return for deposit," dynamic wave logo, red and white, NOS, 1970s, EX...$15.00 D

Cardboard, triangle-shaped, NOS, 1950s, M........$65.00 D

Cardboard, twelve bottle, white lettering on red background, 1950s, EX ....$25.00 C

Cardboard, twelve bottles, "Coca-Cola" in script, white on red, NOS, 1951, EX ....$30.00 D

Cardboard, twelve regular size bottles, yellow on red, 1950s, EX ....$20.00 D

Cardboard, 24 bottle case, 1950s, EX ....$50.00 D

Cardboard, waxed, "In 6 Bottle cartons" with "Coca-Cola" button at left, will hold four six pack cartons, NOS, 1940s, M ....$55.00 C

Cardboard case, holds four six packs, EX, $75.00 D.

Cardboard carton display, "Take enough home today," 1950s, 14" x 20" x 8", EX, $235.00 C. *Courtesy of Muddy River Trading Co./Gary Metz.*

Cardboard six pack carrier, 6 for 25¢, red and white, 1939, EX, $60.00 C. *Courtesy of Muddy River Trading Co./Gary Metz.*

Cardboard display rack, "Drink Coca-Cola Take Home a Carton," 1930s, VG, $725.00 B. *Courtesy of Muddy River Trading Co./Gary Metz.*

Cardboard with metal handles, "Drink Coca-Cola" on front, "Have a Coke" "Picnic Cooler" on sides, red with white lettering, 1956, EX, $130.00 C. *Courtesy of Mitchell collection.*

Cardboard, white lettering on red, "Chill ... Serve ..." banner at top by cut out carry handle, twelve bottles, NOS, 1950s, EX ....$25.00 C

Cardboard, white top with red lettering, red button, twelve bottles, NOS, 1960s, NM ....$15.00 C

Cardboard with metal handles, "Drink Coca-Cola" on front, "Have a Coke," "Picnic Cooler" on sides, red with white lettering, 1956, NM ....$155.00 D

Cardboard with top carrying handle, will hold six bottles, "Drink Coca-Cola Delicious and Refreshing," "Serve Ice Cold," 1929, EX..$80.00 D

Cardboard with wire handle, white lettering on red, six bottle, NOS, 1950s, NM......................................$50.00 D

Display case for giant 20" bottles, 1950s, VG ....$180.00 C

Masonite six pack carrier, 1940s, EX ....$85.00 D

Metal and wire Canadian carrier and vendor for 18 bottles "Drink Coca-Cola Iced" on side panels, 1930s, 18 bottle, G ....$285.00 C

Metal and wire 18 bottle, Canadian, 1930 – 1940, red, VG..$295.00 D

Metal for car window, 1940s, white and red, EX ..$75.00 D

Metal vendor's carrier, red with white lettering; embossed on ends, metal loop handle with on front, 1950s, red, VG ....$235.00 C

Miniature six pack, plastic bottles in red and white carton, 1970s, EX ....$20.00 D

Plastic miniature six pack carrying case, red lettering on white, 1970s, EX ....$10.00 D

Plastic six pack carrier, King Size, white lettering, 1950s, red, EX ....$15.00 D

Cardboard six pack, "Serve Ice Cold," 1930s, EX, $135.00 C. *Courtesy of Mitchell collection.*

"Serve Ice Cold" first used in 1931.

Cardboard six pack, red background, 1930s, EX, $155.00 C. *Courtesy of Mitchell collection.*

Metal rack with spring-loaded folding shelves, 1960s, EX, $100.00 B. *Courtesy of Muddy River Trading Co./Gary Metz.*

Metal grocery cart two bottle holder with sign on front "Enjoy Coca-Cola While You Shop, Place Bottles Here," 1950s, EX, $65.00 C. *Courtesy of Mitchell collection.*

Metal carton display rack, 25¢ per six pack, 55" tall, 1930s, VG, $500.00 B. *Courtesy of Muddy River Trading Co./Gary Metz.*

Metal rack with folding metal shelves, 47" tall, 1940 – 1950s, EX, $225.00 B. *Courtesy of Muddy River Trading Co./Gary Metz.*

Metal and wire case carrier with wire handles, red on white, 1950 – 1960s, G $65.00 C. *Courtesy of Muddy River Trading Co./Gary Metz.*

Plastic six pack carrier, regular size, white lettering, 1950s, red, EX ....$15.00 D

12 bottle aluminum carrier with red panel on side, 1950s, EX ....$85.00 C

24 bottle display case, 1950s, VG ....$170.00 C

48 bottle wooden shipping crate, 1910s, 9" x 18" x 25", VG ....$375.00 C

Salesman's sample for bulk case storage, 1960s, 6" x 12" x 13", EX ....$4,500.00 C

Six pack cardboard, French, 1934, G ....$85.00 C

Six pack carton wrapper, July 4th, 1930s, red, white, and blue, EX..$350.00 C

Vinyl 12 bottle, white lettering on red, 1950s, EX..$35.00 D

Metal stadi-
um carrier
with opener,
white letter-
ing on red,
1950s, EX,
$275.00 D.
*Courtesy of Rare
Bird Antique Mall/
Jon & Joan Wright.*

Metal three
case bottle rack
with "Place
Empties Here,
Thank You"
sign at top, red,
G, $375.00 C.
*Courtesy of Mike and
Debbie Summers.*

Metal twelve pack,
red lettering on
yellow body,
1920 – 1930s,
G, $325.00
C. *Courtesy of
Mitchell collection.*

Salesman sample,
Meade Merchandis-
ing, bottle rack with
'60s decal that carries
the message "Things
go better with Coke,"
complete with 6 vin-
tage miniature Coke
cases and bottles,
1960s, NM, $2,200.00
B. *Courtesy of Muddy River
Trading Co./Gary Metz.*

**Wire and metal bottle rack built in
three tiers with "Drink Coca-Cola"
button at top, unusual piece, 1940s
– 50s, F, $290.00 B.** *Courtesy of Muddy
River Trading Co./Gary Metz.*

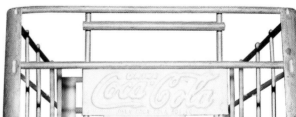

**Wire carrier, case size with embossed aluminum
"Drink Coca-Cola," 1940s, 24 bottle, EX, $45.00
D.** *Courtesy of Chief Paduke Antique Mall.*

Tin, carton
rack with great
rare sign at top,
hard to find,
1930s, 5' tall,
NM, $825.00 B.
*Courtesy of Muddy
River Trading
Co./Gary Metz.*

**Wire and metal statium carrier with
"Drink Coca-Cola Iced" signs on each
side, will hold 24 bottles or cups of the
delicious Coca-Cola, fair, $450.00 B.** *Cour-
tesy of Muddy River Trading Co./Gary Metz.*

Wooden, "Drink Coca-Cola in Bottles," with cut out carrying handle, wings at end, 1940s, yellow, G..........$95.00 C

Wooden six pack, "Six bottles for 25¢ plus deposit," 1940s,
red, EX ....$150.00 C

Wire case holder, sign on top, "Drink Coca-Cola Take enough home," EX, $165.00 D. *Courtesy of Patrick's Collectibles.*

Wire case rack with "Take some Coca-Cola home today" sign at top of rack, metal wheels on bottom, EX, $285.00 C.

Wooden six pack carrier with bottle separators, "Pause ... Go refreshed," white on red, 1930s, EX, $450.00 B. *Courtesy of Muddy River Trading Co./Gary Metz.*

Wooden six pack with wooden handle featuring a cut out hand hold, 1940s, EX, $165.00 C. *Courtesy of Mitchell collection.*

Wooden six pack with wood and wire handle, wings on side of carrier, 1930 – 1940s, yellow, EX, $115.00 C. *Courtesy of Mitchell collection.*

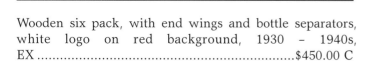

Wooden six pack, with end wings and bottle separators, white logo on red background, 1930 – 1940s, EX ....$450.00 C

Wooden six pack, with hand in bottle and wings logo on both ends, G ....$125.00 C

Wooden with dovetail corner joints, "Refresh yourself Drink Coca-Cola in Bottles," black lettering, 1920s, VG, $275.00 C. *Courtesy of Bill Mitchell.*

Airline Coca-Cola cooler with stainless steel cooler, white lettering on red, 1950s, G, $325.00 B. *Courtesy of Muddy River Trading Co./Gary Metz.*

Cooler, metal with dynamic wave, "It's the real thing," 18" x 13" x 16½", G, $165.00 D. *Courtesy of Patrick's Collectibles.*

The slogan "It's the real thing" first appeared in 1942 and was revived in 1969.

Cooler, wood and metal with tin sides, "Serve yourself ... Please pay the clerk," 32" x 29" x 2¼" F, $1,700.00 B. *Courtesy of Collectors Auction Services.*

Ball park vendor complete with canvas straps and opener, has divider and is insulated, 1940s – 1950s, VG, $300.00 C. *Courtesy of Mitchell collection.*

Stadium backpack and premix vendor with carrying strap and cup dispenser, 1950s, G, $525.00 B. *Courtesy of Muddy River Trading Co./Gary Metz.*

Stainless steel drink and picnic cooler with front lettering "Drink Coca-Cola in bottles" with opener on side, G, $95.00 C. *Courtesy of Sam and Vivian Merryman.*

Airline style painted cooler with stainless liner, with opener on end, white lettering on red, 1950s, NM ....$400.00 C

Airline, with top handle, 1950s, red, NM ....$450.00 C

Aluminum, 12 pack, 1950s, 12 pack, EX ....$125.00 D

Aluminum, 12 pack, 1950s, 12 pack, G ....$85.00 C

Brochure from Progress Refrigerator Company that was distributed to bottlers, 1953, EX ....$25.00 C

Dispenser, fountain, red with white lettering, 1940s, EX..$475.00 D

Floor chest, embossed, yellow and white lettering on red background with bottle at left side, 29" x 32½" x 22", G ....$750.00 C

Floor, large, resembling a large picnic cooler, 1950s, red, NM ....$3,200.00 C

Glascock table top cooler chest type wet box, very sought after, 1930s, red and white .... $400.00 C
Restored ....$1,600.00 C

Hemp Model 9022 picnic, white "Drink" on red, metal latch and handle, NOS, 1950s, M.....................$525.00 D

Insulated stadium vendor, no strap or opener, red, 1930s, F ....$175.00 C

Metal picnic, small, "Drink Coca-Cola in Bottles," 1950s, G...$115.00 C

Floor chest, embossed, yellow and white lettering on red background with bottle at left side, 29" x 32½" x 22", VG, $950.00 B. *Courtesy of Muddy River Trading Co./Gary Metz.*

Glascock salesman's sample, complete with under cooler case storage metal, NM, $1,500.00 C. *Courtesy of Mitchell collection.*

Floor cooler, with base, in form of picnic cooler, 1950s, 17" x 12" x 39", EX, $3,100.00 B. *Courtesy of Muddy River Trading Co./Gary Metz.*

Junior stainless steel cooler, 1950s, 12" x 9" x 14", EX, $650.00 B. *Courtesy of Muddy River Trading Co./Gary Metz.*

Metal picnic, small, "Drink Coca-Cola in Bottles," 1950s, VG, $135.00 C. *Courtesy of Mitchell collection.*

The first standardized cooler made especially for Coca-Cola was produced by Glascock Brothers in 1929, and cost to the bottlers was $12.50.

Glascock junior size cooler complete with cap catcher, 1929, EX, $1,800.00 C. *Courtesy of Mitchell collection.*

Vinyl cooler with zip top and vinyl handle, dynamic wave logo on bottom, 13" x 13" x 9", EX, $40.00 C. *Courtesy of Sam and Vivian Merryman.*

Metal, Progress Refrigerator Company, Louisville, Kentucky, featuring "Things go better ..." logo embossed on front, with lift top lid, metal handles with opener under handle, white lettering on red background, F....$125.00 D

Plastic covered metal, by Royal Mieco Inc. Clinton, Oklahoma, metal handles featuring "Drink" opener on side, white on red, G ....$95.00 C

Metal picnic, with bottle in hand decal, 1940 – 1950s, 13" x 12" x 8", NM ....$130.00 D

Metal picnic, with bottle in hand decal, 1940 – 1950s, 13" x 12" x 8", F...$55.00 C

INTRODUCING
Victor
Counter Coolers
FOR
COCA-COLA

DRINK
Coca-Cola
IN BOTTLES

MODEL C-31

Available in two big sizes—31 and 45 case capacity. These famous Victor Dry Counter Coolers are made especially for bottlers of Coca-Cola*... the last word in self-service merchandisers. Think of it! The Victor Model C-31, pictured above, occupies only 15.2 square feet of floor space and its capacity is 31 cases.

For use in any location—either self-service or under the counter. Can be used as a service counter when equipped with service counter

top. Removable, rust-proof, heavy wire dividers can be adjusted to accommodate any storage arrangement. Meets all health codes. Glide-back lids permit instant service and easy access to each section. Victor Counter Coolers for Coca-Cola are equipped with hermetically sealed condensing units protected by five year warranty on the sealed mechanism.

"Coca-Cola" and its abbreviation "Coke" are the registered trademarks which distinguish the product of The Coca-Cola Company.

DESIGNED FOR *Greater Sales* ... CONSTRUCTED FOR LONG, *Service-Free Life!*

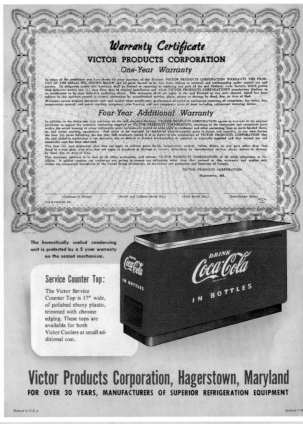

Warranty Certificate
VICTOR PRODUCTS CORPORATION
One-Year Warranty

Four-Year Additional Warranty

VICTOR PRODUCTS CORPORATION

Hagerstown, Md.

The hermetically sealed condensing unit is protected by a 5 year warranty on the sealed mechanism.

Service Counter Top:
The Victor Service Counter Top is 17" wide, of polished ebony plastic, trimmed with chrome edging. These tops are available for both Victor Coolers at small additional cost.

DRINK
Coca-Cola
IN BOTTLES

Victor Products Corporation, Hagerstown, Maryland
FOR OVER 30 YEARS, MANUFACTURERS OF SUPERIOR REFRIGERATION EQUIPMENT

Informational leaflet for the Coca-Cola counter cooler Victor C-31, 8½" x 11", four page foldout, 1950s, EX, $20.00 C.

Victor Dry Counter Coolers for COCA-COLA

furnish ample reserve stock where you need it most... IN THE COOLER!

SPECIFICATIONS

Cooling Capacity: Model C-31, thirty-one cases of Coca-Cola. Model C-45, forty-five cases of Coca-Cola.

Outside Dimensions: Model C-31: 75½" wide, 29" deep, 40" high. Model C-45: 98½" wide, 29" deep, 40" high.

Exterior Shell: Heavy gauge cold rolled steel, bonderized against rust for perfect finish and long life.

Interior Shell: Heavy gauge galvanized steel; resists rust, cleans easily.

Insulation: High efficiency Fiberglas 3 inches thick; keeps temperatures and operating costs down.

Compressor: Model C-31, ⅓ H.P. hermetically sealed Tecumseh unit. Model C-45, ½ H.P. hermetically sealed Tecumseh unit. (Service cord is not furnished with ½ H.P. units. Electrical connection to junction box is required to comply with Underwriters, CSA and local codes.)

Cooling Coil: Oversize, self-defrosting finned coil, forced convection type; gives rapid heat removal.

Fan Motor: Lifetime oiled heavy duty motor, directly connected to four blade fan, forces a constant stream of cold air over each bottle cooling top bottles FIRST. Fan motor 110 volt, 60 cycle, single phase current.

Lids: Disappearing lids glide on tempered brass track; allow full use of cooler during rush periods.

Dividers: Removable, rust-proof, heavy wire dividers can be adjusted to provide the desired size storage compartment in each section. Facilitates proper rotation of stocks during peak output of sales.

Apron: Stainless steel apron on service side prevents cabinet from being marred by bottles and cases; gives protection at point of greatest use.

Crown Catcher: Special removable crown catchers at each end of cabinet. Large capacity, leak-proof crown containers can be emptied in a jiffy... no mess on floor.

Kick Plate: Black enamel inset around base gives greater comfort to both dealers and customers; prevents finish from being scratched.

Drain: ¾" drain outlet—plus directional elbow—in left hand front end makes cabinet easy to clean and keep clean.

Approximate Shipping Weight When Crated: Model C-31, 680 lbs. Model C-45, 825 lbs.

Warranty: 5 year warranty.

Counter Tops: Additional accessory—constructed of heavy plywood covered with Formica and trimmed in chrome edging.

All specifications and descriptions are subject to change without notice.

Victor

OUTSTANDING FEATURES

★ Exclusive Victor design, controlled forced air cooling system chills top bottles first and unbelievably fast.

★ Lids glide back. No lifting strain. Easy access to bottles with greatest chill exposure.

★ Unmatched temperature recovery after loading warm bottles.

★ Super cooling capacity, assuring efficient normal operation *even in prolonged high temperatures.*

★ Big capacity per square foot of floor space.

★ Designed for merchandising. Increases impulse buying at point of sale.

Stainless Steel Apron Protects Point of Greatest Use

Heavy Gauge Cold Rolled Steel Bonderized

Heavy Fiberglas Insulation

Coldest Bottles Always on Top

Two Crown Pullers

Glide Back Lids

Two Removable Crown Catchers

Recessed Kick Plate

Baked on Enamel Finish

Sealed Compressor Protected by a 5 Year Warranty

Model C-45 45 Case Capacity

Model C-31 31 Case Capacity (See Cover)

Salesman's sample Glascock double case cooler "Serve Yourself ... Please Pay the Clerk," 10½" x 13" x 8", 1929, EX ....$5,700.00 C

Vinyl picnic with fishtail logo, shaped like a box with a fold-over top and strap, "Refreshing New Feeling," NM ....$50.00 D

Vinyl cooler bag featuring "drink" fishtail on front, red & white, 1960s, 1" x 10" x 6", G ....$85.00 D

Westinghouse Master electric chest cooler, dispenses 144 bottles fairly common, 1930 – 1940, red, EX ....$550.00 D

Westinghouse Master electric chest cooler, dispenses 144 bottles, fairly common, 1930 – 1940, red, NM ..$795.00 C

Metal cooler in original cardboard box, all original with galvanized interior and tray, red, 17" x 12" x 19", EX $375.00 B. *Courtesy of Collectors Auction Services.*

Metal round cooler, with "Drink Coca-Cola" decal on the outside and a zinc liner on the inside, white on red, 8" x 9", 1940s, VG, $250.00 B. *Courtesy of Muddy River Trading Co./Gary Metz.*

Salesman's sample of Westinghouse wet cooler, white on red, EX, $2,550.00 C.

Metal unused Cavalier cooler in original box, 1950s, NM, $275.00 B. *Courtesy of Muddy River Trading Co./Gary Metz.*

Salesman's sample sale aid shaped like box cooler, EX, $175.00 C. *Courtesy of Mitchell collection.*

Salesman's sample counter dispenser with original carrying case and complete presentation unit, light inside lights up glasses, very rare, 1960s, 4½"w x 6½"d x 6¾"h, EX, $2,500.00 B. *Courtesy of Muddy River Trading Co./Gary Metz.*

Picnic cooler with original hand- and-bottle decals on each side, with bail handle, red, 1940s, 8" x 12" x 13", EX, $100.00 B. *Courtesy of Muddy River Trading Co./Gary Metz.*

Stadium vendor, "Have a Coke," 16" x 10" x 21", VG, $195.00 C. *Courtesy of Muddy River Trading Co./Gary Metz.*

Stainless steel picnic cooler, "Drink Coca-Cola" on front in red, 1950s, six pack, EX, $425.00 B. *Courtesy of Muddy River Trading Co./Gary Metz.*

Wooden cooler for iced bottles, with the original zinc lined tub, red on yellow, 1920s, 38" x 20" x 35", F, $950.00 B. *Courtesy of Muddy River Trading Co./Gary Metz.*

Cavalier C-27 vending machine, 18" x 22" x 41", 1940 – 1950s, EX, $1,400.00 B.
Courtesy of Muddy River Trading Co./Gary Metz.

Cavalier cooler, holds two cases, and works on the honor system since it wasn't equipped with a vending mechanism, red, silver, and white, 18⅛" x 18½" x 40¾", 1940 – 1950s, EX, $1,595.00 D.
Courtesy of Riverside Antique Mall.

Cavalier wet box, with embossing on inside of lid and on all sides, open to the back, white on red, EX, $695.00 D.

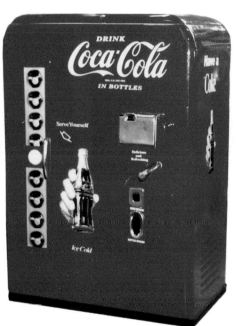

Cooler, lift-top fiberglass, built to resemble a Vendo V-81 vending machine, new, EX, $350.00 C.

Bottle cooler, wet box, wood by Mengel, "Drink Coca-Cola Delicious Refreshing," 1920s, 32" x 38", yellow and red, EX..$1,700.00 B

Cavalier Coca-Cola vending machine, model 96, vends 96 bottles and precools 17 bottles, 1950s, EX ....$950.00 C

Cavalier 10 case giant chest electric cooler, dispenses 240 bottles, 1940 – 1950, red and stainless steel, EX ..$575.00 D

Cavalier 10 case giant ice chest type cooler, dispenses 256 bottles, 1940 – 1950, red, EX ....$600.00 D

Cavalier C-27, chest type machine that looks more like an upright, dispenses 27 bottles, uncommon, can be difficult to locate but most collectors could find one with a few contacts, 1940 – 1950s, 18" x 41" x 22", red, VG ..$1,100.00 C

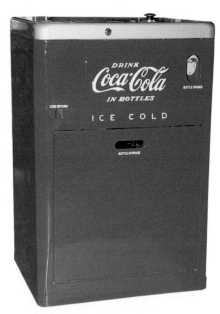

GBV (Glasco Bottle Vendor) dry box with slider top and front left cap catcher, Muncie, Indiana, red and white, 35½" x 20" x 40", 1950 – 1960s, EX, $895.00 D.

Glasco single lid dry box with single hinge lid and decal lettering, white on red, 32" x 18" x 41", F, $625.00 C. *Courtesy of Riverside Antique Mall.*

Vendo model #23, also known to collectors as the spin top machine, comes in standard and deluxe model, which has the silver top, vends 23 bottles and precools 7, with drop door in front for storage, 1940 – 1950s, 24" x 36" x 21", EX, $1,395.00 D.

Vendo model 44, restored, red and white, 1950s, 16" x 57½" x 15½", NM, $2,400.00 B. *Courtesy of Collectors Auction Services.*

Vendo coin changer with keys and "Have a Coke" sign under glass, 12" x 15", F ....$350.00 D

Vendo model 39, a top entry drum type box with the coin mechanism on top, vends 39 bottles and precools 42 bottles, not highly sought after in the past, but a nice machine whose value will increase, white lettering on red, 1940s, 34½"w x 34"h x 27½"d, EX ....$900.00 C

Vendo model 56, similar to the model 81, but without fluorescent tube in door, and the door on most versions has to be opened to observe selection, red and white, 1950s, 25"w x 52"h x 18¾"d, F ....$650.00 D

Vendo model 56, similar to the model 81, but without fluorescent tube indoor, and the door on most versions has to be opened to observe selection, red & white, 1950s, 25"w x 52"h x 18¾"d, VG ....$950.00 D

Cavalier C-51, upright that will dispense 51 bottles with a precooling shelf under the dispensing unit, 1950s, red, EX ....$550.00 C

Cavalier CS-72, 24¾" x 21⅞", 1950s, EX ....$1,850.00 C

Cavalier CS-72, upright that dispenses 72 bottles, will dispense many brands and sizes of bottles, still fairly easy to find, 1950s, red and white, EX..........................$675.00 C

Cavalier model C-51, with embossed "Ice Cold" and "Coca-Cola" on front door, 24¾" x 20¼" x 65", 1950s, EX ....$875.00 B

Jacobs vending machine model #26, upright shaped like a mailbox, very sought after but also the most common Jacobs machine, 1940 – 50s, red, EX ....$1,600.00 C

Vendo model 83 vending machine, not in great demand due in large part to the fact they are so heavy, red and white, 1940s, 32½"w x 63"h x 18" d, G........................$450.00 D

Vendo 39 vending machine, chest type with top drum and coin entry box, 1940s, 34½"w x 34"h x 27¼"d, F ....$350.00 D

Vendo V-23, box cooler that will vend 23 bottles, made in a standard and deluxe version, fairly easy to find, 1940 – 50s, red and silver, G ....$600.00 C

The Vendo Company introduced its coin changer due to the huge demand for nickels for vending machines, shortly following WWII.

Vendo coin changer with keys, reproduction sign, EX, $625.00
B. *Courtesy of Muddy River Trading Co./ Gary Metz.*

Vendo V-39, a fairly common machine, dispenses 39 bottles and precools 20 bottles, 1940 – 1950s, 27"w x 58"h x 16"D, NM, $2,995.00
D. *Courtesy of Patrick's Collectibles.*

Vendo model HA56-B with front opening door, red and white, 1960s, EX, $795.00 D.
Courtesy of Riverside Antique Mall.

Vendo V-81, much sought after for home use due to its compact design and ability to dispense different size bottles, 1950s, 27" x 58" x 16", white on red, VG, $1,300.00 C.
Courtesy of Mike and Debbie Summers.

Vendo V-23, box cooler that will vend 23 bottles, made in both a standard and deluxe version, fairly easy to find, 1940 – 1950s, red and silver, NM ....$1,550.00 D

Vendo V-39, box type cooler that will vend 39 bottles and will precool slightly more than this number, 1940s, red, EX ....$675.00 C

Vendo V-44, an upright box that is highly sought after by collectors, will dispense 44 bottles, 1950s, red and white, EX ....$1,850.00 C

Vendo V-56, upright, will dispense 56 bottles, 1950s, red and white, EX..$1,600.00 D

Vendo V-56, upright, will dispense 56 bottles, 1950s, red and white, VG...$1,200.00 C

Vendo V-59 top chest cooler, electric, dispenses 59 bottles, not very sought after by collectors, 1940s, red, EX ....$575.00 C

Vendo V-80, upright, will dispenses 80 bottles, not aggressively sought after so still relatively easy to find and easy to buy, 1950s, red and white, EX ....$450.00 D

Vendolator 72, dual chute machine with very large embossed Coca-Cola logo, dispenses 72 and pre-cools 6, 1950s, 25"w x 58"h x 15"d, G, $1,500.00 D. *Courtesy of Patrick's Collectibles.*

Vendolator model Dual 27, successor to the table top version of this machine, dispenses 27 bottles while precooling 27, 1950s, 25½"w x 52"h x 17½"d, NM, $2,195.00 D. *Courtesy of Patrick's Collectibles.*

Victor C-45A salesman's sample chest cooler, cardboard, 1940 – 1950s, G, $175.00 C. *Courtesy of Mitchell collection.*

Westinghouse ten case master, electric "dry" box, lid hinges in middle and opens side to side instead of front to back, cools 240 bottles, stacked, 1950s, 30½"w x 36"h x 45", NM, $1,850.00 D. *Courtesy of Patrick's Collectibles.*

Westinghouse Model 42T with embossed "Here's a Coke For You" on sides, holds 42 bottles, red and white, 25" x 20" x 53½", 1950s, EX, $2,295.00 D. *Courtesy of Riverside Antique Mall.*

Vendo 81 Coca-Cola vending machine, one of the most sought after machines due in part to its compact design, original unrestored, red and white, 1950s, 27"w x 58"h x 16"d, NM ....$2,000.00 C

Vendo V-81, dispenses 81 bottles, upright, this machine is also sought after by collectors but is still fairly easy to find, 1950s, red and white, G ....$850.00 C

Vendo V-81, dispenses 81 bottles, upright, this machine also sought after by collectors but is still fairly easy to find, 1950s, red and white, NM.............................$2,000.00 C

Vendo V-83, dispenses 83 bottles, very common, 1940 – 1950, red, EX..$650.00 C

Vendo #83 with electric coin mechanism, because of the size and weight of these machines they aren't as popular as other models, 32½" x 18" x 63", 1940 – 1950s, EX ....$550.00 C

Vendolator 27, known as the table top, this machine would sit on a desk or special stand, dispenses 27 bottles, still fairly easy to find, 1940s, 24" x 27" x 19", red, F ....$775.00 C

Vendolator 27, known as the table top, this machine would sit on a desk or special stand, dispenses 27 bottles, still fairly easy to find, 1940s, 24" x 27" x 19", red, NM ....$1,950.00 C

Vendolator 33, upright that dispenses 33 bottles, relatively common, 1950s, red, EX ....$650.00 D

When Westinghouse introduced its line of coolers in 1934, the Glascock coolers' popularity began to diminish.

Westinghouse salesman's sample, standard box, metal, EX, $2,200.00 C. *Courtesy of Mitchell collection.*

Westinghouse WE-6, salesman's sample, 1940 – 50s, 4⅜" x 4" x 3", G, $450.00 C. *Courtesy of Mitchell collection.*

Zinc lined wet box for cooling and dispensing, "Help Yourself Drink Coca-Cola Deposit in Box 5¢," wood exterior, 1920s, $325.00 C. *Courtesy of Muddy River Trading Co./Gary Metz.*

Vendolator 44, upright that dispenses 44 bottles, not hard to find, 1950s, red and white, EX ....$1,200.00 B

Vendolator 72, upright will dispense 72 bottles, will serve only 6½ oz. bottles, 1950s, red, EX....................$895.00 C

Westinghouse 3 Case Junior electric chest box, dispenses 75 bottles, 1940 – 1950s, red, EX ....$850.00 D

Westinghouse 3 Case Junior, water cooled chest box, 1940 – 1950s, red, G ....$400.00 C

Westinghouse 3 Case Junior, water cooled chest box, 1940 – 1950s, red, NM ....$1,150.00 C

Westinghouse 6 Case Master dispenses 140 bottles, chest box, electric, 1940s, red and stainless steel, G ..$475.00 D

Westinghouse 6 Case Master wet chest type box dispenses 144 bottles, 1940s, red, EX ....$450.00 D

Westinghouse model 42, embossed "Here's a Coke For You" on sides, early models were solid red, red and white, 1950s, 25"w x 53½"h x 20"d, NM ....$1,200.00 D

Westinghouse model 96, vends 96 bottles and will dispense both regular and King Size bottles, 1950s, 25"w x 75"h x 19½"d, NM ....$1,000.00 C

Westinghouse salesman's sample, featuring open front, white on red, VG ....$1,400.00 D

Westinghouse Standard ice chest, dispenses 102 bottles, 1930s, red, EX ....$425.00 C

Bottle shaped, AM/FM, plastic, 1970s, EX, $45.00 C. *Courtesy of Mitchell collection.*

Vending machine design, upright, 1980s, EX, $95.00 C. *Courtesy of Mitchell collection.*

Can with the dynamic wave, 1970s, EX, $45.00 C. *Courtesy of Mitchell collection.*

Vending machine design, upright, 1960s, G, $165.00 C. *Courtesy of Mitchell collection.*

Vending machine design, upright, J. Russell, 1970s, EX, $125.00 C. *Courtesy of Mitchell collection.*

Cooler, prices on these vary greatly, some will go into the thousands, while others fall below the book price, remember condition, 1950s, red, VG, $850.00 C. *Courtesy of Muddy River Trading Co./Gary Metz.*

Cooler-shaped crystal with ear piece, if all parts including instructions present, increase price, EX, $225.00 C. *Courtesy of Mitchell collection.*

Vending machine, upright, 1950s, F, $200.00 C. *Courtesy of Mitchell collection.*

Extremely rare and hard to find, radio designed to resemble an airline cooler, top lifts to reveal controls, red and white, 1950s, G, $3,800.00 B. *Courtesy of Muddy River Trading Co./Gary Metz.*

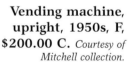

Vending machine design, upright, with dynamic wave, 1970s, EX, $125.00 C. *Courtesy of Mitchell collection.*

Bottle-shaped, 1933, VG ....$3,500.00 B

Cooler, lights up and plays, 1950s, EX ....$900.00 C

Cooler, lights up and plays, 1950s, G ....$300.00 C

Tall bottle radio, all original, 24", 1933, EX, $5,500.00 B. *Courtesy of Muddy River Trading Co./ Gary Metz.*

Anniversary style dome, 1950s, 3" x 5", EX, $850.00 C. *Courtesy of Mitchell collection.*

Boudoir, leather with gold logo at bottom, "Drink Coca-Cola So Easily Served," 1910, 3" x 8", $1,500.00 B. *Courtesy of Muddy River Trading Co./Gary Metz.*

Celluloid desk, Hilda Clark seated at table holding a glass in a holder, clock is in lower left portion of piece, working, rare and hard to find, 1901, 5½" x 7¾", EX, $8,500.00 C.

Counter, light-up, "Drink Coca-Cola Please Pay When Served," yellow numbers on black background, 19¼" x 9", VG, $775.00 C.

Counter, light-up, clock and sign, restored, 1950, $850.00 C. *Courtesy of Muddy River Trading Co./Gary Metz.*

Counter, light-up clock, "Drink ..." is reverse painted, "Lunch with us" is painted on face, seen in several variations, red, white, green, and black, 19½" x 5" x 9", 1940s, EX, $925.00 B. *Courtesy of Collectors Auction Services.*

Counter, light-up neon, "Pause ... Drink Coca-Cola," showing bottle spotlighted, restored, rare and hard-to-find piece, 1930s, EX, $5,500 C. *Courtesy of Mitchell collection.*

Dome, white lettering "Drink Coca-Cola" in red center, 1950s, 6" x 9", EX ....$1,100.00 C

Electric, plastic white background, 1970s, EX ....$85.00 C

Light-up advertising by Modern Clock Advertising Company in Brooklyn, N.Y., aluminum case with plastic face, 1950s, 24" diameter, red on white, VG..............$375.00 D

Clocks

Desk, leather composition with "Drink Coca-Cola in Bottles 5¢" at top center over clock works and smaller bottles at lower right and left corners, 1910, 4⅓" x 6", EX, $1,300.00 C.

Counter light-up, "Serve Yourself" base with "Drink ..." and clock on sign body, 1950s, 9" x 20", EX, $850.00 D.
Courtesy of Pleasant Hill Antique Mall & Tea Room/Bob Johnson.

"Drink Coca-Cola in Bottles," wooden frame, 1939 – 1940, 16" x 16", G, $200.00 C.
Courtesy of Muddy River Trading Co./Gary Metz.

"Drink Coca-Cola 5¢ Delicious, Refreshing 5¢," Baird Clock Co., 15 day movement, working, 1896 – 1899, EX, $6,500.00 B.

"Drink Coca-Cola" red and white plastic, round, EX, $450.00 C.
Courtesy of Mitchell collection.

Gilbert pendulum with original finish, 1930s, VG, $1,200.00 B. *Courtesy of Muddy River Trading Co./Gary Metz.*

Gilbert regulator with Gibson girl decal on glass, 1910, EX, $6,000.00 B. *Courtesy of Muddy River Trading Co./Gary Metz.*

Ingraham with restored regulator on bottom glass, some fade in to clock face, 1905, VG, $950.00 B. *Courtesy of Muddy River Trading Co./Gary Metz.*

Light-up counter top, "Serve Yourself," 1940 – 1950s, VG ....$750.00 B

Light-up, "Drink Coca-Cola in Bottles," button in center with white on red, numbers are black on white, by Swihart, 1950s, 15" diameter, EX ....$400.00 D

Light-up fishtail with green background, "Drink Coca-Cola" in white lettering on red fishtail background, 1960s, VG ....$195.00 C

Light-up fishtail with white background, 1960, EX ....$195.00 C

208

Gilbert regulator key wind clock, found in bottlers' offices, this particular clock was in the old Jackson St. plant in Paducah, Kentucky, worn lettering on the face is normal, the gold on the glass is in exceptional condition; this clock was removed from the bottler's office early and has changed hands only three times, 1920 – 30s, EX, $2,000.00 C. *Courtesy of Al and Earlene Mitchell.*

Glass and metal light-up clock, with red spot center, 14½" diameter, EX, $550.00 B. *Courtesy of Collectors Auction Services.*

Light-up clock made by Modern Clock Advertising Company in Brooklyn, N.Y., aluminum case with solid plastic face that lights up, 1950s, 24" diameter, EX, $550.00 B. *Courtesy of Muddy River Trading Co./Gary Metz.*

Light-up fishtail clock, NOS, 1960s, EX, $275.00 B. *Courtesy of Michael and Debbie Summers.*

Light-up glass front clock with "Drink Coca-Cola" in red fishtail in center, NOS, in original box, 1960s, M, $550.00 B. *Courtesy of Muddy River Trading Co./Gary Metz.*

Neon clock with rainbow panel from 9 to 3 o'clock, "Drink Coca-Cola, Sign of good taste," red and white, 1950s, 36" across, NM, $1,550.00 B. *Courtesy of Muddy River Trading Co./Gary Metz.*

Maroon, on wings, 1950s, 17½" diameter, EX, $350.00 C.

Light-up glass front, white lettering in center on red button, 1950s, NM ....$600.00 C

Light-up round on top of rectangular shaped base, crinkle painted with the message "It's Time To Take Home A Carton", 1930 – 1940s, EX ....$5,500.00 C

Light-up round with "Drink Coca-Cola" in red on white background with bottle above number 6, 1950s, VG..$450.00 D

Maroon, on wings with Sprite Boy on each end, it's hard to find these with wings still attached, even harder to find them with the Sprite Boy on the ends, 1950s, EX ....$850.00 C

Metal and plastic construction dot logo at 4 and 5, "Things Go Better With Coke" where 10 and 11 should be, 16" x 16", EX ....$125.00 C

Metal framed electric with silhouette girl above number 6, 1930 – 1940, 18" diameter, EX ....$825.00 C

Metal framed glass front by Lackner, has bottle in circle at top of number 6, 1940s, 16" x 16", M................$950.00 C

Neon, bottle on octagon with logo, metal case with yellow border, 1942, 16" x 16", EX ....$1,250.00 B

Neon, octagonal, featuring Silhouette Girl logo on center disc, "Ice Cola Cola Coca-Cola," 1941, G ....$1,300.00 B

Neon clock with spotlighted bottle at 6 o'clock, square, green wrinkle on outer case, 1930s, 16", EX, $825.00 B. *Courtesy of Muddy River Trading Co./Gary Metz.*

Neon, octagonal, "Ice Cold Coca-Cola," Silhouette Girl, 1940s, 18", VG, $1,600.00 B. *Courtesy of Muddy River Trading Co./Gary Metz.*

Plastic clock with dynamic wave contour, 1970s, EX, $40.00 B. *Courtesy of Muddy River Trading Co./Gary Metz.*

Plastic and metal light up advertising clock with bottom message panel, "Roller Skate for fun," 1950s, 25" x 55", EX, $500.00 B. *Courtesy of Muddy River Trading Co./Gary Metz.*

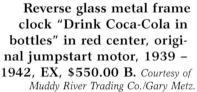

Plastic electric, with wood grain effect, 1970s, EX, $15.00 B. *Courtesy of Muddy River Trading Co./Gary Metz.*

Plastic and metal, "Things go better with Coke," 16" x 16", EX, $95.00 C.

Reverse glass metal frame clock "Drink Coca-Cola in bottles" in red center, original jumpstart motor, 1939 – 1942, EX, $550.00 B. *Courtesy of Muddy River Trading Co./Gary Metz.*

Rocking bottle clock made by Swihart Products, red and green on white background, 1930s, 20", G, $750.00 C. *Courtesy of Mitchell collection.*

Swihart electric, unusual size, 1960s, 8" x 6½", EX, $350.00 B. *Courtesy of Muddy River Trading Co./Gary Metz.*

Neon surrounded by rainbow banner from 9 to 3, "Drink Coca-Cola Sign of Good Taste" on rainbow panel, 1950s, 24" diameter, NM .... $2,700.00 C

Plastic body electric with fake pendulum and a light-up base with "Coca-Cola" in base, 1970s, G .... $45.00 D

Round Silhouette Girl with metal frame, 1930 – 1940s, 18" diameter, VG, $775.00 C. *Courtesy of Mitchell collection.*

Small china, with Coca-Cola in red on face, story is these were given to a few of the better soda fountains, G, $3,500.00 C. *Courtesy of Mitchell collection.*

Telechron, red dot in hour positions with white background and white wings, 1948, 36" wing span, VG, $475.00 C. *Courtesy of Mitchell collection.*

Travel, German-made with brass case, 1960s, 3" x 3", $135.00 C. *Courtesy of Mitchell collection.*

Plastic body, white background with red lettering and "Coca-Cola" written in lower right hand corner, 1960s, 16" x 16", EX...$135.00 D

Plastic pocket watch, 1970s, EX.........................$35.00 C

Plastic pocket watch shape, "Drink Coca-Cola," 18" diameter, EX...$45.00 D

Pocket watch, with second hand dial at bottom, VG .... $85.00 C

Reproduction Betty, 1974, VG ....$50.00 D

Reproduction plastic regulator style, 1972, EX....$50.00 D

Round, pulsating Silhouette Girl, cut number 6 on dial, fairly rare, 1930s, 18" diameter, EX...............$2,900.00 C

Wood framed with "Drink Coca-Cola in Bottles" in white on red background, 1930s, 16" x 16", EX ....$425.00 C

Wood framed with Silhouette Girl at bottom center, 1930s, 16" x 16", EX ....$850.00 B

Wooden regulator, pendulum, oak case, key wound "Drink Coca-Cola In Bottles" in black on white face, 1980s, 23"h, M..$225.00 C

Wall, spring-driven pendulum, "Coca-Cola, The Ideal Brain Tonic," Baird Clock Co., 1891 – 1895, 24" tall, EX, $5,000.00 B.

Wooden Welch Octagon School House, 1901, EX, $1,700.00 B. *Courtesy of Gene Harris Antique Auction Center, Inc.*

Bottle shaped, 1950s, EX, $150.00 C.

Bakelite and metal, 1950s, black, EX, $55.00 D.
Courtesy of Chief Paduke Antiques.

Bottle shaped, EX, $50.00 C.
Courtesy of Mitchell collection.

"Coca-Cola Bottles" key style, 1930s, EX, $55.00 C.

Bottle stopper and opener, "Glascock Bros. Mfg. Co., Coca-Cola Quality Coolers," 1919 – 1920s, EX, $95.00 C. *Courtesy of Antiques, Cards & Collectibles.*

"Drink Bottled Coca-Cola" saber shaped opener, 1920s, EX, $200.00 C.

"Coca-Cola" block print cast iron wishbone, 1900s, EX, $120.00 D.

Top, from left: Corkscrew, wall mounted, 1920s, EX, $85.00 C; Corkscrew, wall mounted, 1950s, EX, $35.00 C; Cast "Drink Coca-Cola" wall mount, 1930s, EX, $10.00 C.

Center: Wall mounted metal "Drink Coca-Cola," also has been referred to as bent metal opener, 1950, EX, $20.00 C.

Bottom: Opener, formed hand version, several versions exist, circa 1930s, $25.00 C; Opener, over the top "Drink Coca-Cola," several versions, circa 1940s, $30.00 C.
Courtesy of Mitchell collection.

Card suit, stainless steel set in marked carrier sleeves, 1970s, EX .... $50.00 C

Cigar box cutter, "Delicious & Refreshing," 1905 – 1915, EX .... $90.00 C

"Drink Coca-Cola™ in Bottles," 1920 – 1940s, EX, $20.00 D.

"Drink Coca-Cola in Bottles" brass key, 1910s, EX, $120.00 C.

"Drink Coca-Cola™ in Sterilized Bottles," lollipop-shaped, 1930s, EX, $100.00 C.

"Drink Coca-Cola™," straight, 1910 – 1950s, EX, $35.00 C.

Top: "Drink Coca-Cola," plastic and metal, red and white, EX, $5.00 C.

Bottom: 75th Anniversary from Columbus Ohio, plastic and metal, 1970s, EX, $20.00 C.

"Drink Coca-Cola" key-shaped with bottle cap facsimile at top, 1920 – 1950s, F, $40.00 C.

Top row: Formed hand, many versions, circa 1940s, $20.00 C; formed hand, many versions, circa 1920s, $25.00 C; formed hand, P, ca. 1940s, $10.00 C.

Second row: ca. 1940s, $25.00 C; formed hand version, circa 1950s, $15.00 C; can piercer, metal, "...Coke," circa 1970s, $10.00 C.

Third row: combination can and bottle, 1980s, $8.00 C; plastic handle can piercer and cap opener, circa 1950s – 1970s, $8.00 C.

Fourth row: 50th Anniversary, 1950s, EX, $55.00 C; Spoon opener, 1920 – 30, 7½", EX, $75.00 C.

Bottom: plastic handle with dynamic wave, 1960s, $8.00 C; metal, "Drink Coca-Cola," $5.00 C.

Courtesy of Mitchell collection.

Fishtail spinner, 1910 – 1930, EX ....$150.00 C

Hand spinner, "You Pay," 1910 – 1920, EX ....$120.00 C

Metal, eagle head, "Drink Coca-Cola," engraved, 1919 – 1920s, EX ....$165.00 C

Flat metal, 1950s, EX, $35.00 C.

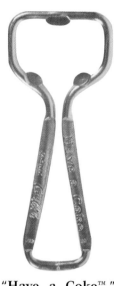

"Have a Coke™," 1950 – 1960s, EX, $12.00 C.

"Have a Coke" beer type, $5.00 C.

"Have a Coke," wire, EX, $3.00 C.

Metal, closely resembling leg, 1920, EX, $210.00 B.

Nashville, Tennessee, celebrating 50th Anniversary, metal, gold plated bottle-shaped with opener at bottom of bottle, 1952, EX, $85.00 C.

Nail puller and crate opener from Piqua Coca-Cola Bottling Co., 1960s, EX, $85.00 C. *Courtesy of Mitchell collection.*

Starr "X" wall mount in original box, 1940 – 1980, EX, $25.00 D.

Metal lion head, 1910 – 1930s, EX ....$160.00 C

Metal, logo at end with "Drink Bottled Coca-Cola," hard-to-find, 1908, EX ....$160.00 C

Metal with a solid handle, "Shirts For the Coke Set," EX ....$20.00 C

Opener and spoon combination, 1930s, NM ....$130.00 D

Steel, black with red background, outing style, 1910 – 1920s, EX ....$100.00 D

Turtle style with four devices, "Drink Coca-Cola in Bottles," 1970s, EX ....$12.00 C

Top: One blade and one opener, "Coca-Cola Bottling Company," 1910s, EX, $300.00 C.

Bottom: "The Coca-Cola Bottling Co.," blade has to be marked Kaster & Co. Coca-Cola Bottling Co., Germany, 1905 – 1915, brass, beware of reproductions, EX, $425.00 C.
Courtesy of Mitchell collection.

Pearl handle with corkscrew blade and opener, 1930s, EX, $135.00 C.
Courtesy of Mitchell collection.

Two blade, "Drink Coca-Cola," G, $45.00 D.

Two blade pen knife, "Enjoy Coca-Cola," all metal, EX, $25.00 D.

Small metal utility with a cutting blade, an opener, and a nail file with key chain, "Enjoy Coca-Cola," EX, $12.00 C.

Stainless steel with one blade and nail file, 1950 – 1960s, EX, $30.00 C. *Courtesy of Mitchell collection.*

Bone handle combination knife/opener, red lettering, "Drink Coca-Cola in Bottles," 1915 – 1925, EX..$125.00 C

Bonc handle, two blade, "Delicious and Refreshing," 1920, VG ....$110.00 C

Combination Henry Sears & Son, Solingen, one blade with case shaped like boot as opener, "Coca-Cola," 1920s, white, EX..$400.00 D

"Compliments – The Coca-Cola™ Co," 1930s, EX ..$95.00 D

"Drink Coca-Cola™ in Bottles," 1940s, EX ....$85.00 D

Pearl handle, "Serve Coca-Cola™," 1940s, EX ....$175.00 D

Switchblade, Remington, "Drink Coca-Cola in Bottles," 1930s, EX ....$225.00 D

"The Coca-Cola™ Bottling Co." embossed on side, 1940s, EX...$55.00 D

Truck shaped from seminar, 1972, EX ....$35.00 D

"When Thirsty Try a Bottle" embossed on sidc with bottle, 1910, EX ....$350.00 D

In the early years of Coca-Cola, most bottlers operated only in the summer months when demand for their product was high.

Bulb type handle, large, 1920s, VG, $65.00 C.
Courtesy of Mitchell collection.

Ice pick and bottle opener, 1920s, VG, $45.00 C.
Courtesy of Mitchell collection.

Squared wooden handle advertising "Coca-Cola in Bottles" and "Ice-Coal Phone 87," 1930 – 1940s, EX, $35.00 C. *Courtesy of Mitchell collection.*

Wooden handle, 1960s, EX, $12.00 C. *Courtesy of Mitchell collection.*

Wooden handle, bottle opener in the handle end, 1930, EX, $40.00 C.
Courtesy of Mitchell collection.

❧ Ashtrays ❧

Ashtray with bottle lighter featuring "Drink" logo from Canadian bottler, red and white, 1950s, NM, $250.00 B. *Courtesy of Muddy River Trading Co./Gary Metz.*

From Mexico, Wave logo, 1970s, EX, $5.00 D.

Bronze colored, depicting 50th Anniversary in center, 1950s, EX, $75.00 C. *Courtesy of Mitchell collection.*

Glass from Dickson, Tennessee, EX, $20.00 C. *Courtesy of Mitchell collection.*

"High in energy, Low in calories," tin, 1950s, EX, $30.00 C. *Courtesy of Mitchell collection.*

Metal with molded cigarette holder, EX, $35.00 D. *Courtesy of Mitchell collection.*

Bottle, 1950s, EX ....$100.00 D

Ceramic, celebrating the Chattanooga Bottling Co. 75th Anniversary, World's First Bottler, 6½" diameter, 1974, EX ....$25.00 C

"Drink Coca-Cola™," round, 1960, EX ....$5.00 D

"Drink Coca-Cola™," round with scalloped edge, 1950s, EX ....$10.00 C

Glass, with gold lettering, three raised cigarette rests, EX ....$20.00 C

Left: Top match pull Bakelite, rare, 1940s, EX, $1,200.00 C.

Right: Bottle lighter, 1950s, EX, $145.00 C.
Courtesy of Mitchell collection.

Set of four, ruby red, price should be doubled if set is in original box, 1950s, EX, $425.00 C.
Courtesy of Mitchell collection.

Metal, "Coke adds Life to Everything Nice," 4" x 5", 1970s, EX ....$12.00 C

"Support Your Fireman, Compliments of Coca-Cola," tin rectangular, EX ....$225.00 C

"The pause that refreshes & J.J. Flynn Co.," square glass, red round center, 1950s, EX ....$70.00 D

"Things go Better with Coke™," square metal, 1960s, red, EX..$15.00 D

Bakelite lighter and pen holder, 1950s, EX, $185.00 C. *Courtesy of Mitchell collection.*

"Drink Coca-Cola," 1950s, EX, $30.00 C. *Courtesy of Mitchell collection.*

Musical, 1970s, EX, $200.00 C. *Courtesy of Mitchell collection.*

Round with diamond-shaped pattern, "Enjoy Coca-Cola," 1960s, $45.00 C. *Courtesy of Mitchell collection.*

Can-shaped, with dynamic wave, M, $40.00 C. *Courtesy of Mitchell collection.*

Bottle-shaped, fairly common, without the lighter it's known as "the pill box," 1950, M, $45.00 C. *Courtesy of Mitchell collection.*

Dispose-a-lite in original box, 1970s, EX ....$20.00 D

"Enjoy Coca-Cola" on bottom, flip top, gold plate, NM ....$85.00 D

Executive award, 1984, NM...............................$35.00 D

Gold Sygnus standup, 1962, EX........................$145.00 D

Musical, red "Drink" on white dot, EX ....$155.00 D

Red lettering on the diagonal with gold-tone background, 1962, EX ....$135.00 D

Silver with embossed bottle, flip top, M ....$45.00 D

Book, 50th Anniversary, 1936, EX, $15.00 C. *Courtesy of Mitchell collection.*

Book, "A Distinctive Drink in a Distinctive Bottle," 1922, EX, $125.00 C. *Courtesy of Mitchell collection.*

Book, "Have a Coke," 1950s, VG, $5.00 C. *Courtesy of Mitchell collection.*

Book, "Have a Coke," bottle in hand, 1940 – 1950s, VG, $12.00 C. *Courtesy of Mitchell collection.*

Left: Book for Westinghouse coolers for the Bottlers of Coca-Cola, G, $8.00 C.

Right: Book from the Coca-Cola Bottling Co. at Fulton, Kentucky, EX, $8.00 C.

Courtesy of Mitchell collection.

Top: Book from 1982 World's Fair at Knoxville, Tennessee, 1982, EX, $5.00 D.

Bottom: Book from New York World's Fair, 1964, $12.00 C. *Courtesy of Mitchell collection.*

Left: Book, "King Size Coke," 1959, VG, $5.00 C.

Right: Book, "Vote for A. A. Nelson, Railroad Commissioner," VG, $5.00 C.

Courtesy of Mitchell collection.

Book with bottle on cover, 1910 – 1920s, VG......$75.00 D

Book with woman on front, 1910s, VG ....$95.00 C

Matchbook holder, celluloid, 1910, EX..............$300.00 C

Matchbook holder, "Compliments of The Coca-Cola Co. Coca-Cola Relieves Fatigue," 1907, EX ....$350.00 C

Matchbook holder, "Drink Coca-Cola at Soda Fountains 5¢," 1907, EX...$350.00 C

Match strikes, porcelain, French, NM ....$275.00 C

Porcelain match striker, "Drink Coca-Cola, Strike matches here," 1939, NM, $400.00 B. *Courtesy of Muddy River Trading Co./Gary Metz.*

Holder, tin, "Drink Coca-Cola in Bottles," 1940s, F, $375.00 C. *Courtesy of Mitchell collection.*

"Drink Coca-Cola in bottles" first used in 1910.

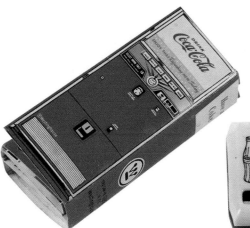

Left: Book, is mock-up of Westinghouse cooler, $85.00 C.

Right: Safe & strikes, 1930s, EX, $295.00 C. *Courtesy of Mitchell collection.*

Matchbook holder with matches, metal, 1959, EX, $175.00 C. *Courtesy of Mitchell collection.*

Safe, "Drink Coca-Cola in Bottles," 1908, EX ..$700.00 C

Striker, "Drink Coca-Cola, Strike Matches Here," beginning to be a scarce item, 1939, red, white, and yellow, VG ....$275.00 C

Striker, porcelain, "Drink Coca-Cola Strike Matches here," English, yellow and white lettering with red background and black match strike field, NM......................$500.00 C

Paper program for the 37th National Convention in Miami, Florida, Oct. 10 – 13, 1955, American Legion, Drink Coca-Cola, 1955, VG, $40.00 C.

Left: "Please put empties in the rack," green and white, $10.00 D.

Center: "Things go better with Coke," red lettering on white background, round, $8.00 D.

Right: "Things go better with Coke," red and white, square with scalloped edges, M, $8.00 D.
Courtesy of Mitchell collection.

Clockwise from top left: Foil showing lady with a bottle, square, M, $5.00 C; foil showing a street car scene, M, $5.00 C; foil showing party tray and cooler, square, M, $5.00 C; foil showing hand and bottle with the Earth behind square, M, $5.00 C.
Courtesy of Mitchell collection.

Metal, "Drink Coca-Cola," EX ....$10.00 D

Metal featuring the Sprite Boy, many collectors specialize on Sprite Boy items, driving the demand and value up, 1940 – 1950s, EX ....$75.00 C

Metal, Hilda Clark artwork, EX ....$8.00 D

Metal with Juanita, 1984, EX.............................$10.00 D

Metal with likeness of Golden Gate Bridge, 4" square, 1940s, EX ....$8.00 C

Metal with Santa Claus, white.............................$8.00 D

Plastic with dynamic wave, "Enjoy Coca-Cola," red, 1970s, EX .... $10.00 D

"Please Put Empties In The Rack", 1950s, EX ......$5.00 C

Aluminum, 1960s, green, EX...................................$5.00

Cardboard, "Go with Coke," 1960s, red and white, EX ....$8.00 D

"Drink Coca-Cola ice cold," with Silhouette Girl, 1940s, M ....$20.00 C

Left: Bottle bag, the distinctive Coca-Cola glass, EX, $12.00 C.

Right: Bottle bag, used in the days of "wet" coolers to keep the customer dry, 1931, EX, $25.00 C. *Courtesy of Mitchell collection.*

Bottle protector, 1932, VG, $15.00 C. *Courtesy of Mitchell collection.*

Paper, with button sign that reads "Drink Coca-Cola Delicious and Refreshing" with graphics of man and woman at sandwich counter, message below graphics reads "Makes a light lunch refreshing," 1940s, EX, $12.00 C. *Courtesy of Sam and Vivian Merryman.*

Dispenser for no drip protectors, unmarked, red, 1930s, 4¼" x 8" x 2¾", EX, $95.00 C. *Courtesy of Bill Mitchell.*

Tin no drip protector dispenser with two original sleeves, in original box with mounting instructions, super find, hard to locate, 6½" x 5", EX, $170.00 B. *Courtesy of Autopia Advertising Auctions.*

"A Great Drink...With Good Things To Eat," 1938, NM ....$10.00 C

Bottle protector, 1934, EX ....$10.00 C

Bottle protector, 1944, EX ....$10.00 C

Bottle protector, 1948, EX ....$10.00 C

Featuring a couple dancing, 1946, NM...............$15.00 C

"In Bottles" protector, 1930, NM ....$20.00 C

Paper bottle protector, 1946, EX.........................$10.00 C

Rear view of man drinking from a bottle, 1936, NM ....$10.00 C

"The Pause That Refreshes," featuring three bottles, 1936, NM ....$10.00 C

Menu Boards

Cardboard and wood in tin frame menu board for pricing 6½ and 12 oz. Coke, red on black, 1950s, 25" x 15", G, $175.00 D. *Courtesy of Muddy River Trading Co./Gary Metz.*

Cardboard menu board, "Sign of Good Taste," with bottle on each side of board, difficult to locate in cardboard, 1959, 19" x 28" NM, $250.00 C. *Courtesy of Muddy River Trading Co./Gary Metz.*

Chalkboard, painted metal, made in U.S.A, American Art Works, Inc., Coshocton, Ohio, 1940, 19¼" x 27", F, $225.00 D.

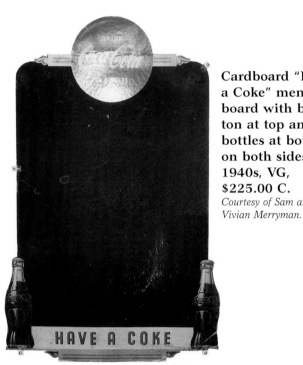

Cardboard "Have a Coke" menu board with button at top and bottles at bottom on both sides, 1940s, VG, $225.00 C. *Courtesy of Sam and Vivian Merryman.*

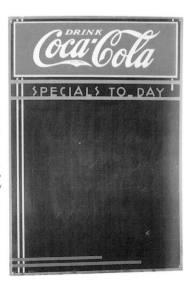

"Drink Coca-Cola Specials Today," 1930s, G, $185.00 C. *Courtesy of Muddy River Trading Co./ Gary Metz.*

Heavy plastic menu board with original box and letters, clock in center, 57" x 16", 1960s, NM, $1,000.00 B. *Courtesy of Muddy River Trading Co./Gary Metz.*

Cardboard stand-up, "Refreshing You Best," 1950s, EX ....$175.00 C

Kay Displays, 1940 – 1950s, 3' x 1', NM ....$2,400.00 B

Kay Displays, wood with
metal trim, "Drink Coca-
Cola," 1940s, EX, $675.00
C. *Courtesy of Mitchell collection.*

*Wooden Kay
Displays signs
were made
during WWII
to conserve
metal.*

Kay Displays, wood
and metal with
button at center,
1930s, EX, $650.00
C. *Courtesy of Muddy River
Trading Co./Gary Metz.*

Metal board with
menu strips with
button between the
wings, 1950s, 60" x
14", NM, $2,300.00
B. *Courtesy of Muddy River
Trading Co./Gary Metz.*

Metal and
wood,
"Drink Coca-
Cola" in
white letter-
ing inside
red fishtail
on green
background,
metal menu
strips, 1950s,
VG, $250.00
C. *Courtesy of
Mitchell collection.*

Metal board with "Drink
Coca-Cola" oval at top
"Specials To-day," at top
of writing surface, black,
red, green, and yellow,
1932, EX, $450.00 D.
Courtesy of Riverside Antique Mall.

Metal board with
"Drink Coca-Cola"
tag at top, black,
red, and white,
EX, $200.00 C.
*Courtesy of Riverside
Antique Mall.*

Kay Displays, "Drink" on spotlight with full glass and
gold tone slots on both sides, 1940 – 1950s, 36" x 12",
EX ....$500.00 C

Light-up design with clock, 1960s, EX ....$145.00 C

Metal, "Drink Coca-Cola Delicious and Refreshing," Silhouette Girl in lower right corner, 1930s, VG....$275.00 C

225

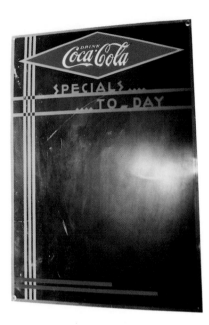

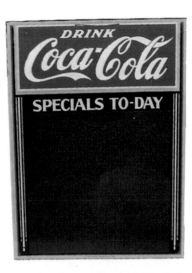

Metal board with silhouette girl in lower right corner, "Delicious and refreshing," green, red, yellow, and white, 1939, EX, $450.00 D. *Courtesy of Riverside Antique Mall.*

Metal, "Drink Coca-Cola," in diamond at top with "Specials To-day" on lines below, black, red, yellow, green, and white, 1931, VG, $450.00 D. *Courtesy of Riverside Antique Mall.*

Metal, Canadian, "Drink Coca-Cola Specials To-day," embossed, scarce and difficult to locate, 1938, 17" x 24", NM, $650.00 B. *Courtesy of Muddy River Trading Co./Gary Metz.*

Plastic menu board with dynamic wave logo at top, 12½" x 16½", EX, $40.00 C. *Courtesy of Sam and Vivian Merryman.*

Metal, painted single-sided board with fishtail top, "Made in USA Robertson 4-59," 19½" x 28", 1959, G, $125.00 C. *Courtesy of Collectors Auction Services.*

Metal, French Canadian board, embossed, 1938, 17" x 24", F ....$145.00 D

"Refresh Yourself" with bottle and cap lower right corner, 1930, 20" x 28", VG ....$450.00 D

Tin, arched top embossed with fishtail design at top, NM, $375.00 B. *Courtesy of Muddy River Trading Co./Gary Metz.*

Plywood Kay Displays menu board with "Drink" logo at top, 1930 – 1940s, 20" x 37", G, $325.00 B. *Courtesy of Muddy River Trading Co./Gary Metz.*

Wood and metal Kay Displays menu board, rare and hard to find, 1940s, F, $550.00 C. *Courtesy of Muddy River Trading Co./Gary Metz.*

Tin, die cut, "Drink Coca-Cola Be Refreshed," Canadian, 1950, EX, $325.00 C. *Courtesy of Muddy River Trading Co./Gary Metz.*

Wood and masonite Kay Displays menu board featuring a 16" button at top center, manufactured to resemble leather, 17" x 29", EX, $525.00 B. *Courtesy of Muddy River Trading Co./Gary Metz.*

Tin, "Drink Coca-Cola" at extreme top with "Specials Today" under that and on top of blackboard section, 1934, 20" x 28", VG ....$350.00 C

Tin, "Specials Today, Coca-Cola" oval at top and bottle in lower right corner, blackboard for easy menu changes, 1929, 20" x 28", F ....$150.00 C

Wave logo at top, 1970s, 20" x 28", M ....$85.00 D

❧ Door Pushes ❧

Door push, porcelain, Canadian, yellow and white lettering on red, 31" x 3½", EX, $75.00 C. *Courtesy of Collectors Auction Services.*

Great pair of nearly perfect pushes identical, with fishtail design, "Drink Coca-Cola Be Really Refreshed," 1960s, NM, $875.00 B. *Courtesy of Muddy River Trading Co./Gary Metz.*

Metal, painted push bar, "Drink Coca-Cola, Refresh Yourself In Bottles," with "Thanks–Call Again" on reverse, G, $375.00 C. *Courtesy of Bill Mitchell.*

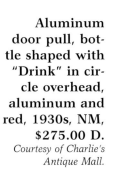

Porcelain construction, in nearly perfect condition, "Ice Cold Coca-Cola In Bottles," 1940s – 50s, 30" wide, M, $1000.00 B. *Courtesy of Muddy River Trading Co./Gary Metz.*

Aluminum door pull, bottle shaped with "Drink" in circle overhead, aluminum and red, 1930s, NM, $275.00 D. *Courtesy of Charlie's Antique Mall.*

Plastic bottle shaped pull for use on the newer machines, EX, $100.00 C. *Courtesy of Sam and Vivian Merryman.*

Porcelain "Coke is it" with two wave logo boxes, white on red, 1970s, NM, $95.00 B. *Courtesy of Muddy River Trading Co./Gary Metz.*

Porcelain "Ice Cold Coca-Cola In Bottles," 1930s, 30" x 2½", NM, $300.00 B. *Courtesy of Muddy River Trading Co./Gary Metz.*

Porcelain and wrought iron, "Drink Coca-Cola," 1930s, EX, $425.00 C. *Courtesy of Mitchell collection.*

Aluminum bottle, 1930 – 1940, NM.................$285.00 D

Aluminum door plate with diagonal lettering "Coke Is It!" 4" x 10", 1970s, EX ....$75.00 C

"Drink Coca-Cola/Ice Cold/In Bottles," porcelain, red and white lettering on red and white background, 35" long, NM ....$260.00 C

Metal and plastic, "Have a Coke!" on door attachment, 1930, NM ....$155.00 D

Metal and plaster, "Drink Coca-Cola Delicious Refreshing," 1930 – 1940s, EX ....$150.00 C

Porcelain and wrought iron, adjustable, "Drink Coca-Cola" in center, 1930s, G ....$265.00 C

Coca-Cola is now sold in nearly 200 countries.

Left: Porcelain door pull plate, with "Pull ... Refresh Yourself," with button facsimile at bottom, green, red, and white, 4" x 8", 1950s, EX, $450.00 B.

Right: Porcelain door push, "Refresh Yourself" with button artwork, green, red, and white, 4" x 8", 1950s, NM, $525.00 B.

Courtesy of Muddy River Trading Co./Gary Metz.

Porcelain door push in French "Merci Revenez Pour un Coca-Cola," yellow, white, and red, 3½" x 13½", NM, $160.00 B.
Courtesy of Muddy River Trading Co./Gary Metz.

Porcelain door plate, "Come in! Have a Coca-Cola," Canadian, yellow, white, and red, 4" x 11½", NM, $320.00 B.
Courtesy of Muddy River Trading Co./Gary Metz.

Porcelain door push, "Thanks Call Again for a Coca-Cola," Canadian, yellow, white, and red, 3½" x 13½", NM, $325.00 B.
Courtesy of Muddy River Trading Co./Gary Metz.

Porcelain door push, unusual horizontal message "Prenez un Coca-Cola," yellow, white, and red, 6½" x 3¼", NM, $120.00 B.
Courtesy of Muddy River Trading Co./Gary Metz.

Porcelain, "Come In! Have a Coca-Cola," yellow and white lettering on red background, 3½" x 11½", NM ..$290.00 C

Porcelain, horizontal, "Have a Coca-Cola," yellow and white lettering on red background trimmed in yellow, 6½" x 3½", VG ....$275.00 C

Porcelain, "Ice Cold in Bottles," red on white, 1960s, 30", EX ....$325.00 C

Porcelain, "Iced Coca-Cola here," yellow and white on red, Canadian, 1950s, 30", NM ....$225.00 D

Porcelain, "Iced Coca-Cola Here," yellow and white lettering on red background, 1950s, 31", EX.............$225.00 C

Porcelain, "Ice Cold Coca-Cola In Bottles" on front with "Thank You, Call Again" on reverse side, white lettering on red background, 1930s, 25" x 3¼", NM, $475.00 B. *Courtesy of Muddy River Trading Co./Gary Metz.*

Porcelain "Take Some Coca-Cola Home Today," white lettering on red, 1950s, 34" long, NM, $525.00 B. *Courtesy of Muddy River Trading Co./Gary Metz.*

"Refreshing Coca-Cola New Feeling," 1950 – 60s, EX, $175.00 C. *Courtesy of Mitchell collection.*

Steel with heavy paint featuring wave logo, white on black with red and white logo, 1970 – 1980s, NM, $75.00 B. *Courtesy of Muddy River Trading Co./Gary Metz.*

Tin push plate with Silhouette Girl in yellow spotlight, "Drink Coca-Cola delicious refreshing," red with white and yellow lettering, 1939, 28" x 3½", NM, $500.00 B. *Courtesy of Muddy River Trading Co./Gary Metz.*

Porcelain, oversized, outdoor style, with original box, 1942, 18" x 54", NM ....$1,700.00 B

Porcelain, "Thanks Call Again For A Coca-Cola," yellow and white lettering red background, 4" x 11½", VG ....$275.00 C

Porcelain, "Thanks Call Again for a Coca-Cola," yellow and white lettering on red, Canadian, 1930s, EX......$235.00 C

Porcelain, vertical, "Thanks Call Again for a Coca-Cola," yellow and white lettering on red background, 3½" x 13½", NM ....$350.00 C

Tin, arched top embossed with fishtail design at top, NM ....$375.00 B

Tin, die cut, "Drink Coca-Cola Be Refreshed," Canadian, 1950, EX ....$300.00 C

Tin, "Refresh Yourself," 1940 – 1950, 3" x 6", G ....$275.00 C

Tin, "Refresh Yourself," 1940 – 1950, 3" x 6", NM ....$350.00 D

Tin, silhouette, 1939 – 1941, 33" x 3½", EX ......$385.00 D

Above: "Big Wheel," "Drink Coca-Cola," add $30.00 if MIB, 1970, EX, $75.00 C.

Left: Buddy L #5646 GMC with all original accessories in box, 1957, yellow, EX, $675.00 C.

Courtesy of Muddy River Trading Co./Gary Metz.

Above: Buddy L, "Enjoy Coca-Cola," complete with hand truck that mounts in side compartment, add $20.00 if MIB, 1970, EX, $95.00 C.

Right: Buddy L #5546 International in original box with all accessories, 1956, NM, $725.00 B.

Courtesy of Muddy River Trading Co./Gary Metz.

Bank, wooden van with stamped logo, driver, and cases, 1980s, 7", EX ....$35.00 C

Barclay open bed, even load, 1950, 2", yellow, EX ....$175.00 C

Bedford, Oinky, even load, open body, 1950s, 4½", red and white, NM ....$325.00 C

Berlist Stradair of France, 1960s, 4¼", EX ....$325.00 C

Buddy L #420C, 1978, G ....$45.00 C

Buddy L #591-1350, steel, Japan, 1980s, 11", EX ....$125.00 C

Buddy L #666 set, 15 pieces, 1980s, M ....$55.00 D

Buddy L #4969, scarce tractor-trailer rig, 1970s, NM ....$125.00 C

Buddy L #4973 set, 7 pieces, 1970s, NM ....$85.00 C

Buddy L #5215, 1970s, NM ....$50.00 C

Buddy L #5215 H, big tires, pressed steel, 1980s, red and white, M ....$40.00 C

Buddy L #5216 plastic A-frame, will hold eight cases, in original box, 1962, yellow, EX ....$375.00 C

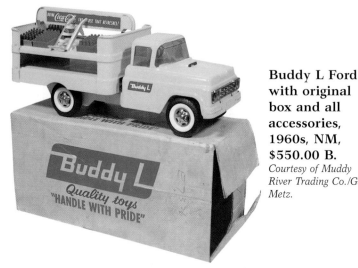

Buddy L Ford with original box and all accessories, 1960s, NM, $550.00 B. *Courtesy of Muddy River Trading Co./Gary Metz.*

Buddy L with cases and bottles, 1960s, EX, $325.00 C.

Cargo style with working headlights and tail-lights, 1950, VG, $300.00 B. *Courtesy of Muddy River Trading Co./Gary Metz.*

Gas, made in Germany, model #426-20, a rare and desirable tin wind-up litho with great detailing with a full load of tin and plastic cases, 1949, yellow, EX, $2,600.00 B. *Courtesy of Muddy River Trading Co./Gary Metz.*

Marx #991 with gray cab and frame in original box, 1953, yellow and gray, NM, $900.00 B. *Courtesy of Muddy River Trading Co./Gary Metz.*

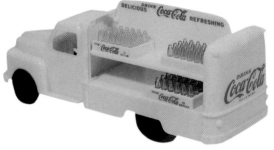

Marx Ford style, 1950s, yellow, EX, $375.00 B. *Courtesy of Muddy River Trading Co./Gary Metz.*

Buddy L #5426, pressed steel, 1960, 15", NMIB..$500.00 B

Buddy L #5426 truck, steel, Ford style with chrome grille, 1960s, yellow, NM ....$125.00 C

Buddy L #5646, GMC loader with case loading line, 1950s, yellow ....$450.00 C

Buddy L, 5-piece set, 1981, NM ....$135.00 C

Budgie even load, 1950, 5", yellow, EX ....$450.00 D

Chevy delivery, tin, Smokeyfest Estb. 1930, 1995, MIB ....$250.00 C

Corgi, Jr. double decker bus, 1974, 3", EX ....$30.00 D

Corgi, Jr. featuring contour logo, 1982, NM ....$35.00 D

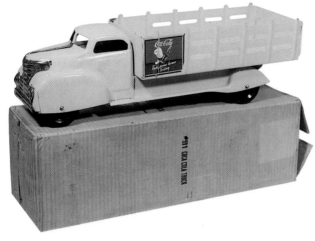

Marx #991 with Sprite Boy decal on side, in original box, 1951, yellow, NM, $625.00 B. *Courtesy of Muddy River Trading Co./Gary Metz.*

Marx, if in MIB condition with original box this value would nearly double, 1950, G, $275.00 C.

Marx, metal, 1950s, yellow, VG, $450.00 C.

Marx, plastic with original six Coca-Cola cases, Canadian, 1950s, red, EX, $525.00 B. *Courtesy of Muddy River Trading Co./Gary Metz.*

Durham Industries van in original packaging, 1970 – 1980s, NM...$30.00 D

El Camino, given away at convention in Ohio, plastic, 1995, red and white, MIB ....$20.00 C

Goodies van, Canadian, contour logo, 1970s, 12", M...$110.00 C

Lemerzarugyar plastic van, friction, 7", silver, MIB ....$105.00 C

Lemerzarugyar van, Hungary, plastic friction, 1970s, red, MIB..$215.00 D

London, "Drink Coca-Cola" decal on side, 1960s, EX ....$265.00 C

Marx #21 open side, 1950s, yellow, EX ....$450.00 D

Marx #21, open divided double decker bed, 1954, 12½", yellow and red, NM...$285.00 D

Marx #1090, tin, open bed, 1956, 17", yellow and red, EX ....$450.00 B

Matchbox, tractor-trailer, Super King, 1978, NMIB ....$55.00 D

Matchbox with even load bed, "Drink Coca-Cola," 1960s, 2", yellow, EX ....$75.00 D

Matchbox with staggered load bed, "Drink Coca-Cola," 1960s, yellow, EX ....$155.00 D

Maxitoys/Holland metal van with open sided driver's seat, 1980s, 11", yellow and black, EX..$300.00 D

Maxwell Co., plastic delivery van, India, 1970s, EX..$55.00 D

Metalcraft #171 A-frame, 1932, red and yellow, EX..$900.00 D

Metalcraft #171 pressed steel, rubber wheels, A-frame, 1932, red and yellow, NMIB ....$2,500.00 B

Model T, cast iron, 1980s, M, Warning: Fantasy item..$10.00 C

Marx, stake, yellow bed with red cab and frame with Sprite Boy decal on side of bed, 1950, G, $300.00 C. *Courtesy of Muddy River Trading Co./Gary Metz.*

Maxitoys made in Holland, hard to find since only 500 were made, 1980s, 11" long, NM, $300.00 B.

Plastic Marx Canadian truck with six plastic cases, wooden wheels, in original box, hard to find, red, 1950s, 11", G, $1,400.00 C.

Metalcraft with rubber tires, if this item were MIB price could go up by as much as $400.00, 1930s, G, $750.00 C. *Courtesy of Mitchell collection.*

Model T, scale kit in original box, 1970s, MIB ....$65.00 C

Osahi, Japan, van, tin and plastic, friction, 1970s, EX ....$85.00 C

Panel type, AMBO with smooth tires, tin litho, 1960s, EX ....$550.00 D

Plastic Fun Mates from Straco, wind-up, 1970s, EX ....$40.00 D

Plastic, smooth tire, 1940 – 1950s, yellow, EX ..$115.00 D

Renault, solid metal, 1970s, red, NM.................$65.00 D

Renault, solid metal, 1970s, yellow, NM ....$65.00 D

Rico Sanson-Junior with contour logo, 1970s, 13½", red, EX ....$55.00 D

Rosko friction motor, beverage delivery, 1950, 8", EX ....$475.00 C

Sanyo/A. Haddock Co route, battery operated, in original box, 1960s, yellow, white, red, VG ....$275.00 D

Siki Eurobuilt, Mack tractor trailer, die cast, 1980s, 12½", MIB..$55.00 D

Siku-Oldtimes, metal, 1980s, 5¼", EX ....$45.00 D

Smith-Miller A-frame, wood and aluminum, rubber tires, 1944, 14", red, EX..$1,600.00 D

Smith Miller, metal, GMC #2 of 50 stamped on bottom, with six original cases of 24 green bottles in original box, #1 is in the Smith Miller Museum, rare, 1979, red, EX...$1,700.00 B

Smith-Miller, wood and metal with bottle logos on bed, 1947 – 1953, 14", red, EX ....$695.00 D

Smokeyfest Estb. 1930, 1995, G ....$45.00 C

Straco, plastic Wee People, Hong Kong, 5½", EX...$50.00 D

Supervan, plastic, 1970s, 18" x 11", NM...........$110.00 D

Tin van, "Drink Coca-Cola, Delicious, Refreshing," Japanese, 1950, 4", yellow ....$165.00 D

Tin, even load, Japanese, 1950s, 4", yellow, EX..$150.00 D

Tin Lineman, friction power, 1950s, VG...........$200.00 D

Metal tractor trailer with spotlight carton on the trailer, in box, but the box is a bit rough, EX, 225.00 C. *Courtesy of Sam and Vivian Merryman.*

Sanyo truck made in Japan, distributed by Allen Haddock Company in Atlanta, Georgia, with original box, battery operated, 1960s, 12½" long, EX, $325.00 B. *Courtesy of Muddy River Trading Co./Gary Metz.*

VW van with friction motor by Taiyo, 1950s, 7½" long, VG, $235.00 C. *Courtesy of Mitchell collection.*

Vending machine style ¹⁄₂₅-scale model kit, 1970, MIB, $75.00 C.

Tootsie Toy van copy, die cast metal, white lettering, 1986, M ....$25.00 D

Uni Plast, Mexican #302, van with contour logo, plastic, 1978 – 1979, red, NM ....$30.00 D

Van, cardboard, Max Headroom, 1980s, 6", NM ....$20.00 D

Winrose, Atlanta Convention, 1994, MIB.........$165.00 D

Buddy Lee composition doll with original uniform bearing the original Lee tag, 1950s, 12" tall, EX, $875.00 B. *Courtesy of Muddy River Trading Co./Gary Metz.*

Clockwise, from top: Bang gun with Santa in sleigh, 1950s, M, $20.00 C.

Bang gun with clown, yellow, red, and white, 1950s, $20.00 C.

Bang gun, "It's the real thing," M, $20.00 C. *Courtesy of Mitchell collection.*

Baseball Hall of Fame information featuring both National and American League from 1901 to 1960, baseball-shaped, 1960, G, $95.00 C. *Courtesy of Muddy River Trading Co./Gary Metz.*

Buddy Lee doll in homemade uniform with original patches worn by "Aunt" Earlene Mitchell's father when he worked for Coca-Cola in Paducah, Kentucky, 1950s, EX, $600.00 C. *Courtesy of Mitchell collection.*

American Flyer kite, bottle at tail end of kite, 1930s, EX ....$400.00 C

American Flyer train car, "Pure As Sunlight," a complete train set with track and original box would push this price to around $4,500.00, 1930s, red and green, EX ....$1,500.00 C

Barbie doll, first in Fashion series, "Soda Fountain Sweetheart," styled after an advertisement in 1907, 1996, EX ....$125.00 C

Barbie doll, second in Coca-Cola Fashion series, "After the Walk," 1997, EX...$125.00 C

Barbie doll, third in Coca-Cola Fashion series, "Summer Daydreams," a facsimile from a 1913 Coca-Cola calendar, 1998, EX ....$125.00 C

Bean bag, "Enjoy Coca-Cola," with dynamic wave, 1970s, red, VG ....$30.00 C

Bicycle, EX ....$775.00 D

Boomerang, 1950s, EX...$40.00 C

Buddy L can car, 1970s, EX...$75.00 D

Bus, cardboard double decker with dynamic contour logo, Sweetcentre, 1980s, red, M ....$55.00 C

Lionel train in original box, engine has dynamic wave logo at cab, the cars advertise Fanta, Tab, Sprite, and the caboose has a large wave logo, 1970s, EX, $425.00 C. *Courtesy of Sam and Vivian Merryman.*

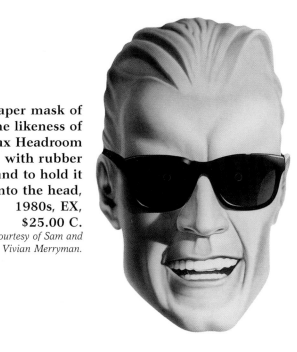

Paper mask of the likeness of Max Headroom with rubber band to hold it onto the head, 1980s, EX, $25.00 C. *Courtesy of Sam and Vivian Merryman.*

Puzzle with 2,000 pieces featuring a potpourri of Coca-Cola items, EX, $55.00 C. *Courtesy of Mitchell collection.*

Caboose with wave logo, 1970s, 6½" long, EX..$65.00 D

Car kit, Bill Elliott's thunderboat with logo, plastic, 1:24 scale ....$20.00 C

Car, tin Taiyo Ford taxi, friction power, "Refresh With Zest," 1960s, 9", white and red, NM ....$250.00 D

Corvette, die cast, convention banquet gift, 1993, NRFB ....$35.00 C

Dart board with "Drink Coca-Cola" in center, 1950s, EX..$95.00 D

"Express Cafe Snackbar," plastic and tin, "Drink Coca-Cola" button on front and advertisement on back, 1950 – 1960s, NM ....$175.00 C

Fanny pac, Jeff Gordon, shaped like pace car, logo, M ....$20.00 D

Friction car by Taiyo, 1960s, red and white, EX ....$250.00 B

Jump rope with whistle in one handle, "Pure as Sunlight" on other handle, 1920s, G $375.00 C

Kit Carson stagecoach, EX ....$150.00 C

Lionel train complete with original box and transformer, 1970s, VG ....$225.00 C

Marbles in bag that were given away with every carton, 1950, EX ....$55.00 C

Model airplane with Coca-Cola circle for wings, 1960s, red and white, EX ....$65.00 D

Pedal car, metal and rubber, 1940 – 1950s, 19" x 36", M ....$1,800.00 B

Pedal car, white lettering, 1940 – 1950, 19" x 36", red, EX..$1,300.00 B

Roller skates, embossed "Drink Coca-Cola in Bottles" on the face with "Pat. Aug 16, 1914" under first line, probably from the St. Louis Bottling Company, 1914, VG, $900.00 B. *Courtesy of Muddy River Trading Co./Gary Metz.*

Shopping basket, child's size with grocery graphics printed on both sides of basket liner, complete with contents, 1950s, EX, $425.00 C. *Courtesy of Mitchell collection.*

Train, Express Limited, still in original box with all components present, box shows a little shelf wear but nothing that detracts from the display, 1960s, EX, $450.00 C. *Courtesy of Sam and Vivian Merryman.*

Train tank car, HO gauge, "Enjoy Coca-Cola," 1980s, EX, $55.00 C. *Courtesy of Mitchell collection.*

Yo-yo, wooden, EX, $110.00 C. *Courtesy of Mitchell collection.*

Picnic cooler, plastic, 6", EX.............................$100.00 C

Play town hamburger stand made of wood, metal, and plaster in original box, very desirable piece, 1950s, EX ....$375.00 C

Puzzle, jigsaw in original can, 1960, EX.............$75.00 D

Puzzle, wire, with "Drink Coca-Cola in Bottles" on flat portion of puzzle, 1960s, EX ....$45.00 D

Stove, "Drink Coca-Cola with Your Meals," 1930s, green, EX ....$2,200.00 C

Train tank car HO gauge, "Enjoy Coca-Cola," 1980s, G..$25.00 C

Tic-Tac-Toe with bottle pawns, 1950s, EX.........$125.00 C

Top, plastic, "Coke Adds Life To ... Fun Times," 1970s, VG...$15.00 C

Whistle, plastic, "Merry Christmas Coca-Cola Bottling, Memphis Tennessee, 1950, EX..........................$30.00 C

Whistle, thimble-shaped, 1940s, EX ....$70.00 C

Whistle, tin, "Drink Coca-Cola," 1930, red and yellow, VG...$135.00 D

Whistle, wood, "Drink Coca-Cola," 1940s, EX ....$80.00 D

Yo-yo, Russell Championship, "Drink Coca-Cola" on side, 1960, EX ....$45.00 D

Yo-yo, wooden, VG ....$85.00 C

Metal bank, can shaped, with diamond design with money slot in top, NM, $85.00 C. *Courtesy of Sam and Vivian Merryman.*

Plastic bank, vending machine shaped, if found in original box value will climb to $250.00 C, 1950s, EX, $125.00 C. *Courtesy of Mitchell collection.*

"Play refreshed" introduced in 1948.

Metal truck bank still in original box, message of "Advertising Dept" on side, new, NM, $35.00 C. *Courtesy of Sam and Vivian Merryman.*

Metal can shaped bank with the dynamic wave logo, foreign market, EX, $95.00 C. *Courtesy of Sam and Vivian merryman.*

Metal truck bank still in original box, new, NM, $45.00 C. *Courtesy of Sam and Vivian Merryman.*

Bank, bottle cap with slot in top, plastic, 1950s, M ....$30.00 C

Bank, dispenser shaped, plastic, if this is in original box double the price, 1960s, VG ....$95.00 C

Metal bank, vend-
ing machine shaped
with coin slot on
top, 1940s, 2¼" x
3", EX, $150.00 C.
*Courtesy of Mitchell collec-
tion.*

Pig bank, plastic with the message "Drink
Coca-Cola Sold Everywhere," EX, $35.00
C. *Courtesy of Sam and Vivian Merryman.*

Plastic church bank with the
message "You'll feel right at
home drinking Coca-Cola," EX,
$135.00 C. *Courtesy of Sam and Vivian
Merryman.*

Truck delivery box
van with dynamic
wave on side, NM,
$35.00 C. *Courtesy of
Sam and Vivian Merryman.*

Bank, dispenser shaped with glasses, add $200.00 if in
original box, metal, 1950s, VG ....$375.00 C

Bank, plastic cooler shaped, there is a reproduction of this
that has two sets of five horizontal lines on the face, plus
bottles on both sides of the bottom slot, 1950s,
EX ....$125.00 C

Baseball glove, left-handed, MacGregor, 1970, EX, $200.00 C. *Courtesy of Mitchell collection.*

Ball and cap game, wooden, 1960s, EX, $40.00 C. *Courtesy of Mitchell collection.*

Checkers, wooden, Coca-Cola name in script on top, 1940 – 1950s, EX, $45.00 C. *Courtesy of Mitchell collection.*

Checkers, modern, 1970s, EX, $65.00 C. *Courtesy of Mitchell collection.*

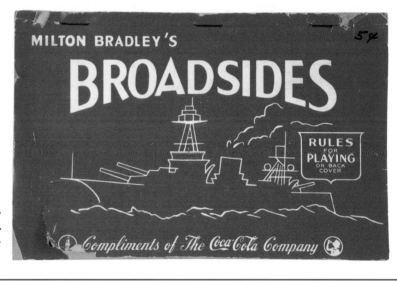

Broadsides, Milton Bradley, 1940 – 1950s, G, $125.00 C. *Courtesy of Mitchell collection.*

Baseball bat, 1950s, EX $175.00 C

Baseball bat, wooden, featuring Coca-Cola at end, 1968, EX...$55.00 D

Baseball glove, left-handed, 1920s, EX ....$350.00 C

Bingo card, "Drink Coca-Cola" in center spot, 1950s, EX...$20.00 D

Bingo card with slide covers, "Play Refreshed Drink Coca-Cola From Sterilized Bottles," 1930s, EX ....$55.00 D

Broadsides, Milton Bradley, 1940 – 1950s, F......$100.00 C

Canned Wizzer Coke game, EX ....$10.00 D

Checkers, dominos, cribbage board, two decks of cards, and a bridge score pad in a carrying box, 1940s, VG..$200.00 D

Chinese Checkers board with Silhouette Girl logo, 1930 – 1940s, EX ....$95.00 D

Cribbage board, 1940s, EX ....$60.00 D

Dart board, 1940s, EX ....$100.00 C

Dart board, 1950s, EX ....$55.00 D

Dart set of three darts, 1940 – 1950s, EX ....$125.00 C

Dominos, wooden in original box, 1940 – 1950s, VG ....$50.00 D

Dominos, wooden in original box 1940 – 50s, EX, $65.00 C. *Courtesy of Mitchell collection.*

Flip game, early, showing boy drinking from a bottle with a straw, 1910 – 1920s, VG, $875.00 C. *Courtesy of Mitchell collection.*

Flying disc, plastic with dynamic wave logo on top, "Coke adds life to having fun," 1960s, EX, $12.00 C. *Courtesy of Mitchell collection.*

Game box, contains two decks of 1943 cards unopened, plus marbles, dominos, chess, and checkers, 1940s, NM, $475.00 D. *Courtesy of Muddy River Trading Co./Gary Metz.*

Football, miniature, 1960s, black and white, EX ....$10.00 D

Flying disc, plastic with dynamic wave logo on top, "Coke adds life to having fun," 1960s, NM ....$15.00 C

Game of Steps to Health, based on the Malden Health Series, cardboard tri-fold board game, prepared and distributed by The Coca-Cola Company of Canada, Limited, 1940 – 1950s, EX ....$135.00 C

Horse Race, in original box, EX ....$350.00 C

Magic kit, 1965, EX ....$175.00 D

Playing cards, Arkansas Chapter "Holiday Happening" in plastic, 1995, EX ....$35.00 C

Playing cards, Atlanta Christmas, 1992, EX ....$50.00 D

Playing cards, Atlanta Christmas, 1993, EX ....$45.00 D

Playing cards, Atlanta, Georgia, convention cards, 1990s, NRFB ....$30.00 D

Playing cards, beach scene, 1960, M ....$95.00 D

Playing cards, "Coca-Cola adds music to my life," 1988, EX ....$50.00 D

Playing cards, bottle on ice man, 1958, M ....$85.00 C

Playing cards, "Coke Refreshes You Best," girl with bowling ball, 1961, M ....$75.00 C

Playing cards, "Coke Refreshes You Best," 1961, M ....$70.00 C

Playing cards, couple at beach with surf board, 1963, M..$100.00 C

Playing cards, couple playing tennis, 1979, EX ..$40.00 D

Playing cards, couple playing tennis, 1979, M ....$45.00 D

Playing cards, couple sitting and resting under tree in planter, 1963, M, ...$100.00 C

Playing cards, Dearborn Convention, 1993, EX ..$35.00 D

Puzzle in original box with a Coke girl on front enjoying a glass of Coke, 500 pieces, good, $75.00 C. *Courtesy of Sam and Vivian Merryman.*

Poster puzzle with scenes from various cardboard posters, mounted on board, 35" x 43", VG, $100.00 C. *Courtesy of Sam and Vivian Merryman.*

Playing cards, Kansas City Spring Fling, 1993, EX...$65.00 D

Playing cards, Louisville, Kentucky, convention, 1980s, NRFB ....$20.00 C

Playing cards, "Drink Coca-Cola," party scene, 1960, M ....$75.00 D

Playing cards featuring a Coca-Cola bottle, 1963, white and red, EX ....$40.00 D

Playing cards featuring the bobbed hair girl, "Refresh Yourself," in original box, 1928, EX.........................$600.00 C

Playing cards, friends and family, 1980, G..........$30.00 D

Playing cards from Campbellsville, Kentucky, Bottling Co., G ....$50.00 C

Playing cards from the California Chapter of the Cola Clan, 1986, EX ....$125.00 D

Playing cards, girl in circle surrounded by leaves, in original box, 1943, EX ....$105.00 D

Playing cards, girl in pool, "Sign of Good Taste," 1959, EX...$80.00 D

Playing cards, Kansas City Convention, 1995, NRFB ....$25.00 C

Playing cards, model that was used on 1923 calendar, 1977, M ....$50.00 D

Puzzle in original box with graphics of young lovers in front of an old general store with an early Coke cooler, 1000 pieces, EX, $25.00 C. *Courtesy of Sam and Vivian Merryman.*

Many of the games produced by Coca-Cola were for servicemen during the war.

Game in original cardboard box, contains table tennis, bingo, dominos, two decks of cards, chess, checkers, 1940s, EX, $1,200.00 D. *Courtesy of Antiques, Cards & Collectibles/Ray Pelly.*

Coca-Cola and Don Nelson of the Milwaukee Bucks, 1970s, M, $95.00 C.

Mexico, 1971, M, $65.00 C.

"Coca-Cola adds life to everything nice," 1976, M, $30.00 C.

Betty, 1977, M, $30.00 C.

Gold box, 1974, M, $15.00 C.

Dynamic wave trademark, 1985, M, $20.00 D.

Girl sitting in field, 1974, M, $20.00 D.

Bottle and food, 1974, M, $25.00 C. *Courtesy of Mitchell collection.*

Playing cards, "Refreshing New Feeling," featuring couple in front of fireplace, 1963, M ....$80.00 C

Playing cards, Smokeyfest Chapter, 1994, EX......$30.00 C

Playing cards, Smokeyfest Chapter, 1995, EX......$35.00 C

Playing cards, snowman in a bottle cap hat, 1959, M ....$85.00 D

Playing cards, woman with tray of bottles, 1963, M ....$60.00 C

Pool cue, dynamic wave logo, EX......................$60.00 C

Pool cue with dynamic contour logo, EX ....$40.00 D

Puzzle, bottles in tub, 1950s, 12" x 18"...............$85.00 D

Puzzle, jigsaw, "An Old Fashioned Girl," in original box, 1970 – 1980s, NM ....$20.00 D

Puzzle, jigsaw, Coca-Cola Pop Art, in sealed can, 1960, NM ....$25.00 C

Puzzle, jigsaw, Hawaiian beach, rare, in original box, NM ....$165.00 C

Puzzle, jigsaw, in original box, "Crossing The Equator," NM ....$135.00 D

Playing cards, Elaine, 1915, EX, $1,150.00 C.
Courtesy of Mitchell collection.

Playing cards, double deck in container similar to eight-pack holder, 1970s, EX, $65.00 C.
Courtesy of Mitchell collection.

Playing cards, complete with Joker and Bridge scoring cards, featuring girl with bottle, 1928, NM, $2,500.00 B.
Courtesy of Muddy River Trading Co./Gary Metz.

Playing cards, friends and family, 1980, M, $55.00 C.

Playing cards from Campbellsville, Kentucky, Bottling Co., M, $65.00 C.
Courtesy of Mitchell collection.

Lady at party with a bottle, 1951, M, $80.00 C.

Girl at beach, 1956, M, $85.00 C.

Girl putting on ice skates, 1956, M, $80.00 C.

"Refresh," 1958, M, $85.00 C.

Cowgirl in hat with a bottle, 1951, M, $80.00 C.

"Drink Coca-Cola In Bottles," 1938, M, $135.00 C.

1943, EX, $210.00 C.

Lady with dog and bottle, 1943, EX, $235.00 C. *Courtesy of Mitchell collection.*

Puzzle, jigsaw, Teen Age Party, NM ....$75.00 D

Puzzle, miniature, in box, 1983, NM ....$20.00 D

Puzzle, wooden blocks that spell "Ice Cold Coca-Cola," 15", NM ....$300.00 D

Games

In 1943, two decks of aircraft spotter cards were issued at a cost of 33¢ each; one deck had a nurse on back; the other had an operator ...

Top row, left to right: Santa Claus, 1979, M, $30.00 C.

Sprite Boy and bottle, 1979, M, $45.00 C.

"Coke Is It," 1985, M, $25.00 C.

Red and white, 1986, M, $25.00 C.

Bottom row, left to right: Hamilton King Coca-Cola girl on the cover, 1977, M, $25.00 C.

"Have a Coke and a Smile," double check, 1979, $40.00 C.

Kansas City Spring Fling '82, M, $55.00 C.
Courtesy of Mitchell collection.

...The diamond suit had German planes, clubs bore the Italian and Japanese planes. The United States planes were on the spade suit, with British planes on the hearts.

Score keeper, cardboard, keeps score of runs, hits, and errors by both teams, by score wheels, 1900s, VG, $135.00 C.
Courtesy of Mitchell collection.

Left to right: Spotter lady, 1943, M, $125.00 C; Blue wheat, 1938, M, $155.00 C; Great Bend, Kansas, EX, $175.00 C; Military nurse in uniform, 1943, EX, $135.00 C; Woman in circle, 1943, M, $100.00 C; "Drink Coca-Cola in Bottles," 1938, red wheat, M, $155.00 C; "Drink Coca-Cola in Bottles," 1938, green wheat, EX, $150.00 C; Woman in uniform with wings below photo, 1943, EX, $150.00 C. *Courtesy of Mitchell collection.*

Record chart, baseball-shaped, National League Hall of Fame, 1960, EX ....$155.00 D

Ring toss game with Santa Claus at top of handle, VG ....$35.00 D

Shanghai, MIR...$20.00 D

Steps to Health with original playing pieces and envelope, 1938, 11" x 26", NM ....$145.00 D

Tower of Hanoi, EX..$225.00 D

Bottle earrings still on display card, NM, $20.00 C. *Courtesy of Sam and Vivian Merryman.*

Left: Case, snap lid with raised bottle in center, all metal, EX, $75.00 C.

Right: Money clip, compliments Coca-Cola Bottling Works, Nashville, Tennessee, EX, $55.00 C.
Courtesy of Mitchell collection.

Charm bracelet, NFL with charms, 1960s, EX, $125.00 C. *Courtesy of Mitchell collection.*

Charm bracelet with bottle and glass charms, EX, $130.00 C. *Courtesy of Mitchell collection.*

Cuff links, gold finish, "Enjoy Coca-Cola," glass shaped, 1970s, EX, $65.00 C. *Courtesy of Mitchell collection.*

Belt and buckle, "All Star Dealer Campaign Award," 1950 – 1960s, M ....$35.00 D

Brooch, "Drink Coca-Cola," EX ....$40.00 D

Button, pin lock, bottle is hand club pen, VG ....$20.00 C

Coca-Cola Bottlers convention pin, shield-shaped, 1912, EX...$500.00 D

Coca-Cola Bottling Company annual convention pin, 1915, red, white, blue, EX..$600.00 D

Coca-Cola Bottling Company annual convention pin, 1916, EX...$600.00 D

Coca-Cola 100th anniversary wrist watch, featuring a diamond chip at 12 o'clock, NM ....$120.00 B

Compact with 50th Anniversary spot on front center, 1950s, red, M ....$60.00 D

Hat pin from driver's uniform, "Drink Coca-Cola," 1930, EX..$175.00 D

Key chain, 50th Anniversary, G .... $35.00 C

Match safes, for wood matches, "Drink Coca-Cola in Bottles" on side in cameo, EX ....$350.00 C

Match safes, for wood matches, "Drink Coca-Cola," F ....$175.00 C

Money clip, "All Star Dealer Campaign Award," 1950 – 1960s, NM...$35.00 D

Money clip, bottle in horseshoe, EX....................$40.00 C

Key chain, 1900s, EX, $135.00 C.
Courtesy of Mitchell collection.

Watch fob with likeness of Duster Girl, Coca-Cola logo on reverse side, 1911, EX, $800.00 B.
Courtesy of Muddy River Trading Co./Gary Metz.

Key chain, compliments of Coca-Cola Bottling Works, Nashville, Tennessee, in original box with Merry Christmas card inside, VG, $75.00 C. *Courtesy of Mitchell collection.*

Tie tack, 30-year service award still in box, NM, $45.00 C. *Courtesy of Sam and Vivian Merryman.*

Money clip, "Coca-Cola" in white lettering on gold plate, EX ....$30.00 C

Money clip, "Enjoy Coca-Cola" with dynamic wave on silver plate, VG ....$30.00 D

Money clip, gold plate with "Drink Coca-Cola" button in center, F ....$35.00 C

Money clip, silver plate, "Enjoy Coca-Cola," dynamic wave with knife.. $30.00 C

Money clip, 50th year, from the Coca-Cola Bottling Co., Piqua, Ohio, EX...................................$45.00 C

Necklace with bottle, EX ....$85.00 C

Pledge pin, bottle-shaped, EX ....$30.00 D

Raquel Welch bracelet, EX................................$50.00 C

Service pin, 5 year, EX..$75.00 C

Service pin, 10 year, EX.....................................$85.00 C

Service pin, 15 year, EX.....................................$90.00 C

Service pin, 20 year, EX.....................................$95.00 C

Service pin, 30 year, EX...................................$135.00 D

Service pin, 50 year, as you might expect this pin is hard to find and is extremely rare, EX ....$425.00 C

Tie clasp, "Drink Coca-Cola," 1960s, VG ....$20.00 C

Tie clasp with bottle on chain, 1940s, VG......... $40.00 D

Watch fob, 50th Anniversary, EX ....$85.00 C

Watch fob, brass, "Drink Delicious Coca-Cola in Bottles," girl drinking from bottle with straw, 1912, EX ..$195.00 C

Watch fob, brass swastika (this was a good luck symbol until the 1930s when the Nazi connection made it an ugly form), 1920s, EX ....$175.00 C

Watch fob, brass with gold wash, "Relieves Fatigue" on front, "Drink Coca-Cola Sold Everywhere 5¢" on back, 1907, EX ....$165.00 C

Watch fob, brass with red enamel lettering, 1900s, EX ....$155.00 C

Watch fob, brass with red enamel lettering, "Drink Coca-Cola," 1920s, EX ....$150.00 C

Watch fob, bulldog, 1920s, EX ....$110.00 C

Watch fob, "Coca-Cola 5¢," applied paper label bottle ....$75.00 C

Watch fob, "Drink Delicious Coca-Cola in Bottles," brass with black enamel, EX.....................................$175.00 C

Watch fob, Duster Girl, 1911, G ....$300.00 D

Watch fob, Hilda Clark in center, EX ....$125.00 C

Watch fob, horseshoe-shaped with paper label bottle in center, 1905, EX ....$950.00 D

Watch fob, oval, girl drinking from a bottle with a straw, 1910, 1¼" x 1¾", EX ....$800.00 D

Watch fob, round celluloid girl in bonnet with red ribbon, 1912, EX...$1,800.00 D

Watch fob, with swastika, 1915 ....$150.00 C

Wrist watch, in original metal tin, NM ....$55.00 D

Apron, cloth with the message "Drink Coca-Cola" on the front, two pockets, EX, $55.00 C.
Courtesy of Sam and Vivian Merryman.

Apron, cloth, "Be Really Refreshed" with button on chest portion, 1950s, white, VG, $35.00 C.
Courtesy of Mitchell collection.

Backpack, "Official soft drink of the 1984 Olympics," never used, 1984, EX, $20.00 C. *Courtesy of Sam and Vivian Merryman.*

Bandanna, Kit Carson, 1950s, 20" x 22", red, EX, $75.00 C. *Courtesy of Mitchell collection.*

Belt, web construction with metal slide buckle trimmed in red outline with the message "Enjoy Coke," NM, $15.00 C.
Courtesy of Sam and Vivian Merryman.

Apron, "Enjoy Ice Cold Coke" on bib, 1941, EX ....$65.00 C

Apron with double pockets with a bottle, "Pause Refresh, Ice Cold In Bottles." 1930s, EX ....$85.00 C

Bandanna, Kit Carson, new, white, EX, $25.00 C. *Courtesy of Mitchell collection.*

Belt, web construction with metal slide buckle that has graphics of the dynamic wave on the front, and the message "Enjoy Coke," 1960s, NM, $20.00 C. *Courtesy of Sam and Vivian Merryman.*

Bowler's shirt, red and white, "Things go better with Coke," 1960s, EX, $30.00 C. *Courtesy of Mitchell collection.*

Belt, white leather with harness style buckle and the message "Enjoy Coke," 1960s, EX, $20.00 C. *Courtesy of Sam and Vivian Merryman.*

Cap, felt beanie, 1930 – 1940s, 8" diameter, VG, $45.00 C. *Courtesy of Mitchell collection.*

Coke uniform with round drink patch, 38 regular, VG, $125.00 C.

Brown uniform necktie with dynamic wave squares, EX, $12.00 C. *Courtesy of Sam and Vivian Merryman.*

Apron, salesman's sample, "Drink ... In Bottles," EX ....$55.00 C

Apron with red change pockets, "Drink Coca-Cola," 1950 – 1960s, VG ....$35.00 C

Bandanna, Kit Carson, new, white, VG ....$20.00 C

Cowboy hat; this item was an employee incentive award item, still in original box in unused condition, NM, $150.00 C. *Courtesy of Sam and Vivian Merryman.*

Draw string "it's the real thing" pants, EX, $15.00 C. *Courtesy of Sam and Vivian Merryman.*

Driver's cap with round "Drink" patch and hard bill, hats like this are becoming hard to locate, EX, $125.00 C. *Courtesy of Sam and Vivian Merryman*

In 1925, standard employee uniforms were created.

Driver's shirt, short sleeve, white with green stripes and large back patch with white background, VG, $45.00 C. *Courtesy of Mitchell collection.*

Driver's shirt, short sleeve, 1960s, VG, $60.00 C. *Courtesy of Mitchell collection.*

Driver's folding cap, 1950s, VG, $70.00 C. *Courtesy of Mitchell collection.*

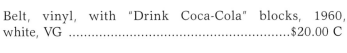

Belt, vinyl, with "Drink Coca-Cola" blocks, 1960, white, VG .... $20.00 C

Bow tie, white "Coca-Cola" on red, NM .... $40.00 C

Cowboy hat, convention, 1937, EX .... $235.00 C

251

Hat for soda attendant with round "Drink Coca-Cola" logo on both sides, NOS, NM, $55.00 B. *Courtesy of Autopia Advertising Auctions.*

Golf shirt with logo over pocket, VG, $35.00 C. *Courtesy of Sam and Vivian Merryman.*

Hat, soda person, white and red cloth, 1940, EX, $30.00 C. *Courtesy of Mitchell collection.*

Kerchief, "The Cola Clan," with Silhouette Girl from Coca-Cola Collectors' banquet, 1970s, white and red, EX, $35.00 C. *Courtesy of Mitchell collection.*

Hat, soda person, EX, $25.00 C. *Courtesy of Mitchell collection.*

The term "soda jerk" wasn't coined until the 1940s.

Patch, "Drink Coca-Cola in Bottles" with yellow and white lettering, 1960s, red, EX, $8.00 C. *Courtesy of Mitchell collection.*

Patch, "Coca-Cola," red outline and lettering on white background, VG, $8.00 C. *Courtesy of Mitchell collection.*

Patch, large, back, "Enjoy Coca-Cola," with yellow and white lettering, 1950 – 1960s, red, EX, $15.00 C. *Courtesy of Mitchell collection.*

Patch, small shirt, "Drink Coca-Cola," with red and black lettering, 1960s, EX ....$15.00 C

Painter's hat, 1950s, F ....$20.00 C

Souvenir from 1983 Kentucky State Fair, has punch out Coke coupon, turns into sun visor with the message "Coke is it!", white on red, 1983, EX, $25.00 C.

Suspenders, white with red lettering that carries the message "Enjoy Coke," with metal snap closures, these were company issued to employees, NM, $35.00 C. *Courtesy of Sam and Vivian Merryman.*

T-shirt with large "Coca-Cola Winning University" on front, G, $10.00 C. *Courtesy of Sam and Vivian Merryman.*

Uniform belt, web with metal slide buckle, with lettering "Enjoy Coca-Cola" over dynamic wave, EX, $20.00 C. *Courtesy of Sam and Vivian Merryman.*

Uniform coat, brown with red and square dynamic wave logo patch, nicknamed the hunting coat, original Riverside manufacturer's tag, EX, $55.00 C. *Courtesy of Sam and Vivian Merryman.*

Uniform jacket with original Riverside tag, embroidered Central States Bottling Co., EX, $45.00 C. *Courtesy of Sam and Vivian Merryman.*

Uniform pants and shirt, green with wave patch over pocket, EX, $65.00 C. *Courtesy of Sam and Vivian Merryman.*

Uniform pants and shirt, green pants and white shirt with wave patch, EX, $45.00 C. *Courtesy of Sam and Vivian Merryman.*

Uniform pants and shirt, new still in original packing by Riverside, green pants, white shirt with green and red collar, NM, $65.00 C. *Courtesy of Sam and Vivian Merryman.*

Uniform, pants and shirt, still in original wrapping, made by Riverside, with dynamic wave patch, NM, $75.00 C. *Courtesy of Sam and Vivian Merryman.*

Vest for company uniform with the dynamic wave logo patch on front, EX, $35.00 C. *Courtesy of Sam and Vivian Merryman.*

Uniform vest, quilted with square wave patch, original Riverside tag, EX, $35.00 C. *Courtesy of Sam and Vivian Merryman.*

Vest for company uniform with the dynamic wave logo patch on front, EX, $35.00 C. *Courtesy of Sam and Vivian Merryman.*

Above and right: Vest for company uniform, large "Drink ... in bottles" on back and smaller round "Drink" patch over left pocket, EX, $65.00 C. *Courtesy of Sam and Vivian Merryman.*

Woman's swim suit, red with white Coke lettering, VG, $20.00 C. *Courtesy of Sam and Vivian Merryman.*

Coin purse with gold lettering engraved in leather "When thirsty try a bottle," "Coca-Cola Bottling Company" with a paper label bottle to the left of lettering, 1907, maroon, EX, $100.00 C.
Courtesy of Mitchell collection.

Left: Leather, black, 1920s, EX, $100.00 C.

Right: Leather, "Drink Coca-Cola, Delicious, Refreshing," 1920s, EX, $85.00 C.
Courtesy of Mitchell collection.

Left: Coin purse with snap closures, leather, arrow, "Whenever you see an arrow think of Coca-Cola," 1909, VG, $175.00 C.

Right: Coin purse with snap closure top, leather, reads "Compliments of Coca-Cola Bottling Co., Memphis, Tenn.," 1910 – 1920s, VG, $185.00 C.
Courtesy of Mitchell collection.

Plastic, "Enjoy Coca-Cola," 1960s, black, EX, $15.00 C.
Courtesy of Mitchell collection.

Coin purse, leather with gold embossed lettering, "Drink Coca-Cola in Bottles Delicious Refreshing" with gold colored rounded metal snap, 1910, black, EX ....$165.00 C

Coin purse, leather with silver colored rounded metal snap top and silver embossed lettering, 1920s, black, EX ....$175.00 C

Embossed wallet with bottle on front, 1920s, black, EX ....$55.00 C

Leather with gold embossed lettering, 1907, black, EX ....$95.00 C

Tri-fold with calendar and photo sleeves, leather, gold embossed lettering, 1920s, black, EX ....$75.00 C

Tri-fold with calendar, leather with gold embossed lettering, 1918, black, EX...$85.00 C

Coca-Cola distributed the first Sundblom Santa Claus in 1931 using a model named Lewis Prentiss, whom they paid $3 an hour....

... It is generally believed that after Prentiss died of a heart attack in 1946, Haddom Sundblom used himself as a model for Santa.

1954 calendar, "Me, too!" with 1953 Santa cover sheet, full pad, owner recorded high and low temperatures of each day, VG, $150.00 B. *Courtesy of Muddy River Trading Co./Gary Metz.*

1954 calendar, reference edition with full pad featuring Santa with a bottle, EX, $125.00 C. *Courtesy of Mitchell collection.*

1956 calendar, famous flower paintings, reference version, EX, $35.00 C. *Courtesy of Mitchell collection.*

1957 calendar, reference edition of flower prints with Santa on front, M, $35.00 C. *Courtesy of Mitchell collection.*

1961 calendar, reference with Santa sitting in an easy chair holding a glass that's being filled by an elf, M, $45.00 C. *Courtesy of Mitchell collection.*

Banner, horizontal paper, Santa Claus, "The gift for thirst," 1952, G ....$50.00 C

Black Rushton doll holding a bottle, one of the harder dolls to find, 1970s, 16" tall, EX ....$230.00 C

Cardboard cut out, "Free Decorations in cartons of Coke," Santa standing on ladder in front of Christmas tree with a small girl on stool at bottom of ladder, 1960s, EX ....$30.00 C

Cardboard cut out, "Free new Holiday Ideas in cartons of Coke," Santa standing on ladder with small child playing with a jack-in-the-box on floor, 1960s, 36", EX .. $45.00 C

Cardboard cut out, "It's the real thing. Coke Stock up for the Holidays," featuring Santa standing in back of elves decorating a Christmas tree, 1970s, VG ....$45.00 C

Cardboard cut out, Santa Claus, "Greetings," ribbon on bottom, G ....$350.00 C

1965 calendar, reference edition with Santa and children, M, $40.00 C. *Courtesy of Mitchell collection.*

1963 calendar, reference edition with Santa Claus, holding a bottle, in middle of electric train display in front of Christmas tree with helicopter flying around his head, M, $50.00 C. *Courtesy of Mitchell collection.*

1964 calendar, reference featuring Santa standing by a fireplace with his list and a bottle, M, $30.00 C. *Courtesy of Mitchell collection.*

In December 1949, there were 28 Santa Claus advertisements in National Geographic.

1966 calendar, Santa Claus standing on ladder with a bottle and a Christmas ornament in front of a Christmas tree, M, $30.00 C. *Courtesy of Mitchell collection.*

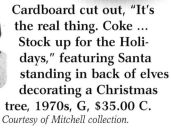

1967 calendar, reference edition with Santa Claus sitting at desk with a bottle, EX, $25.00 C. *Courtesy of Mitchell collection.*

1970 calendar, reference edition featuring Santa with a bottle, M, $20.00 C. *Courtesy of Mitchell collection.*

Cardboard cut out, "It's the real thing. Coke ... Stock up for the Holidays," featuring Santa standing in back of elves decorating a Christmas tree, 1970s, G, $35.00 C. *Courtesy of Mitchell collection.*

Bottle hanger, Santa Claus holding a bottle with information card about "Twas the Night Before Christmas," fold out story inside, 1950s, M, $25.00 C. *Courtesy of Mitchell collection.*

Bottle hanger, Santa Claus in refrigerator full of bottles being surprised by small child, 1950s, EX, $35.00 C. *Courtesy of Mitchell collection.*

Cardboard cut out, Santa Claus trying to quiet small dog in front of Christmas tree, while holding a bottle, 1960s, EX ....$95.00 C

257

Cardboard cut out, Santa Claus, "Greetings from Coca-Cola," 1946, 6" x 12", EX, $225.00 C. *Courtesy of Mitchell collection.*

Cardboard cut out, Santa Claus in front of an open refrigerator door holding a bottle, this folds in the middle, easelback, 1948, 5' tall, F, $235.00 C. *Courtesy of Mitchell collection.*

Cardboard cut out, Santa Claus, "The gift for thirst," 1953, 9" x 18", EX, $225.00 C. *Courtesy of Mitchell collection.*

Cardboard cut out showing small boy peering around a door facing at Santa who's opening a bottle, easelback, 3-dimensional, 1950s, VG, $230.00 C. *Courtesy of Mitchell collection.*

Cardboard cut out, "Things go better with Coke," Santa and little boy with dog, 1960s, 36", EX, $45.00 C. *Courtesy of Mitchell collection.*

Cardboard cut out, "Things go better with Coke," scenes of people over Santa's head, 1960s, 36", EX, $50.00 C. *Courtesy of Mitchell collection.*

Cardboard cut out, "Things go better with Coke," scenes of people over Santa's head, 1960s, 36", VG ....$35.00 C

Cardboard cut out, "Things go better with Coke," Santa and little boy with dog, 1960s, 36", G ....$30.00 C

Cardboard poster with graphics of Santa holding a bottle of Coke, 1940s, 43" x 32", EX, $1,000.00 B. *Courtesy of Muddy River Trading Co./Gary Metz.*

Cardboard die cut hanging sign "Christmas Greetings," 1932, NM, $4,200.00 B. *Courtesy of Muddy River Trading Co./Gary Metz.*

Cardboard easel back Santa cutout, message reads, "Host for the Holidays ... Take enough Coke Home," 1952, 13" x 24", EX, $500.00 B. *Courtesy of Muddy River Trading Co./Gary Metz.*

Cardboard Santa Claus Santa Packs blank price sign, NOS, NM, $35.00 C. *Courtesy of Sam and Vivian Merryman.*

Cardboard stand up Santa Claus holding three bottles in each hand with a button behind Santa, 1950s, VG, $200.00 C. *Courtesy of Mitchell collection.*

Cardboard stand up Santa Claus resting one arm on a post while holding a bottle with the other, a holly Christmas wreath is shown in the rear, 1960s, EX, $95.00 C. *Courtesy of Mitchell collection.*

Cardboard truck sign featuring Santa with both hands full of Coke bottles "Santa's Helpers," 1960s, 66" x 32", G, $125.00 B. *Courtesy of Muddy River Trading Co./Gary Metz.*

Cardboard stand up, Santa Claus resting one arm on a post while holding a bottle with the other, a holly Christmas wreath is shown in the rear, 1960s, VG ....$75.00 C

Cardboard poster, artwork of Santa with bottle, "Sign of Good Taste ... anytime!" EX, $95.00 C. *Courtesy of Bill Mitchell.*

Christmas card with possible origin of Santa clothing on reverse side, VG, $75.00 C. *Courtesy of Mitchell collection.*

Carton stuffer Santa Claus, "Good taste for all," EX, $70.00 C. *Courtesy of Mitchell collection.*

Cardboard Santa hanger, "Add Zest to the Season," Canadian, 1949, 10½" x 18½", EX, $900.00 B. *Courtesy of Muddy River Trading Co./Gary Metz.*

Carton stuffer Santa Claus, "Good taste for all," VG .... $50.00 D

Doll, Rushton, holding a bottle, 1960s, 16" high, EX .... $145.00 C

Hanging display sign, cardboard, "Serve Coke and add Punch to your Holidays," Santa at bottom of sign holding a glass, 1958, EX .... $45.00 C

Light hanger, 1960, EX .... $35.00 C

Paper hanger, Season's Greetings with Santa and helicopter, 1962, 16" x 24", NM .... $425.00 B

Christmas serving tray, there are many variations of this tray, 1973, EX, $20.00 D.

Display topper, cardboard, "Stock up for the Holidays," Santa holding a bottle behind a six pack, 1950s, EX, $150.00. *Courtesy of Mitchell collection.*

Cut out Santa Claus on stool holding wooden rabbit, EX, $125.00 C. *Courtesy of Mitchell collection.*

Porcelain, large animated, Santa holding a book that has good boys and girls list, new, EX, $125.00 C. *Courtesy of Mitchell collection.*

Porcelain, large, Santa holding a bottle and a string of lights standing beside a small wooden stool with a striped package sitting on the top step, new, EX, $145.00 C. *Courtesy of Mitchell collection.*

Paper sign designed for pole mount display with graphics of Santa and information about receiving a collectible Santas Cola cup, 22" x 30", NM, $15.00 C. *Courtesy of Sam and Vivian Merryman.*

Porcelain, large animated, Santa holding a bottle and holds up a finger to quiet a small porcelain dog, new EX ....$120.00 C

Poster, cardboard, "Coke adds life to Holiday Fun," lettering on sign in front of Santa, 1960s, EX ....$45.00 C

Poster, cardboard cut out, "Free for your tree Holiday Decorations in Cartons of Coke," Santa seated at desk with a bottle, 1960s, VG ....$55.00 C

Poster, cardboard, "A Merry Christmas calls for Coke," Santa seated in green easy chair while elves bring him food, 1960s, 16" x 24", VG, $65.00 C. *Courtesy of Mitchell collection.*

Poster, cardboard, "Bring Home The Coke," Santa at his work bench, 1956, 14" x 28", EX, $225.00 C. *Courtesy of Mitchell collection.*

Poster, cardboard, "Coke adds life to Holiday Fun," lettering on sign in front of Santa, 1960s, EX, $35.00 D. *Courtesy of Mitchell collection.*

Poster, cardboard, "Extra Bright Refreshment," Santa beside a Christmas tree with a six pack in front, 1955, 16" x 27", VG, $65.00 D. *Courtesy of Mitchell collection.*

Poster, with graphics of Santa trying to keep a small dog from waking a sleeping boy and girl, with message and price space at bottom, 30½" x 47", EX, $45.00 C. *Courtesy of Sam and Vivian Merryman.*

Poster, cardboard, cut out, "Season's Greetings," Santa sitting in the middle of a train set with a white helicopter flying around his head, 1962, 32" x 47", EX ....$375.00 C

Poster, cardboard, "Extra Bright Refreshment" Santa beside a Christmas tree with a six pack in front, 1955, 16" x 27", EX ....$85.00 C

Poster, cardboard, "Get your Santa Collector's Cup," Santa holding a glass, EX, $20.00 C. *Courtesy of Mitchell collection.*

Poster, cardboard, "real holidays call for the real thing," Santa holding a Christmas wreath, 1970s, 36" tall, EX, $35.00 D. *Courtesy of Mitchell collection.*

Poster, cardboard, "The More the Merrier," Santa sitting in front of Christmas tree with sacks of toys and Coca-Cola and Sprite in front of him, 1970s, EX, $30.00 C. *Courtesy of Mitchell collection.*

Poster, cardboard, vertical, "The gift for thirst, Stock up for the Holidays," children with presents and a hatless Santa with a bottle, EX, $75.00 C. *Courtesy of Mitchell collection.*

Poster, large, cardboard, "Holiday Refreshment Starts Here Enjoy Coca-Cola," Santa pointing to the lettering with one hand and holding a bottle with the other, EX, $55.00 C. *Courtesy of Mitchell collection.*

Poster, paper, "The pause that refreshes," Santa in his workshop, EX, $20.00 C. *Courtesy of Mitchell collection.*

Poster, cardboard, "Get your Santa Collector's Cup," Santa holding a glass, G .... $10.00 C

Poster, cardboard, "Real holidays call for the real thing," Santa holding a Christmas wreath, 1970s, 36" tall, G .... $20.00 C

Poster, paper, "Coke adds life to Holiday Fun," Santa beside fireplace holding a bottle, EX, $25.00 C. *Courtesy of Mitchell collection.*

Royal Orleans porcelain figurine featuring Santa seated holding a child and a bottle while a small boy kneels at a dog sitting up, one in a limited set of six, 1980s, $130.00 C. *Courtesy of Mitchell collection.*

Royal Orleans porcelain figurine featuring Santa holding a bottle and looking at a globe, one part of a six series set, 1980, EX, $195.00 C. *Courtesy of Bill Mitchell.*

Royal Orleans porcelain figurine featuring Santa hushing a small dog and holding a bottle, one in a limited six part series, 1980, EX, $140.00 C. *Courtesy of Mitchell collection.*

Poster, paper, "Coke adds life to Holiday Fun," Santa beside fireplace holding a bottle, NM ....$40.00 C

Poster, paper, "The pause that refreshes," Santa in his workshop, EX ....$30.00 C

Royal Orleans Santa plate, first plate, 1983, MIB...$85.00 C

Santa doll in black boots, original, 1950s, 16", EX ....$175.00 C

Royal Orleans porcelain figurine featuring Santa standing beside a sack of toys and drinking from a glass, part of a six piece limited edition set, 1980, EX, $150.00 C. *Courtesy of Mitchell collection.*

Royal Orleans porcelain figurine with Santa holding a book in front of a fireplace that has a bottle on the mantel, part of a limited six-part series, all six pieces together MIB $1,500.00, 1980s, EX, $130.00 C. *Courtesy of Mitchell collection.*

Santa cardboard poster, "Coke adds life to Holiday Fun" with artwork of Santa holding list and bottle, 1960s, 36" x 20", EX, $95.00 C. *Courtesy of Bill Mitchell.*

Santa Claus playing cards, 1979, M, $30.00 C.

Sign, cardboard, double sided hanging, "Things go better with Coke," Santa and a couple kissing, 1960, 13½" x 16", EX, $55.00 C. *Courtesy of Mitchell collection.*

Sign, cardboard, "Santa's Helpers," Santa holding six bottles, 1950s, VG, $110.00 D. *Courtesy of Mitchell collection.*

Sign, cardboard rocket, "Drink Coca-Cola Festive Holidays," die cut dimensional Santa, 1950s, 33" tall, VG, $325.00 C. *Courtesy of Mitchell collection.*

Wreath, cardboard, Santa holding six bottles, 1958, EX, $45.00 C. *Courtesy of Mitchell collection.*

Sign, cardboard rocket, "Drink Coca-Cola Festive Holidays," die cut dimensional Santa, 1950s, 33" tall, EX .... $375.00 D

Sign, cardboard, "The More the Merrier," Santa sitting in front of Christmas tree with sacks of toys and Coca-Cola and Sprite in front of him, 1970s, NM .... $45.00 D

The Sprite Boy was conceived by the D'Arcy advertising agency in St. Louis in 1941. He was first used in advertising Coca-Cola in January 1942 and continued selling Coca-Cola until phased out in 1957 – 1958.

1945 pocket calendar, with Sprite Boy looking around bottle on left side, EX, $55.00 C. *Courtesy of Mitchell collection.*

1946 calendar, Sprite Boy on cover with two months and a scene on each page, framed under glass, EX, $1,350.00 C. *Courtesy of Bill Mitchell.*

Birthday card for Coca-Cola employees featuring the Sprite Boy, the message reads "A Treat in store...for your Birthday," unused, EX, $20.00 C. *Courtesy of Sam and Vivian Merryman.*

Cardboard die cut of Sprite Boy with bottle cap hat presenting an icy cup of Coke, 37½" x 29", EX, $250.00 C. *Courtesy of Sam and Vivian Merryman.*

Cardboard, case insert with Sprite Boy, "Take some home," 10" x 13", 1944, NM, $220.00 B. *Courtesy of Muddy River Trading Co./Gary Metz.*

1946 calendar, Sprite Boy on cover with two months and a scene on each page, VG ....$900.00 C

Booklet, Profitable Soda Fountain Operation, with Sprite Boy logo on back, 1953, EX...............................$85.00 D

Cardboard, cup sign with Sprite Boy, 1950s, 15" x 12", EX ....$95.00 C

Cardboard fan on wooden handle, with Sprite Boy, "Have a Coke," 1950s, VG ....$55.00 D

Cardboard poster, Sprite Boy of Woolworth, Pennsylvania, 11" x 14", EX...$100.00 D

Cardboard, promotional sign for cups featuring Sprite Boy, 1940s, 15" x 12", F...$375.00 D

Cardboard sign, die cut, string hanger featuring Sprite Boy with bottle cap hat, "Drink Coca-Cola, Be Refreshed," Canadian, 1950s, 11" wide, NM ....$2,200.00 D

Cardboard sign, "Now Family Size too!," Sprite Boy advertising Coca-Cola all on yellow background, 1955, 16" x 27", VG ....$165.00 D

Cardboard sign, "Now Family Size too!," Sprite Boy advertising Coca-Cola all on yellow background, 1955, 16" x 27", EX ....$195.00 C

Cardboard sign, Sprite Boy advertising the ice cold 12 oz. king size bottle, 1957, M ....$400.00 C

Coupon, Free Coke with Sprite Boy, 1950s, VG ..$20.00 D

Cardboard, die cut, Sprite Boy sign featuring a six pack, 34" x 43", G, $375.00 C.

Cardboard cut out sign featuring Sprite Boy and Santa Claus with reindeer, has original easel back attachment, 1940s, 26" x 52", EX, $525.00 B. *Courtesy of Muddy River Trading Co./Gary Metz.*

Cardboard, "Have a Coke," sign featuring Sprite Boy advertising King Size, has a hanger and easel back attachment, 1957, 18" square, EX, $170.00 B. *Courtesy of Muddy River Trading Co./Gary Metz.*

Cardboard, horizontal poster, featuring Sprite Boy advertising family size too, in original wooden frame, 1955, 36" x 20", EX, $550.00 B. *Courtesy of Muddy River Trading Co./Gary Metz.*

Cardboard fold out fan with Sprite Boy from the Coca-Cola bottler at Memphis, Tennessee, 1951, F, $65.00 C. *Courtesy of Mitchell collection.*

Cardboard poster, featuring Sprite Boy and a six pack, probably part of another larger sign, 41½" x 27½", 1946, EX, $525.00 B. *Courtesy of Muddy River Trading Co./Gary Metz.*

Cardboard fan on wooden handle, with Sprite Boy, "Have A Coke," 1950s, EX, $85.00 C. *Courtesy of Mitchell collection.*

Cardboard poster, featuring Sprite Boy displaying two bottle sizes, 1955, 16" x 27", NM, $225.00 C. *Courtesy of Muddy River Trading Co./Gary Metz.*

Decal, Sprite Boy looking around a large bottle, 13" x 13", EX ....$325.00 C

"Delicious, Refreshing," blotter with Sprite Boy and a bottle, 1951, EX ....$35.00 D

Die cut cardboard Sprite Boy light pull, featuring Sprite Boy holding bottle, 10" x 15", EX.....................$250.00 C

Glass sign, decal mounted on glass and framed, Sprite Boy, advertising bottles sales, note bottle cap hat as opposed to fountain hat, 13" x 13", NM ....$425.00 D

"Have a Coke" coaster with Sprite Boy, 1940s, M ..$15.00 C

Magazine, Sprite Boy at soda fountain wearing soda fountain hat, 1949, G ....$30.00 D

Marx #991, pressed steel truck, Sprite Boy decal, 1950s, gray, MIB ....$1,000.00 D

267

Cardboard fan with wooden handle, Sprite Boy, "Bottles, Bottles Who's got the Empty Bottles?," Paducah Coca-Cola Bottling Company, Inc., 1950s, EX, $140.00 **C.** *Courtesy of Mitchell collection.*

Cardboard fan with wooden handle, Sprite Boy, "A way to win a welcome wherever you go," Starr Bros. Coca-Cola Bottling Company, Mt. Vernon, Illinois, 1950s, $115.00 C. *Courtesy of Mitchell collection.*

Cardboard poster, "Now! King Size too!", Sprite Boy with a six pack of king size Coca-Cola and a six pack of regular Coca-Cola, 1955, 16" x 27", G, $145.00 **C.** *Courtesy of Mitchell collection.*

Cardboard sign, promotional sign for cups featuring Sprite Boy, 1940s, 15" x 12", F, $375.00 D. *Courtesy of Muddy River Trading Co./Gary Metz.*

Hat, soda person, paper fold-up, featuring Sprite Boy, 1950s, VG, $30.00 C. *Courtesy of Mitchell collection.*

"Have a Coke" coaster with Sprite Boy in bottle cap hat, M, $12.00 D. *Courtesy of Mitchell collection.*

Marx #991, pressed steel truck, Sprite Boy decal, 1950s, red and yellow, G ....$150.00 D

Marx, stake truck, Sprite Boy, 1940s, yellow, EX ....$650.00 B

Masonite, Sprite Boy in arrow through cooler, 1940s, G..$750.00 D

Metal, bag holder, painted, "For Home Refreshment Coca-Cola," Sprite Boy, 36" x 17", EX ....$675.00 C

Metal bag rack, "For Home Refreshment" with Sprite Boy pointing to Coca-Cola logo, 36" x 17", 1940 – 1950s, VG...$350.00 C

Metal button sign, 12", with wings, Sprite Boy on ends and lettering of Sundaes and Malts in between, 1950s, 12" x 78", VG..$1,100.00 C

Metal button sign, 12", with wings, Sprite Boy on ends and lettering of Sundaes and Malts in between, 1950s, 12" x 78", F ....$600.00 D

Napkin with Sprite Boy, 1950s, M ....$18.00 D

Paper poster, "Now! King Size Too!," Sprite Boy between two six packs, 1955, 36" x 20", NM ....$225.00 C

Paper, Sprite Boy, "Come In, Have a Coke," framed under glass, NM...$225.00 C

Paper, Sprite Boy, "Come In, Have a Coke," framed under glass, F ....$95.00 D

Paper, "We have Coca-Cola 5¢," Sprite Boy, rare, soda fountain hat on Sprite Boy, 1944, 22" x 7", NM ....$600.00 C

Magazine ad, Sprite Boy looking at Santa in front of opened refrigerator, 1948, EX, $40.00 C.

Magazine ad, Sprite Boy at soda fountain wearing soda fountain hat, 1949, VG, $35.00 C.

The Sprite Boy is most often seen with the bottle cap hat promoting bottle sales, but he is also seen advertising fountain sales with a "soda jerk" hat.

Masonite sign with Sprite Boy in arrow through cooler, 1940s, EX, $850.00 C. *Courtesy of Mitchell collection.*

Masonite, Kay Displays sign featuring a metal button in center of wings that have a Sprite Boy decal on each end, 1940s, 78" x 12", EX, $850.00 B. *Courtesy of Muddy River Trading Co./Gary Metz.*

Metal, horizontal, "Drink Coca-Cola," Sprite Boy in spotlight, red background outlined in yellow with white lettering, 57" x 18", VG, $500.00 D.

Metal bag holder, painted, "For Home Refreshment Coca-Cola," Sprite Boy, 36" x 17", VG, $550.00 D.

Pencil box, pencil-shaped, Sprite Boy, 1948, NM ....$150.00 D

Printer's block with Sprite Boy, 1940s, M...........$40.00 C

National Geographic, back cover, "Travel Refreshed" with Santa and Sprite Boy, 6⅞" x 10", 1949, G, $12.00 C.

National Geographic, with vending machine and Sprite Boy, 1950, G, $8.00 C.

Paper, "Come in ... we have Coca-Cola 5¢," Sprite Boy with glasses, 1944, 25" x 8", VG, $350.00 B.
Courtesy of Muddy River Trading Co./Gary Metz.

Napkin holder with Sprite Boy panel on side, "Have a Coke 5¢," 1950, VG, $725.00 C.
Courtesy of Gary Metz.

School book cover with Sprite Boy, 1940 – 1950s, G ....$10.00 C

Sprite Boy, blotter, 1947, EX ....$95.00 B

Sprite Boy coloring book, issued by the Coca-Cola bottling plant in Gulfport, Mississippi, with pages that promote Coke, Tab, Mello-Yello, and Fanta, 22 pages, 1980s, EX ....$10.00 C

Sprite Boy, paper window sign with a copyright of 1950, Snyder & Black, NOS, 11⅛" x 26⅛", 1950s, NM........$235.00 C

Sprite Boy blotter with a bottle in the snow, 1953, NM ....$30.00 D

Sprite Lucky Lymon, talking vinyl figure holding a can of Sprite, says "I like the way you make me laugh, I like the Sprite in you," a West Coast offering and hard to find, 7" tall, NM...$10.00 C

Tin, French "Buvez" sign featuring Sprite Boy in spotlight on right side, 1948, 54" x 18", NM ....$850.00 B

Tin, rack sign with Sprite Boy decal, yellow on red, 1940s, 16" x 23", NM ....$375.00 C

Wood and masonite, "Beverage Department" with Sprite Boy, 1950s, G ....$625.00 B

Paper blotter with Sprite Boy and a bottle of Coke, 7¾" x 3½", EX, $25.00 C. *Courtesy of Sam and Vivian Merryman.*

Paper, Sprite Boy, "Come In Have a Coke," framed under glass, EX, $175.00 C. *Courtesy of Mitchell collection.*

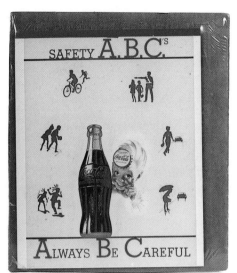

Paper tablet, "Safety ABC's," with graphics of the Sprite Boy in bottle cap hat, EX, $18.00 C. *Courtesy of Sam and Vivian Merryman.*

Porcelain, single sided Sprite Boy sign with spotlight on boy, French, white and yellow on red, 17½" x 54", 1954, EX, $210.00 B. *Courtesy of Collectors Auction Services.*

Porcelain, "Buvez Coca-Cola," with Sprite Boy in spotlight, French, 1940s, 58" x 18", EX, $750.00 B. *Courtesy of Muddy River Trading Co./Gary Metz.*

Paper window sign with graphics of Sprite Boy with bottle cap hat advertising "6 bottles 25¢," still has original stick-ons, probably NOS, 1950, 25" x 10", NM, $300.00 B. *Courtesy of Autopia Advertising Auctions.*

Wood and masonite, "Beverage Department" with Sprite Boy, 1950s, NM...$1,200.00 C

Wood, "Sundae/Malt," button logo and Sprite Boy, 1950s, 12" x 78", EX ....$975.00 C

Writing tablet featuring Sprite Boy and safety ABC's, 1950s, VG ....$12.00 C

Writing tablet featuring Sprite Boy and safety ABC's, 1950s, G ....$10.00 C

Sprite Boy play-ing cards and bottle, 1979, M, $45.00 C.

School book cover with Sprite Boy, 1940 – 1950s, EX, $12.00 C. *Courtesy of Mitchell collection.*

Sprite Boy ball game with glass cover and metal back, VG, $150.00 C. *Courtesy of Mitchell collection.*

Sprite Boy Double Six Domino set in original vinyl case, 1970s, EX, $40.00 C. *Courtesy of Mitchell collection.*

Tin, button sign with Sprite Boy decal, white, 1950s, 16", NM, $775.00 B. *Courtesy of Muddy River Trading Co./Gary Metz.*

Tin, button, Sprite Boy sign advertising 5¢ Cokes, white back-ground, 16", 1950s, EX, $775.00 B. *Courtesy of Muddy River Trading Co./Gary Metz.*

Tin, rack sign with Sprite Boy decal, red background, 16" x 23", 1940 – 1950s, EX, $300.00 B. *Courtesy of Muddy River Trading Co./Gary Metz.*

Tin, round button Sprite Boy sign with bottle and button, embossed edge, string hung, 1940s, 12¾" diameter, EX, $775.00 C.

Wood and masonite, Kay Displays, sign advertising Sundaes and Malts with 12" button in center and Sprite Boy on each end, 1950s, 6'6" x 1', EX, $1,050.00 B. *Courtesy of Muddy River Trading Co./Gary Metz.*

Wood, Sprite Boy, "Welcome Friend," 1940, 32" x 14", EX, $550.00 C. *Courtesy of Mitchell collection.*

Wood Kay Displays sign with a 12" button in center of two wings that has graphics of Sprite Boy at each end with a bottle of Coke, 1940s, 3' x 1', NM, $1,300.00 B. *Courtesy of Muddy River Trading Co./Gary Metz.*

Festoons

Five-piece Square Dance back bar display with the original envelope, 1957, 18" x 11', G, $1,400.00 B.
Courtesy of Gary Metz.

Autumn Leaves, five-piece festoon, designed for use on a soda fountain back bar, 1927, G, $1,000.00 C.
Courtesy of Muddy River Trading Co./Gary Metz.

Nine-piece back bar display, hard to find, complete with original envelope and instruction card, 1958, 12' long, NM, $1,600.00 B. *Courtesy of Muddy River Trading Co./Gary Metz.*

"Add Zest," five pieces with girls, 1951, EX ....$1,500.00 C

Autumn leaves, 1922, NM ....$2,000.00 C

"Birthstones," ribbon with 12 birthstones, 1960s, EX ....$350.00 C

Cardboard, "Balloons" featuring couple in clowns suits, hard to find item, 1912, EX............................$5,600.00 C

Cardboard, cut out, orchid festoon component, 1939, 30" x 18", G ....$250.00 C

Cardboard, die cut, festoon centerpiece featuring soda jerk, scarce, 1931, G ....$1,600.00 C

Cardboard, festoon backbar display, girl's head, five pieces, 1951, NM ....$1,250.00 C

Cardboard, festoon elements featuring man and woman with magnolias, great graphics, 1938, EX..........$700.00 C

Cardboard, festoon unit "Shop Refreshed" featuring couple with a glass of Coke, 1950s, 29" x 14", EX........$280.00 C

"Fans," girl in center lifting glass, flanked by couple toasting on ends, 5 pieces, 1927, EX $4,700.00

Leaf pattern with girl in center, five pieces with original envelope, 1927, NM ....$4,500.00 C

Locket, five pieces with original envelope, 1939, NM ....$1,800.00 C

Petunia, five pieces with original envelope, 1939, NM......$1,800.00 C

Snow bough and icicle, five pieces, in original envelope, 1937, NM ....$4,500.00 B

Swan, five pieces with original envelope, 1938, EX ....$1,800.00 C

Theme of parasols, 1918, NM ....$2,100.00 C

Three pieces of a five-piece back bar display featuring girls' heads, 1951, VG ....$900.00 C

Heavy stock paper, framed and matted under glass, 96" x 20", 1918, EX, $4,500.00 B.
Courtesy of Muddy River Trading Co./Gary Metz.

People in period dress from 1886 to 1951, 1951, NM, $1,200.00 B.
Courtesy of Muddy River Trading Co./Gary Metz.

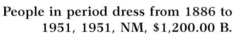

State tree complete with original display envelope, 1950s, EX, $750.00 C.
Courtesy of Mitchell collection.

Two sided, "The Pause that Refreshes," five piece, 1930s, VG, $775.00 B.
Courtesy of Muddy River Trading Co./Gary Metz.

Verbena, center piece only shown, price is for complete 5-piece set with ribbons, $1,500.00 B.
Courtesy of Muddy River Trading Co./Gary Metz.

Lily Pads festoon, 5 piece, 1935, EX, $2,600.00 B.
Courtesy of Muddy River Trading Co./Gary Metz.

Wild rose, five pieces with original envelope, 1938, VG ....$1,400.00 C

Wood flower, three pieces with original envelope, 1934, NM ....$1,800.00 C

"World-Time," globe and time zone clocks, 1953, EX ....$1,100.00 C

Masonite three-piece festoon with the message "howdy partner ... pause ... refresh," EX, **$850.00 B.** *Courtesy of Muddy River Trading Co./Gary Metz.*

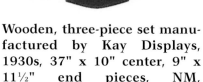

Wooden, three-piece set manu-factured by Kay Displays, 1930s, 37" x 10" center, 9" x 11½" end pieces, NM, **$2,800.00 B.** *Courtesy of Muddy River Trading Co./Gary Metz.*

Parasols, five-piece festoon, originally placed on a soda foun-tain back bar, 1927, G, **$4,700.00 B.** *Courtesy of Muddy River Trading Co./Gary Metz.*

Wooden, three piece Kay Displays made of plywood and metal, featuring embossed icicles, displayed at Weidelich Pharmacies until it closed in the early 1960s, 1936, 36" x 20" center, 36" x 18" end pieces, G, **$4,000.00 B.** Close-up of soda attendant shown at right. *Courtesy of Muddy River Trading Co./Gary Metz.*

Counter dispenser, bolt-on, 1940 – 1950s, VG, $750.00 D. *Courtesy of Patrick's Collectibles.*

Cup dispenser of heavy metal construction in triangle shape, 26" tall, EX, $425.00 B. *Courtesy of Muddy River Trading Co./Gary Metz.*

Coca-Cola was first served by soda fountain manager Willis Venable at Jacobs Pharmacy.

Dispenser with porcelain base, frosted glass body and lid, white lettering on red base, 1920s, 17" tall, NM, $6,200.00 B. *Courtesy of Muddy River Trading Co./Gary Metz*

Dispenser, toy, with original glasses, "Drink Coca-Cola," 1950s, EX, $175.00 C. *Courtesy of Mitchell collection.*

Dispenser, fountain, red with white lettering, 1940s, EX ....$475.00 D

Dispenser, refills from top, red metal with cream lettering, 1950s, VG ....$375.00 D

Dispenser, soda fountain, red and white, 1940 – 50s, EX ....$675.00 D

Dole counter-top dispenser, white and red, 14½" x 11½" x 25", G, $675.00 B. *Courtesy of Muddy River Trading Co./Gary Metz.*

Plastic and metal, three-head dispenser for Sprite and Coke, "Have a Coke" on side, red and white, VG, $275.00 D.

Plastic toy dispenser, played with but still has all the original parts, red and white, 1970s, VG, $110.00 C.

Syrup dispenser, ceramic, complete, marked "The Wheeling Pottery Co.," 1896, VG, $5,500.00 B. *Courtesy of Muddy River Trading Co./Gary Metz.*

Syrup dispenser, reproduction made of hard rubber, 1950s, EX, $350.00 B. *Courtesy of Muddy River Trading Co./Gary Metz.*

Dispenser, soda fountain, red sides with chrome lid, two tops, 1930s, EX ....$675.00 D

Dispenser, "Drink" on panel sides, image of two glasses over the spigot, 1960s, red and white, EX ....$45.00 D

Dispenser, plastic "Drink Coca-Cola" with dynamic wave logo on tank, 1970s, red and white, EX ....$50.00 D

Axe, "For Sportsmen," "Drink Coca-Cola," 1930, EX, $950.00 C. *Courtesy of Mitchell collection.*

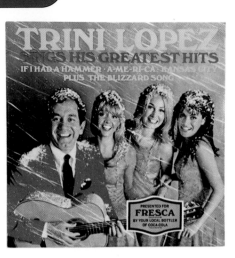

45rpm record, Trini Lopez, with dust cover advertising Fresca, 1967, EX, $25.00 C. *Courtesy of Mitchell collection.*

Bookmark, celluloid, "Drink Coca-Cola at Soda Fountains 5¢," 1898, F, $600.00 C.

Bookmark, paper, "Drink Coca-Cola Delicious and Refreshing" featuring Lillian Nordica at stand table with a glass, 1900s, 2¼" x 5¼", NM, $1,500.00 B. *Courtesy of Muddy River Trading Co./Gary Metz.*

Bookmark, Lillian Nordica, 1904, 2" x 6", EX, $300.00 C. *Courtesy of Mitchell collection.*

Bookmark, celluloid, "Refreshing Drink Coca-Cola Delicious 5¢," 1900s, 2" x 2¼", F, $500.00 C. *Courtesy of Mitchell collection.*

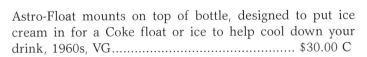

Astro-Float mounts on top of bottle, designed to put ice cream in for a Coke float or ice to help cool down your drink, 1960s, VG... $30.00 C

Badge holder, Bottler's Conference, metal and celluloid, 1943, EX ....$65.00 C

Bell, stamped metal, "Refresh Yourself Drink Coca-Cola In Bottles" on both sides, 1930s, 3¼" tall, NM ......$500.00 B

Bookmark with white cat, Tell City Coca-Cola Bottling Co., Inc., EX, $85.00 D. *Courtesy of Antiques, Cards & Collectibles.*

Bowl, green, scalloped edge Vernonware, "Drink Coca-Cola Ice Cold," 1930s, green, EX, $450.00 C. *Courtesy of Muddy River Trading Co./Gary Metz.*

Bottle lamp, with cap and original marked brass base, very rare and highly desirable, 1920s, 20", NM, $7,200.00 B. *Courtesy of Muddy River Trading Co./Gary Metz.*

Box of straws, with graphics of bottle and straw with the message, "for the pause that refreshes," 1940s, EX, $325.00 B. *Courtesy of Muddy River Trading Co./Gary Metz.*

Box of straws, with graphics of Coke bottle on all four sides, and the message "The pause that Refreshes," 1930s, EX, $575.00 B. *Courtesy of Muddy River Trading Co./Gary Metz.*

Brass book ends in shape of bottle, 1960s, EX, $225.00 B. *Courtesy of Gene Harris Antique Auction Center, Inc.*

Box of straws, graphics of Coke bottle and the message "Delicious and Refreshing," 1930s, VG, $400.00 B. *Courtesy of Muddy River Trading Co./Gary Metz.*

Box of Sweetheart straws with graphics of Coke cup that carries the message "Have a Coke," 1960s, 8½" tall, EX, $210.00 B. *Courtesy of Muddy River Trading Co./Gary Metz.*

Bolo tie, Kit Carson, neckerchief in original mailer envelope, 1950s, EX ....$85.00 C

Bookmark, celluloid oval, "What Shall We Drink? Drink Coca-Cola 5¢," 1906, 2" x 2¼", EX ....$750.00 C

Bookmark, plastic with wave logo, 1970, white and red, EX..$5.00 C

Bumper sticker, "America — You're the real thing," EX...$5.00 C

Bumper sticker extolling the advantages of safe driving because of Coca-Cola, EX ....$5.00 C

Cardboard display of Coca-Cola bottling plant in San Diego, note the streamline architecture; this has been designated a historic cultural monument, 14" x 4½" x 6½", EX ....$75.00 B

Chewing gum jar with thumb nail type lid, 1930s, M ....$500.00 D

Cigar band, 1930, VG ....$45.00 D

Comb, plastic, 1970s, red, EX ....$5.00 D

Cup, paper, red lettering "Things Go Better With Coke" on white square, 1960s, NM...................................$8.00 D

Box of straws that carries the message "Be really refreshed," 1960s, 8½" tall, EX, $250.00 B. *Courtesy of Muddy River Trading Co./Gary Metz.*

"Coke" sandwich toaster with original cord, 1930s, G, $1,500.00 B. *Courtesy of Muddy River Trading Co./Gary Metz.*

Canvas tote bag that carries the message, "Introducing diet Coke," 13½" x 13½", NM, $45.00 C. *Courtesy of Sam and Vivian Merryman.*

Canvas fabric all purpose bag, new, NM, $25.00 C. *Courtesy of Affordable Antiques/Oliver Johnson.*

Cash register topper, "Please Pay When Served," light-up, 1950s, EX, $950.00 B. *Courtesy of Muddy River Trading Co./Gary Metz.*

Card table with bottle in each corner, advertisement sheet under side of table boasts of the fact it's so strong it can hold a grownup standing on it, 1930, VG, $275.00 C. *Courtesy of Mitchell collection.*

Dialing finger, "It's the real thing," 1970s, EX ....$15.00 D

Display bottle, hard rubber, 1948, 4' tall, EX ....$975.00 D

Display bottle, plastic, with embossed logos, 1953, 20" tall, VG...$225.00 D

Dust cover, Lone Ranger, 1971, EX ....$40.00 D

Dust cover, Superman, 1971, EX ....$45.00 D

Fence post topper made from heavy cast iron, used to decorate fence pillars outside bottling plants, has a threaded base, 20" tall, EX ....$500.00 D

Flashlight in original box, 1980, EX....................$40.00 D

Fly swatters, "Drink Coca-Cola In Bottles," EX ..$95.00 D

Glass negative for the 1940s poster featuring the tennis girl, very unusual and rare, 20" x 24", G ....$110.00 D

Cigarette box, 50th Anniversary frosted glass, 1936, EX, $700.00 C. *Courtesy of Mitchell collection.*

Chewing gum display box, held twenty 5¢ packages cardboard, rare, 1920s, VG, $1,500.00 B.

Coke pepsin gum jar with embossed lid, 1905 – 1911, NM, $900.00 B. *Courtesy of Muddy River Trading Co./Gary Metz.*

Cone cup, waxed cardboard with the message "Drink Coca-Cola" on the side, EX, $12.00 C. *Courtesy of Sam and Vivian Merryman.*

Cone cup, waxed cardboard with the message "Enjoy Coca-Cola," EX, $12.00 C. *Courtesy of Sam and Vivian Merryman.*

Globe, leaded glass, round, "Coca-Cola," rare, 1920s, G ....$5,700.00 C

Golf divot remover, metal, EX..............................$5.00 D

Ice bucket, "Drink Coca-Cola In Bottles," 1960s, EX...$20.00 D

Ice tong with metal handle, 1940s, EX.............$250.00 D

Ice tong with wood handle, "Drink Coca-Cola, Greencastle, Ind.," 1920s, EX...$300.00 D

Ice tongs from Coca-Cola Bottling Co., Green Castle, Indiana, has a 3-digit phone number, 1920s, EX......$500.00 D

"Jim Dandy" combination tool that has a screwdriver, button hook, cigar cutter, and bottle opener, rare, 1920, EX..$300.00 D

Jug with paper label in original box, 1960s, one gallon, EX..$40.00 D

Jumbo straws in a box with the fishtail design, "Be Really Refreshed," 1960s, EX ....$75.00 C

Desk pen holder with music box attached, 1950s, EX, $275.00 C.
Courtesy of Mitchell collection.

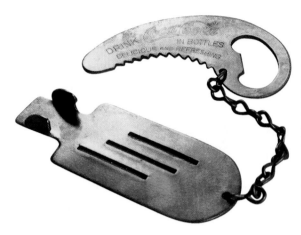

Door lock, metal, "Drink Coca-Cola in Bottles, Delicious and Refreshing," 1930s, EX, $75.00 C.
Courtesy of Mitchell collection.

Fact wheel, United States at a glance, EX, $95.00 C.
Courtesy of Mitchell collection.

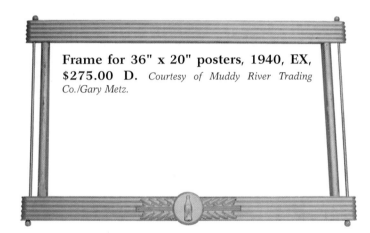

Frame for 36" x 20" posters, 1940, EX, $275.00 D. *Courtesy of Muddy River Trading Co./Gary Metz.*

Letter opener, metal and plastic with bottle on handle, 1950, red and white, EX ....$35.00 D

Letter opener, plastic from Coca-Cola Bottling Co. Dyersburg, Tennessee, clear, EX ....$20.00 C

Letter opener, plastic, white and red, EX ....$5.00 C

Light, hanging adjustable, with popcorn insert on one of four sides, with red and white Coca-Cola advertising on the other panels, 1960s, 18" x 18", M................$525.00 D

Light, octagonal hanging Art Deco motif, believed to have been made for the San Francisco World's Fair Exhibition in 1939, 1930s, 20"w x 24"t, EX ....$1,800.00 D

Light shade for ceiling fixture, milk glass, "Drink Coca-Cola" with red lettering, 1930s, 14" diameter, G ....$600.00 D

Magic lantern slide, hand colored glass, "A Home Run" from Advertising Slide Co., St. Louis, 1970s, EX..........$125.00 D

Magic lantern slide, hand colored slide, "Daddy — here it is," 1920s, EX ....$150.00 D

Magic lantern slide, hand colored glass, "Good Company!" features a couple toasting with Coke bottles, 1920s, EX...$140.00 D

Magic lantern slide, hand colored glass, "People say they like it because ...," 1920s, EX...........................$125.00 D

Magic lantern slide, hand colored glass "Stop at the Red Sign," Coca-Cola Bottling Co, Festus, Missouri, 1920s, EX...$135.00 D

Magic lantern slide, hand colored slide, "Unanimous good taste!," Festus, Missouri, 1920s, EX ....$135.00 D

Message pad shaped like a case of Coke, 1980s, EX..$20.00 D

Mileage meter with home location of Crescent Beach, South Carolina, also has bottom stamp Marion Coca-Cola Bottling Company, 1950s, VG ....$1,000.00 D

Money bag, vinyl zippered, "Enjoy Coca-Cola," 1960s, VG...$12.00 C

Globe, leaded glass, round, "Coca-Cola," rare, 1920s, EX, $10,000.00 D.

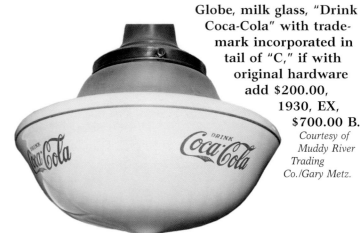

Globe, milk glass, "Drink Coca-Cola" with trademark incorporated in tail of "C," if with original hardware add $200.00, 1930, EX, $700.00 B.
Courtesy of Muddy River Trading Co./Gary Metz.

Key tag, Coca-Cola Bottling Co., Indianapolis, showing 2 cents postage guaranteed, VG, $40.00 C.
Courtesy of Mitchell collection.

Globe, milk glass, from ceiling fixture, "Drink Coca-Cola," 1930 – 1940s, EX, $450.00 C.
Courtesy of Mitchell collection.

Light fixture, rectangular, colored leaded glass, with bottom beaded fringe, "Coca-Cola 5¢," "Pittsburgh Mosaic Glass Co., Inc., Pittsburgh, Pa.," 1910, 11"w x 22" x 7½"h, EX, $12,000.00 C.

Hi-Fi premium record holder for 45rpm records, will hold 90 records, spinner on base for ease of turning to selections, 10" x 10¾", NM, $100.00 B.
Courtesy of Autopia Advertising Auctions.

Music box, cooler shaped, in working order, 1950s, EX..$145.00

Nail clippers, samples with advertising, EX........$20.00 D

Nail file, "Coca-Cola In Bottles" embossed in early script, metal pocketknife style, EX................................$10.00 D

Night light, "It's the real thing" with the dynamic wave logo, rectangular shaped, 1970s, EX....................$25.00 C

Olympic disc in original box, 1980, M................$15.00 D

Paper cigar band with bottle logo, 1930s, EX ......$55.00 C

Pen and pencil set by Cross with logo on pocket clips, in original case, M..$65.00 D

Pen and pencil set in plastic case celebrating the 50th anniversary of Coca-Cola Bottling in Frankfort, Indiana, 1965, EX ....$75.00 D

Pen, baseball bat-shaped, 1940s, white and black, EX..$50.00 D

Metal string holder with six pack in spotlight, "Take Home In Cartons," red, 1930s, 14" x 16", EX, $1,000.00 B. *Courtesy of Muddy River Trading Co./Gary Metz.*

Mileage meter, "Travel refreshed," originating from Asheville, North Carolina, white on red, 1950s, EX, $1,550.00 B. *Courtesy of Muddy River Trading Co./Gary Metz.*

Night lite, "Courtesy of your Coca-Cola Bottler," EX, $5.00 C. *Courtesy of Sam and Vivian Merryman.*

Note pad holder for candlestick phone, price includes phone which also has a courtesy coin box, 1920s, EX, $900.00 B. *Courtesy of Gary Metz.*

NCAA final four commemorative 16 oz. can and pin set, 1994, EX, $20.00 B. *Courtesy of Gary Metz.*

Pencil sharpener, cast metal in shape of bottle, 1930s, VG, $40.00 C. *Courtesy of Mitchell collection.*

Pen, "Drink" and bottle on pocket clip, with prices for specific quantities on barrel, NM ....$55.00 D

Pen, ink, red and white, 1950s, EX ....$45.00 D

Pencil holder, celluloid, 1910, EX......................$135.00 D

Pencil holder, white with red button, 1950s, 5" tall..$300.00 D

Pencil, mechanical, 1930s, EX ....$40.00 D

Pencil sharpener, rectangular, 1960s, EX ....$10.00 D

Pencil sharpener, round, plastic, "Drink Coca-Cola," 1960s, white and red, EX ....$12.00 D

Penlight, push button with wave logo, 1970s, white and red, EX ....$12.00 D

Pepsin gum jar with thumbnail type lid, 1910, EX...$1,600.00 B

Pin set, 100th Anniversary, limited edition, framed under glass, 1986, G..$125.00 C

Plaque for dispenser steel, stepped corners, 1950s, 7" x 3", EX...$75.00 D

Popcorn box, "Drink Coca-Cola," 1950s, EX, $35.00 C. *Courtesy of Mitchell collection.*

Polaroid camera, "Coke adds life to Happy Times," EX, $75.00 C. *Courtesy of Mitchell collection.*

Pin set, 100th Anniversary, limited edition, framed under glass, 1986, EX, $275.00. *Courtesy of Mitchell collection.*

Plastic slant front ink well with black and red fountain pen, 1940 – 1950s, EX ....$350.00 C

Play dollar bill, "Refresh Yourself At The Bar," NM ....$90.00 D

Pocket protector, "Coke adds life to everything nice," 1960s, white and red ....$8.00 C

Pocket protector, vinyl, Union City, Tennessee, 1950s, red and black, G ....$15.00 C

Polaroid camera, "Coke adds life to Happy Times," MIB...$95.00 C

Popcorn bag, Jungleland, 5" x 14", NM ....$12.00 D

Refrigerator water bottle, green glass "Compliments Coca-Cola Bottling Co.," embossed, EX, $135.00 C. *Courtesy of Mitchell collection.*

Ricky Nelson set, consisting of poster and a 45LP, personally autographed, framed, difficult to find these, 1960s, 18" x 14½", G, $575.00 B. *Courtesy of Muddy River Trading Co./Gary Metz.*

Screwdriver, pocket clip set, one straight and one Phillips blade, EX, $10.00 C. *Courtesy of Mitchell collection.*

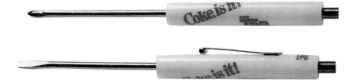

Ruler, 12", wooden, "A Good Rule," very common item, 1920 – 1960, EX, $3.00 C.

Popcorn bucket, "Drink Coca-Cola in Bottles" spot in center, waxed cardboard, 1950s, M ....$15.00 D

Postage stamp carrier, celluloid, 1902, EX ....$500.00 C

Postage stamp holder, celluloid, 1901 – 1902, 1½" x 2½", EX ....$575.00 C

Pot holder, "Drink Coca-Cola every bottle sterilized," red lettering on yellow, 1910 – 1912, G ....$275.00 C

Record album, "The Shadow," 1970, EX..............$35.00 C

Record carrier for 45 rpms, plastic and vinyl, 1960s, 9" x 8", red and white ....$40.00 C

Record dust cover featuring Dick Tracy scenes and the dynamic wave, 1971, EX ....$35.00 D

Record dust cover, Sgt. Preston, 1971, EX ....$35.00 D

Record dust cover, W. C. Field, 1971, EX............$25.00 D

Refrigerator bottle, "Compliments of Coca-Cola Bottling Company" on one side with two horses and riders on the other side, 1940 – 1950s, 9" tall, VG..................$125.00 C

Sewing needle case with packaging featuring the same model that appeared on the 1924 calendar, 1920s, EX, $75.00 C. *Courtesy of Mitchell collection.*

Ruler, 12", plastic with wave logo, 1970, white and red, EX ....$5.00 D

Ruler, 12", wooden, "Coca-Cola refresca en grande," 1950 – 1960s, VG ....$5.00 D

Salt and pepper shaker, thimble-shaped, 1920s, EX..$350.00 D

Sewing needles in Coke packaging, featuring the girl at party with the fox fur, 1920s, EX, $75.00 C. *Courtesy of Mitchell collection.*

Shade, ceiling, milk glass with original hardware, 1930s, 10", EX, $1,500.00 D.

Shade, colored leaded glass, with the chain edge that originally had a border of hanging beaded fringe, "Property of the Coca-Cola Co. to be returned on demand," must be on top band, 1920s, 18" diameter, EX, $5,000.00 C.

Sandwich toaster, "Coke," used at soda fountains to toast sandwiches and would imprint the bread, hard to find, 1930s, EX ....$1,950.00 D

Shoe spoon with wave logo, plastic, 1970s, white and red, EX...$8.00 C

Shade, window, "Drink Coca-Cola, The Pause that Refreshes in Bottles," very rare, 4' x 7', VG ....$3,500.00 C

School set, "Drink Coca-Cola Delicious Refreshing," complete with pencils, rulers, erasers in box, 1930s, red, EX...$80.00 D

Shotgun, model 1500XLT, Coca-Cola Centennial, embossed Coca-Cola on receiver and barrel never fired, 1986, MIB ....$1,500.00 C

Straws in box with titled bottle, G ....$125.00 C

Shaving kit canvas bag with "Enjoy Coca-Cola" and the dynamic wave logo on the front, EX, $25.00 C. *Courtesy of Sam and Vivian Merryman.*

Statue holding bottles of Coca-Cola, "Tell me your profit story, please" on base, 1930 – 1940s, EX, $150.00 C. *Courtesy of Mitchell collection.*

Street marker, brass, "Drink Coca-Cola, Safety First," fairly rare piece, 1920, VG, $175.00 C. *Courtesy of Mitchell collection.*

Superman, original radio broadcast, EX, $25.00 C. *Courtesy of Mitchell collection.*

Tape for reel to reel for radio play, contains 16 advertising spots prepared by McCann & Erickson, Inc., New York, 1970s, $25.00 C. *Courtesy of Mitchell collection.*

String dispenser, tin, red with carton in yellow circle, 12" x 16", EX ....$450.00 C

String holder, curved panels, "Take Home 25¢," six pack in spotlight, 1930s, NM ....$1,000.00 C

Syrup dispenser, reproduction, made of hard rubber, unusual piece, 1950s, EX ....$700.00 C

Tap knob, doubled sided, "Coke," 1960 – 1970, NM ....$25.00 D

Tap knob, enameled double sided, "Drink Coke or Coca-Cola, Ask for it Either Way," 1940 – 1950s, EX ..$85.00 C

Tap knob, one side, "Coca-Cola," 1970 ....$25.00 C

Straws, with front side cut out for dispensing straws and the other three sides with bottle pictured, "Delicious and Refreshing," EX ....$175.00 C

Tape measure, horseshoe-shaped, Coke advertising on side, NM ....$8.00 C

Tin napkin holder, foreign in origin, set up to resemble a box type cooler, 1940s, F, $525.00 B. *Courtesy of Muddy River Trading Co./Gary Metz.*

Thimbles, left: red band, 1920s, EX, $65.00 C. Right: blue band, 1920s, EX, $95.00 C. *Courtesy of Mitchell collection.*

Umbrella, "Drink Coca-Cola ... Be Really Refreshed," F, $575.00 C. *Courtesy of Mitchell collection.*

Uncut sheet of coupons for Coca-Cola, EX, $25.00 C. *Courtesy of Sam and Vivian Merryman.*

Vinyl carrying bag with zipper top and the message "Drink Coca-Cola in bottles," 14" x 5" x 10", EX, $20.00 C. *Courtesy of Sam and Vivian Merryman.*

Telephone, bottle-shaped, new, MIB ....$15.00 D

Telephone, can-shaped, new, MIB ....$25.00 D

Telephone in the shape of a 10 oz. bottle, EX ....$55.00 D

Thimble, aluminum, 1920s, F ....$30.00 D

Thimble, "Coca-Cola," red lettering, M ....$25.00 D

Training kit for sales complete with record, film strips, and charts, 1940s, EX ....$125.00 D

Tumbler, tulip shaped with syrup lines, EX ....$40.00 D

Umbrella, orange, black, and white, "Drink Coca-Cola," 1930s, EX ....$800.00 C

Wall pocket, three-dimensional pressed fiber board, 9" x 13", EX, $650.00 C. *Courtesy of Mitchell collection.*

Wooden bench with original paint that carries the message "Drink Coca-Cola ... Cottages," 1940 – 1950s, F, $850.00 B. *Courtesy of Muddy River Trading Co./Gary Metz.*

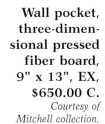

Wooden Kay Displays frame with unusual crest at top, will accommodate 40" x 24" poster, 1930s, F, $175.00 B. *Courtesy of Muddy River Trading Co./ Gary Metz.*

Wooden vertical original Coke frame with crest, gold, 1940s, EX, $300.00 D.

Wooden transistor radio with battery compartment behind back door, Philippines, 1940s, 7"w x 4"d x 5"t, EX, $400.00 C. *Courtesy of Mitchell collection.*

Water cup with handle, tin, "This cup for water but Drink Coca-Cola in Bottles, Coca-Cola Bottling Co. Greencastle, Ind." is printed in black in bottom of cup, rare piece, 1930s, EX ....$135.00 C

Winchester model #94, Coca-Cola Centennial, only 2,500 produced, never fired, 1986, MIB ....$1,300.00 C

Index

*Calendars,
see pages
128 – 129.*

COLLECTOR BOOKS
Informing Today's Collector

DOLLS, FIGURES & TEDDY BEARS

2079	**Barbie** Doll Fashion, Volume I, Eames	$24.95
3957	**Barbie** Exclusives, Rana	$18.95
6022	The **Barbie** Doll Years, 5th Edition, Olds	$19.95
3810	**Chatty Cathy** Dolls, Lewis	$15.95
4559	Collectible **Action Figures**, 2nd Ed., Manos	$17.95
2211	Collector's Ency. of **Madame Alexander Dolls**, 1965 – 1990, Smith	$24.95
4863	Collector's Encyclopedia of **Vogue Dolls**, Stover/Izen	$29.95
5904	Collector's Guide to **Celebrity Dolls**, Spurgeon	$24.95
1799	**Effanbee** Dolls, Smith	$19.95
5611	**Madame Alexander** Store Exclusives & Limited Editions, Crowsey	$24.95
5689	**Nippon Dolls** & Playthings, Van Patten/Lau	$29.95
5253	Story of **Barbie**, 2nd Ed., Westenhouser	$24.95
1513	**Teddy Bears & Steiff** Animals, Mandel	$9.95
1808	Wonder of **Barbie**, Manos	$9.95
1430	World of **Barbie** Dolls, Manos	$9.95
4880	World of **Raggedy Ann** Collectibles, Avery	$24.95

TOYS & MARBLES

2333	Antique & Collectible **Marbles**, 3rd Ed., Grist	$9.95
2338	Collector's Encyclopedia of **Disneyana**, Longest, Stern	$24.95
5681	Collector's Guide to **Lunchboxes**, White	$19.95
4566	Collector's Guide to **Tootsietoys**, 2nd Ed, Richter	$19.95
5360	**Fisher-Price Toys**, Cassity	$19.95
4945	**G-Men and FBI Toys**, Whitworth	$18.95
5593	**Grist's Big Book of Marbles**, 2nd Ed.	$24.95
3970	Grist's Machine-Made & Contemporary **Marbles**, 2nd Ed.	$9.95
5267	**Matchbox Toys**, 3rd Ed., 1947 to 1998, Johnson	$19.95
5830	**McDonald's** Collectibles, Henriques/DuVall	$24.95
5673	Modern **Candy Containers** & Novelties, Brush/Miller	$19.95
1540	Modern **Toys** 1930–1980, Baker	$19.95
5920	Schroeder's Collectible **Toys**, Antique to Modern Price Guide, 8th Ed	$17.95
5908	**Toy Car** Collector's Guide, Johnson	$19.95

JEWELRY, HATPINS, & PURSES

1748	Antique **Purses**, Revised Second Ed., Holiner	$19.95
4850	Collectible **Costume Jewelry**, Simonds	$24.95
5675	Collectible **Silver Jewelry**, Rezazadeh	$24.95
3722	Collector's Ency. of **Compacts**, Carryalls & Face Powder Boxes, Mueller	$24.95
4940	**Costume Jewelry**, A Practical Handbook & Value Guide, Rezazadeh	$24.95
5812	Fifty Years of Collectible Fashion **Jewelry**, 1925-1975, Baker	$24.95
1424	**Hatpins** & Hatpin Holders, Baker	$9.95
5695	**Ladies' Vintage Accessories**, Bruton	$24.95
1181	100 Years of Collectible **Jewelry**, 1850 – 1950, Baker	$9.95
6039	Signed Beauties of **Costume Jewelry**, Brown	$24.95
4850	Unsigned Beauties of **Costume Jewelry**, Brown	$24.95
5696	Vintage & Vogue Ladies' **Compacts**, 2nd Edition, Gerson	$29.95
5923	**Vintage Jewelry** for Investment & Casual Wear, Edeen	$24.95

FURNITURE

3716	American **Oak** Furniture, Book II, McNerney	$12.95
1118	Antique **Oak** Furniture, Hill	$7.95
2132	Collector's Encyclopedia of **American** Furniture, Vol. I, Swedberg	$24.95
3720	Collector's Encyclopedia of **American** Furniture, Vol. III, Swedberg	$24.95
5359	Early **American** Furniture, Obbard	$12.95
1755	Furniture of the **Depression Era**, Swedberg	$19.95
3906	**Heywood-Wakefield** Modern Furniture, Rouland	$18.95
1885	**Victorian** Furniture, Our American Heritage, McNerney	$9.95
3829	**Victorian** Furniture, Our American Heritage, Book II, McNerney	$9.95

INDIANS, GUNS, KNIVES, TOOLS, PRIMITIVES

1868	Antique **Tools**, Our American Heritage, McNerney	$9.95
1426	**Arrowheads** & Projectile Points, Hothem	$7.95
5616	Big Book of **Pocket Knives**, Stewart	$19.95
2279	**Indian Artifacts** of the Midwest, Hothem	$14.95
5685	**Indian Artifacts** of the Midwest, Book IV, Hothem	$19.95
5826	**Indian Axes** & Related Stone Artifacts, 2nd Edition, Hothem	$19.95
6132	Modern **Guns**, Identification & Values, 14th Ed., Quertermous	$14.95
2164	**Primitives**, Our American Heritage, McNerney	$9.95
1759	**Primitives**, Our American Heritage, Series II, McNerney	$14.95
6031	Standard **Knife** Collector's Guide, 4th Ed., Ritchie & Stewart	$14.95

PAPER COLLECTIBLES & BOOKS

4633	**Big Little Books**, A Collector's Reference & Value Guide, Jacobs	$18.95
5902	**Boys' & Girls' Book** Series, Jones	$19.95
4710	Collector's Guide to **Children's Books**, 1850 to 1950, Jones	$18.95
5596	Collector's Guide to **Children's Books**, 1950 to 1975, Jones	$19.95
1441	Collector's Guide to **Post Cards**, Wood	$9.95
2081	Guide to Collecting **Cookbooks**, Allen	$14.95
2080	Price Guide to **Cookbooks** & Recipe Leaflets, Dickinson	$9.95
3973	**Sheet Music** Reference & Price Guide, 2nd Ed., Pafik & Guiheen	$19.95
4733	**Whitman Juvenile Books**, Brown	$17.95

OTHER COLLECTIBLES

5898	Antique & Contemporary **Advertising Memorabilia**, Summers	$24.95
5814	Antique **Brass & Copper** Collectibles, Gaston	$24.95
1880	Antique **Iron**, McNerney	$9.95
3872	Antique **Tins**, Dodge	$24.95
5607	Antiquing and Collecting on the **Internet**, Parry	$12.95
1128	**Bottle** Pricing Guide, 3rd Ed., Cleveland	$7.95
3718	Collectible **Aluminum**, Grist	$16.95
4560	Collectible **Cats**, An Identification & Value Guide, Book II, Fyke	$19.95
5676	Collectible **Souvenir Spoons**, Book II, Bednersh	$29.95
5666	Collector's Encyclopedia of **Granite Ware**, Book II, Greguire	$29.95
4857	Collector's Guide to **Art Deco**, 2nd Ed., Gaston	$17.95
5906	Collector's Guide to **Creek Chub Lures** & Collectibles, 2nd Ed., Smith	$29.95
3966	Collector's Guide to **Inkwells**, Identification & Values, Badders	$18.95
3881	Collector's Guide to **Novelty Radios**, Bunis/Breed	$18.95
4652	Collector's Guide to **Transistor Radios**, 2nd Ed., Bunis	$16.95
4864	Collector's Guide to **Wallace Nutting Pictures**, Ivankovich	$18.95
5929	Commercial **Fish Decoys**, Baron	$29.95
1629	**Doorstops**, Identification & Values, Bertoia	$9.95
5683	**Fishing Lure Collectibles**, 2nd Ed., Murphy/Edmisten	$29.95
5911	**Flea Market Trader**, 13th Ed., Huxford	$9.95
5262	**Fountain Pens**, Erano	$24.95
3819	**General Store** Collectibles, Wilson	$24.95
2216	**Kitchen Antiques**, 1790–1940, McNerney	$14.95
5686	**Lighting Fixtures** of the Depression Era, Book I, Thomas	$24.95
4950	The **Lone Ranger**, Collector's Reference & Value Guide, Felbinger	$18.95
5603	**19th Century Fishing Lures**, Carter	$29.95
5835	**Racing Collectibles**	$19.95
2026	**Railroad** Collectibles, 4th Ed., Baker	$14.95
5619	**Roy Rogers and Dale Evans** Toys & Memorabilia, Coyle	$24.95
1632	**Salt & Pepper Shakers**, Guarnaccia	$9.95
5091	**Salt & Pepper Shakers** II, Guarnaccia	$18.95
3443	**Salt & Pepper Shakers** IV, Guarnaccia	$18.95
5007	**Silverplated Flatware**, Revised 4th Edition, Hagan	$18.95
6040	**Star Wars** Super Collector's Wish Book, Carlton	$29.95
3892	**Toy & Miniature Sewing Machines**, Thomas	$18.95
3977	Value Guide to **Gas Station Memorabilia**, Summers	$24.95
4877	Vintage **Bar Ware**, Visakay	$24.95
5925	The Vintage Era of **Golf Club** Collectibles, John	$29.95
4935	The W.F. Cody **Buffalo Bill** Collector's Guide with Values, Wojtowicz	$24.95

GLASSWARE & POTTERY

4929	**American Art Pottery**, 1880 – 1950, Sigafoose	$24.95
5907	Collector's Encyclopedia of **Depression Glass**, 15th Ed., Florence	$19.95
5748	Collector's Encyclopedia of **Fiesta**, 9th Ed., Huxford	$24.95
5609	Collector's Encyclopedia of **Limoges Porcelain**, 3rd Ed., Gaston	$29.95
1358	Collector's Encyclopedia of **McCoy Pottery**, Huxford	$19.95
5677	Collector's Encyclopedia of **Niloak**, 2nd Edition, Gifford	$29.95
5678	Collector's Encyclopedia of **Nippon Porcelain**, 6th Series, Van Patten	$29.95
5618	Collector's Encyclopedia of **Rosemeade Pottery**, Dommel	$24.95
5842	Collector's Encyclopedia of **Roseville Pottery**, Vol. 2, Huxford/Nickel	$24.95
5921	Collector's Encyclopedia of **Stangl Artware**, Lamps, and Birds, Runge	$29.95
5680	Collector's Guide to **Feather Edge Ware**, McAllister	$19.95
2339	Collector's Guide to **Shawnee Pottery**, Vanderbilt	$19.95
1523	Colors in **Cambridge Glass**, National Cambridge Society	$19.95
4714	**Czechoslovakian Glass** and Collectibles, Book II, Barta	$16.95
5528	Early American **Pattern Glass**, Metz	$17.95
5257	**Fenton Art Glass** Patterns, 1939 – 1980, Whitmyer	$29.95
5261	**Fostoria Tableware**, 1924 – 1943, Long/Seate	$24.95
5899	**Glass & Ceramic Baskets**, White	$19.95
5840	**Heisey Glass**, 1896 – 1957, Bredehoft	$24.95
5691	**Post86 Fiesta**, Identification & Value Guide, Racheter	$19.95
6037	**Rookwood Pottery**, Nicholson/Thomas	$24.95
5924	**Zanesville Stoneware** Company, Rans, Ralston & Russell	$24.95

This is only a partial listing of the books on collectibles that are available from Collector Books. All books are well illustrated and contain current values. Most of our books are available from your local bookseller, antique dealer, or public library. If you are unable to locate certain titles in your area, you may order by mail from COLLECTOR BOOKS, P.O. Box 3009, Paducah, KY 42002-3009. Customers with Visa, MasterCard, or Discover may phone in orders from 7:00–5:00 CST, Monday–Friday, Toll Free 1-800-626-5420, or online at www.collectorbooks.com. Add $3.00 for postage for the first book ordered and 50¢ for each additional book. Include item number, title, and price when ordering. Allow 14 to 21 days for delivery.

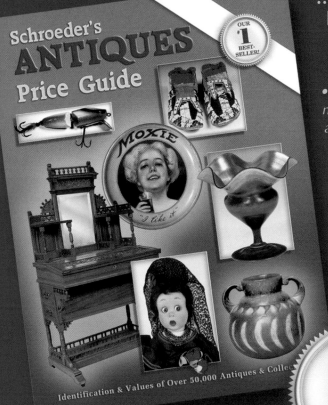

Past Tyme Pleasures

Purveyors of Fine Antiques & Collectibles
Presents Annual Spring and Fall Antique Advertising Auctions

Call / Fax / Email today to be added to our mailing list to receive future auction information.
To receive the next color catalogue and prices realized, send your check for $15 today to:

Past Tyme Pleasures

PMB #204, 2491 San Ramon Valley Blvd., #1   San Ramon, CA 94583
Ph: **925-484-6442**   FAX: **925-484-2551**   CA Bond SD 09017
email: **pasttyme@excite.com**   web site: **www.pasttyme.com**

Sales include 240+ items with a fine selection of rare signs, trays, tins, and advertising items
relating to tobacco, sporting collectibles, breweriana, soda, talc, and general store, etc.

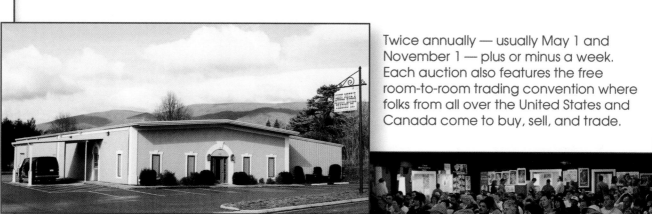

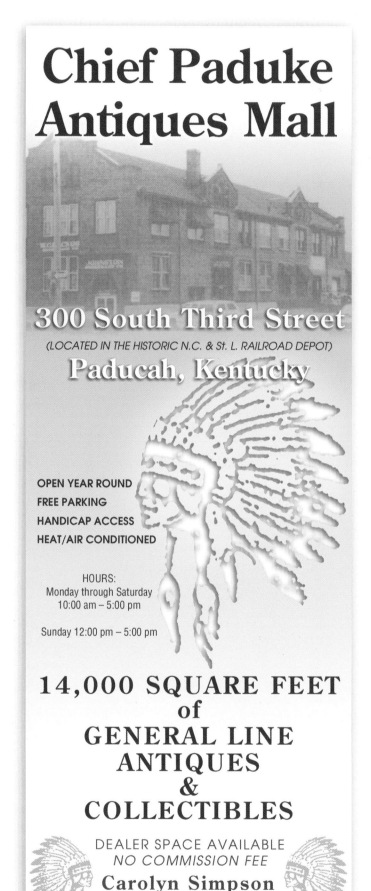

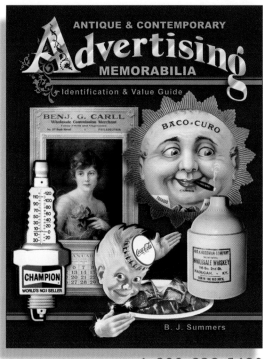

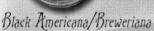